Gambier, James Lord

Notes on the minutes of a Court Martial

Inktank publishing

Gambier, James Lord

Notes on the minutes of a Court Martial

Inktank publishing, 2018

www.inktank-publishing.com

ISBN/EAN: 9783747751053

NOTES,

ON THE

MINUTES

OF A

COURT MARTIAL:

HOLDEN ON BOARD HIS MAJESTY'S SHIP

GLADIATOR,

IN PORTSMOUTH HARBOUR,

On WEDNESDAY, *the 26th day of* JULY, 1809, &c.

ON THE TRIAL, OF

THE RIGHT HONOURABLE

JAMES, LORD GAMBIER;

ADMIRAL OF THE BLUE, &c.

LONDON:
PRINTED FOR J. BUDD, PALL-MALL.

1810.

PREFACE.

IN soliciting the attention of the public, or rather pressing upon their consideration, any point of importance, with a view to obtain their judgment, whether in relation to the interest and honour of the nation, injured by partialities, and endangered by negligence: or whether in relation to the injustice and oppression, experienced by an individual, either from the hand of power, or the iniquitous prejudices of men placed in authority, some explanation is requisite: at once to shew the necessity of the measure; and serve as an apology for the obtrusion.

Shortly after the termination of the Court Martial, held at Portsmouth, on Admiral the Right Honourable LORD GAMBIER, on the subject of his conduct, as Commander in Chief, in the transactions of Basque Roads, and the attack upon the enemy in the Roads of Aix, two Pamphlets, purporting to contain the Proceedings that obtained on that occasion, made their appearance: but as one of them was confessedly defective; and the other evidently garbled; no notice was taken of either.

Shortly afterwards, however, "MINUTES OF "THE COURT MARTIAL," were published: accredited by the name of W. B. Gurney, a gentleman, for whom we entertain much respect; and, as we have well founded reason to believe, at the instance of Lord Gambier. What his Lordship's motives were, in thus introducing those MINUTES to the view, and, as it were, calling for the judgment of the public upon their merits, will not admit of a doubt, when the Sentence*, pronounced by the Court, shall have been perused!

The severity and injustice which those Minutes evidence towards Lord Cochrane: and the favour and affection they breathe towards Lord Gambier, called for those comments, and those elucidations which will be found in the following pages; and which are submitted, in no other spirit, and to no other end, than to diminish the labours of the public, in forming their conclusions, and ultimately deciding upon the matters that those Minutes embrace.—

The Court Martial held on Lord Gambier, is not of that number, which affects only the situation of an individual, who had violated some naval regulations, or failed in the discharge of a minor part of his duty. It is one, in which the public

* Vide the last page of the MINUTES.

are highly interested: one in which the "naval "character is involved;" and with which the honour, and even the existence of the nation, are blended.

It is, therefore, an imperious duty to the public, and to the country, to examine, whether that Court Martial adopted those proceedings, that were calculated to secure the great object, to which their attention had been solemnly directed; and how far it was influenced by those liberal, impartial, and equitable principles, that must govern the acts of every tribunal, of every description: or an appeal to its decrees would be nugatory; and the decrees themselves, a mere mockery and abuse of justice.

To the end proposed, we have selected the more prominent features of the MINUTES before us; and, as far as our judgment is capable of discriminating, fairly and honestly contrasted the Depositions of the several Witnesses, who, from situation, were capable of giving the best information; or who, without any information at all, gave their testimony on points of material consequence.

Having thus submitted the reasons that operated, and our sense of the duty, that compelled us to appear before the public; we have only to entreat, that they will hold in mind, when contemplating the Examinations, allowed by the Court, on subjects which connected with every thing dear to Lord Cochrane, as an officer and a man, that his Lordship was not allowed to be present, when those Examinations were delivering: and, of course, had no opportunity to cross-examine, a right that is granted to every man by the constitution of his Country; and that he was even refused admittance, whilst Lord Gambier's Defence was reading: although that Defence threw out the most injurious insinuations against his honour; and although his Lordship urged his desire to hear its contents, and quoted precedent in support of it—so that, it may be said, the proceedings which took place, in the COURT MARTIAL on ADMIRAL THE RIGHT HONOURABLE LORD GAMBIER, were EX PARTE.

NOTES,

&c. &c.

LORD GAMBIER says, in commencing his Defence; " I have
" to express my satisfaction, that the whole of my conduct, in
" the proceedings of Basque Roads, is now under your conside-
" ration, in consequence of my having applied for this Court-
" Martial; and although I cannot but lament the inconvenience
" occasioned thereby to the service, and to many individuals, I
" trust the necessity of it must be evident to the Members of
" this Court: for either I had to adopt the measure; or, by a
" tacit acquiescence in the insinuations thrown out against me,
" by Lord Cochrane, have compromised not only my own honor,
" but also, that of the brave Officers and Men serving under my
" command," (Minutes of a Court Martial, &c. p. 105.)

Lord Gambier should have shewn where such insinuations were to be traced; for they are no where to be found on the face of the Minutes of the Proceedings of his Lordship's Court-Martial.

In consequence of a suggestion to Lord Cochrane, by the First Lord of the Admiralty, in the course of a private conversation, that it was the intention of his Majesty's Government to move the Thanks of both Houses of Parliament to Lord Gambier, the Officers, Seamen and Marines, that were serving under his Lordship's command in Basque Roads, Lord Cochrane observed, that,

B

in the event of such a measure, he should feel himself bound by his public duty, to object to the Thanks, so far as they would apply to the Commander in Chief [p. 108]. Surely such language, in a private conversation, with the First Lord of the Admiralty, so circumstanced, and from a Member of Parliament, can, by no means, be considered, as conveying " insinuations." It is a fair and manly avowal of Lord Cochrane's opinion on the business of that day, and of the conduct he meant to pursue; furnishing a full and fair opportunity to all, against whom such an opinion was to operate.

In such an affair, a man of a more sedate temper than Lord Gambier discovered on this occasion, we should think, would have managed better, as there was enough of time for reflection. Yet his prudence did not altogether forsake him: And not seeing the fair full honors of a *triumph* in the Basque Road expedition, he proposed to himself the next best honors of an *ovation*. He demanded a Trial by Court Martial! Lord Gambier's motives for demanding this Trial will be found to flow from a source very remote from that which his Lordship assigns; and totally unconnected with any expressions of Lord Cochrane. They have their real origin in vanity and self-love, and not in the honour of the Officers and Men, serving under his command, whom he has identified with himself, and against whom not one single word has been uttered; unless it can be inferred, that Lord Cochrane's objection to the Vote of Thanks to the Commander in Chief, included the brave Officers and Men serving under him. On this subject we will turn to a Letter from Lord Gambier to the Secretary of the Admiralty, in order to establish the fact. " I had flattered myself," says his Lordship, " that I should " have received some signification of an approbation of my con- " duct: understanding, however, that there are some doubts, " and feeling that even a doubt upon such a subject cannot be " entertained consistently with my reputation as Commander in " Chief; I request that you will be pleased to move the Lords " Commissioners of the Admiralty to direct a Court-Martial," (p. 13.) Further, in his written Defence, his Lordship says " I " am warranted in saying, that the service was considered as de- " serving the Thanks of both Houses of Parliament; because in

" a Letter from their Lordships' Secretary, to Lord Cochrane, " dated the 29th of May, which is already before the Court, it " is expressly stated, that it was the intention of his Majesty's " Government to move for such Thanks," (p. 107.)

His Lordship's title to the honours conferred on him for the affair of Copenhagen was still questionable, and very much doubted by the thinking part of the public; and he imagined that " the Thanks of both Houses of Parliament" for his conduct in Basque Roads would set all objections for ever at rest, restore the fading laurels of Copenhagen, and entwine another round his brow. For were it possible that Lord Gambier could be influenced by the words, just quoted, as spoken by Lord Cochrane to the First Lord of the Admiralty, how will he explain the assertion, that a tacit acquiescence on his part, would have compromised not only his own honour, " but that of the brave Officers " and Men serving under his command;" as it is perfectly clear that Lord Cochrane objected to Thanks only " so far as they " should apply to the Commander in Chief?" (p. 108.) Lord Gambier, himself, has subsequently decided this point, and acknowledged the fallacy of his own proposition; for he says, " Lord Cochrane warned the noble Lord at the head of the Ad- " miralty, that if this measure were attempted, he should, if " standing alone, oppose it—thus without specifically objecting " to Thanks being given for the service performed, directing his " hostility *personally at me*, and making his attack as publicly, " though not so fairly as if he had at once exhibited formal " charges," (p. 107.)

Lord Cochrane gave no other " *warning* to the noble Lord at " the head of the Admiralty," than as the same is stated by that noble Lord, in the letter to which we have just referred; and had Lord Gambier reflected on the tendency of the words, in which that " warning" was conveyed, and the spirit, in which they were spoken, with more of his accustomed liberality, and less of that asperity, which we would fain hope does not form a part of his character, he would have given Lord Cochrane credit for the candid avowal of his purposes, at so early a period, instead of concealing them to the moment in which the Vote of

Thanks would have been moved, and then have taken Administration by surprise. Christian charity requires the mildest construction, and in this instance, at least, the disposition of human nature goes hand in hand with the mandate of religion.

Lord Gambier, speaking to his belief, says: "there is not a "precedent to be found in the Naval Annals of Great Britain, of "an Officer of the rank I have the honour to hold, commanding "a fleet, which has performed so important a service as that "accomplished under my direction, approved as that service has "been by the Board of Admiralty, and considered by his Ma-"jesty's Government as even deserving the Thanks of both "Houses of Parliament, being obliged from a sense of what is "due to his own character and honour, as well as to the profes-"sion to which he belongs, to appeal to a Naval Tribunal against "the loose and indirect accusations of an Officer so much his "inferior in rank."—(P. 106.)

Without entering into what, at one particular period, might have been the sentiments of his Majesty's Government towards Lord Gambier, which would be now an unprofitable task, their own acts will best speak their ulterior opinion of his Lordship's conduct, and the light in which they viewed it; and those acts, as they themselves have recorded them, must be received as they appear; and they appear to have been informed by facts and circumstances, the result of their own researches. In the Charges against Lord Gambier, and which were either framed by the Lords of the Admiralty, or at their instance, are these words:—"And whereas by the Log Books and Minutes of Sig-"nals of the Caledonia, Imperieuse, and other ships employed "on that service, it appears that the said Admiral Lord Gam-"bier, on the 12th day of the said month of April, the enemy's "ships being then on shore, and the signal having been made that "they would be destroyed, did for a considerable time neglect or "delay taking effectual measures for destroying them." (P. 2.)

Is there in this passage, which is, in fact, the whole of the Charge, a single word which ingenuity can torture, or a single instance, however construed, that can lead us to infer, that his

Majesty's Government were at all biassed by individual "insinuation," or that his Lordship had been driven to his "appeal to a "Naval Tribunal to defend himself against the *loose* and *indirect* "accusations of an Officer so much his inferior in rank;" as if inferiority of rank meant any thing in a Tribunal of Justice? For the credit of Lord Gambier's understanding, and much more of his heart, we must suppose that an idea, so obnoxious to every principle of justice and of honour, never harboured in his breast. It is too grossly erroneous to be entertained even by the weakest of mankind. And it is equally erroneous, nay, it is an insult to the wisdom and judgment of his Majesty's Government, to suppose that they would have relinquished their declared intention of moving the Thanks of both Houses of Parliament, merely because Lord Cochrane had declared, that, as a Member of Parliament, "he should feel himself bound by his public duty" to meet it with a partial objection.

Lord Gambier may have had his reasons for dwelling, as he has done, upon this fallacy, and upon the equally fallacious doctrine that "a compromise of his honour" would have been a compromise of the honour "of the brave Officers and Men serv- "ing under his command;" but the public, who form, in general, just opinions, and always draw just conclusions, will not suffer such premises to have any weight in the inference they may draw, or on the judgment they shall think proper to pronounce upon this part of his Lordship's Defence. They will, as the Lords of the Admiralty have done, think for themselves; they will not listen to general assertions that are not founded in facts, nor admit those facts that will not bear the strictest scrutiny.

It is an unpleasant labour to any man to correct the inaccuracies of another; but Lord Gambier's Defence abounds with them, and the following passage is of that description:—"Whether Lord Cochrane supposed he might with impunity endeavour to lower me in the opinion of my Country, and of "my Sovereign, signal marks of whose favour had, at that instant, been exclusively conferred upon himself; whether his "Lordship thought to raise his own reputation at the expence of "mine, and whether he expected that his threat would intimidate me to silence, I know not."—(P. 108.)

Lord Cochrane, in giving his evidence upon "what may be "called the prosecution," says: "I admit that the feelings of Lord "Gambier for the honour and interest of his Country were, and "are as strong as my own." (P. 40.)—And is such a statement voluntarily expressed by Lord Cochrane in unison with endeavours to "lower Lord Gambier in the opinion of his Sovereign and his "Country?" Lord Gambier was never within gun-shot of the enemy in the Roads of Aix: Lord Cochrane was closely engaged with them; and Lord Gambier has borne the most honourable testimony of his conduct on that occasion. "I cannot," says his Lordship in his Dispatches to the Admiralty, "speak in sufficient terms of "admiration and applause of the vigorous and gallant attack "made by Lord Cochrane upon the French line of battle ships, "which were on shore, as well as his judicious manner of ap-"proaching them, and placing his ship in a position most ad-"vantageous to annoy the enemy and preserve his own ship, "which could not be exceeded by any feat of valour hitherto "achieved by the British Navy." (P. 66.)

Whence then, was the necessity on the part of Lord Cochrane to be so studiously anxious to "exalt his reputation" by sinister means, such as Lord Gambier insinuates? It was already exalted by a direct and honourable course, as high as the service in which he was employed could possibly raise it, and he had no temptation to seek sinister means by design: nor did it require that service to stamp its worth; it had been long before established. It had not, nor in the nature of things could have, even the most remote connection with the reputation of Lord Gambier.

"The manner in which Lord Cochrane has proceeded towards "his Lordship," and which his Lordship says "he would never per-"mit to any man," has been sufficiently explained. But to finish at once with the accusations, insinuations, and indefinite charges, of which Lord Gambier has declared Lord Cochrane to be the author, we will bring forward the best Evidence that can be produced—the evidence of Lord Gambier himself, and give his Lordship the full benefit of it; premising, that according to his Lordship's own statement, the whole of those Charges, and many others of no better description, that are found wandering through his Lordship's Defence, centre in Lord Cochrane's declaration "that he should feel himself bound by his public duty to oppose "a Vote of Thanks, as far as it may apply to the Commander "in Chief." That Lord Cochrane had a right to make such declaration no man will deny, and Lord Gambier thus unequivocally admits it: "Lord Cochrane, as a Member of Parliament, "may most assuredly support or oppose public measures as he "may think proper." (P. 107.)—And after having thus conceded to Lord Cochrane a right of action, Lord Gambier denies him the right of declaring his intentions to act? The one follows with the other, as a matter of course; and if Lord Gambier should accord with this natural deduction from his own proposition, what becomes of those odious terms which he has so *largely bestowed on,* and so often *reiterated* against Lord Cochrane? Lord Gambier, however, as if aware of having gone too far in the admission of a fact universally recognised, endeavours to *qualify* it, and, to shew that it was changeable, according to circumstances, *instantly* subjoins:—"In the present proceeding, "however, he stands in a situation only as an Officer *serving* "*under my command,* as appears by the following Letter from "the First Lord of the Admiralty." (P. 107.)

Here his Lordship is once more unfortunate; in speaking of Lord Cochrane's situation, he forgets his own—he forgets that his sword, the badge of command, was not in his own possession! and it is not possible to conceive the inducement that could have led to such an apparently inconsistent argument, which contradicts his Lordship's own opinion, and is in itself wholly unfounded? The Letter to which his Lordship refers, contains little more than what passed between Lord Mulgrave and Lord Cochrane, at the time when the latter made the declaration which Lord Gambier had so frequently touched on; unless his Lordship fixes upon that part of the sentence which speaks of Lord Cochrane's professional rank, "*Captain* Lord Cochrane;" but even in that case his Lordship cannot be ignorant, that the Officers in the Army and Navy are addressed and spoken of, in the House of Commons, by the rank they hold; in the very same way as when they are with their ships and corps, or giving evidence before a Court-Martial.

Lord Gambier, clinging to the suggestion he had thrown out, that the honour of the Officers and Men serving under him were completely identified with his own, labours to impress them with the feeling, that they should consider what might be "called or "termed" (P. 91,) his Trial, as a common cause, in which they were equally interested with himself; and to that end, for there is no other apparent object, his Lordship says, that "Lord "Cochrane, on presenting himself to me, after the action, was "general in complaint of the Officers, who commanded the "other ships, but having had equal means with his Lordship of "judging of the conduct of those Officers, I do aver that it "was highly meritorious." (P. 109.)

Upon the liberality of such an assertion, that could serve only, to inflame mens minds and provoke them to acts of violence, comment is unnecessary. His Lordship must have been sensible that those Officers were not on trial; nor in any shape before the Court; and that, so far from having reported them harshly to the First Lord of the Admiralty, Lord Cochrane did by a "tacit "acquiescence" in the then proposed Vote of Thanks, so far as it applied to them and to the men, who had served under Lord Gambier's command, admit the full claim and amount of their merits; and that they were entitled to the high and honourable reward, which the thanks of both Houses of Parliament would confer. No man in his senses, and with any portion of gratitude in his breast, ever doubted the transcendant merits of the Naval Officers, but on the contrary all men speak of them, as rising above their praise.

It was Lord Gambier who indirectly, and for the first time, raised the question; and his subsequent averment in their favour, whilst it can neither add to nor subtract from their worth, is not much in favour of his modesty. His Lordship, however, was not satisfied with making the assertion: he went further, he examined his *own Secretary*, for the purpose of giving it the colouring of support; and here is that gentleman's testimony. "He spoke *generally*" (alluding to a conversation between Lord Gambier and Lord Cochrane,) "of

" *the Sloops* and small vessels, and of a great many of the fire-
" ships, and he particularly noticed the gun-brigs; *small Vessels was the expression.* I am confident that the men of war
" sloops were *intended to be referred to* from the circumstance
" of the Beagle having been mentioned." (P. 179.)

What will the world think of this evidence? So pregnant with insinuation: such a jumble of inconsistency: such a strange jarring between facts, conjecture, and construction; and all equally vague, and nugatory! Will they be of opinion that such Evidence, so featured and complexioned, will bear his Lordship out in the statement, that " Lord Cochrane was general in complaint of *the Officers who commanded the other ships*, engaged at the same time with himself?" Many of the Officers of those " other Ships," commanded Frigates and Ships of the Line: and the witness speaks only of Fire Ships, and Gun Brigs; although his zeal to serve his Lordship is pretty evident from that part of his testimony, in which he deposes confidently, even to what Lord Cochrane had intended: " I am confident, that Sloops were intended to be referred to, from the circumstance of the Beagle having been mentioned." We shall have occasion to speak of Mr. Wilkinson's testimony* more at large: and until then, we observe only that it seems of equal worth with the proposition it was meant to uphold; and clearly demonstrates, that whatever might have been the expressions used by Lord Cochrane, in relation to the small vessels, he was not general in complaint of the " Officers commanding the other Ships engaged at the same time with himself;" and that Lord Gambier's assertion, therefore, to speak of it in the mildest way, is totally unfounded.

* In no part of the Trial is the *candor* of Lord Gambier more conspicuous, *shining* as it is in many parts, than in this, namely the examination of his Secretary, Mr. Wilkinson, page [179.]

———hinc spargere voces
In vulgum amiguas, et quærere conscius arma.

There is more management and delicacy in the evidence of Sir Henry Neale, p. 186. p. 11, 12, 13.

When Lord Cochrane was made acquainted with that assertion (for he was not allowed to be present whilst Lord Gambier's Defence was reading,) and heard that Mr. Wilkinson had been produced to support it, he appears to have felt all the indignation, that a tale of calumny naturally excites in the mind that is conscious of its own rectitude: if we may judge from the following circumstance, which stands recorded upon the face of the Minutes of the Court-Martial.

" The Right Honourable Lord Cochrane called in.

" *President.* Lord Cochrane! I have received the Note which " you addressed to me, and have taken the sense of the Court " upon it. The decision of the Court is, that as the matter to " which your Lordship refers, does not at all bear upon the " Trial of Lord Gambier, they cannot enter into it."

" Lord *Cochrane.* I would request, Sir, that the Letter should " appear, as an official Letter to you; and that it may be entered " upon the Minutes.

" *President.* The Court will take it into their consideration.

" The Court was cleared; Court re-opened.

" *President.* Lord Cochrane! The Court have taken into their " consideration the Note you addressed to them; and have agreed " that it shall be attached to the Minutes."

The Letter was read, and is as follows:

" Sir, Having learnt from my brother Officers, that a report " has gone abroad, that I censured, in general terms, the conduct " of the Officers employed in the Road of Aix, on the 12th of " April, I wish to have an opportunity to declare the truth on " Oath; considering reports, of that nature, highly injurious to " the service of our Country. I am also desirous to lay before " the Court, the Orders given to the fire ships for their guidance;

" as they will tend to elucidate, and clear some of those who " consider that blame has been imputed to them." (P. 228.)

Why the Court-Martial refused compliance with his Lordship's request, upon a subject calculated to do justice to the feelings of those, " who considered that blame had been imputed to " them:" and prevent an injury to " the service of our Country," we cannot divine; unless those motives be ascribed to the act, which we do not even surmise; and which a Court of equity and honour must ever hold in abhorrence.

Some reason, indeed, has been assigned, by the Court themselves; namely, that, as the matter to which Lord Cochrane referred, " did not bear upon the Trial of Lord Gambier, the " Court could not enter into it," But when it is considered, that Lord Gambier had stated, that a tacit acquiescence in the insinuations thrown out against him by Lord Cochrane, would have compromised, not only his own honour, but "*also that of the* " *brave Officers and Men*" serving under his command: and " that Lord Cochrane was general in his complaints *of the Offi-* " *cers* who commanded the other ships engaged at the same " time with himself:" and when it is considered, that Lord Gambier appeared most desirous to establish those positions; and that he, with no common solicitude, examined several witnesses to that end, prefacing his questions as an index, to shew the answer they sought to obtain; thus, for instance, on the Examination of Admiral Stopford. (P. 79, a.)

" *President*. Does your Lordship wish to ask any question of " Admiral Stopford?"

Lord *Gambier*. " With respect to *my own conduct*, I have no " wish; but I think it is due to the Officers *of the fire ships*, to " put a question as to their conduct, which *I aver was highly* " *meritorious*." (P. 79.) When all these circumstances, and a number of others, nearly similar in their nature and tendency, are considered: and when it is further considered, that the Court were in the habit of entering into matters, that positively did not bear upon the Trial of Lord Gambier, nor were in any, the most remote, degree connected with his Defence, as will be established in the most satisfactory manner, on a future stage of these Notes: the reason assigned by the Court for rejecting Lord Cochrane's application, so far from justifying the act, will only serve to magnify the oppression it exercised towards Lord Cochrane, whose name had been frequently brought forward, for the purposes of connecting with it envy, malice, and detraction; in open violence of every principle of justice, which required the whole truth: to the end that the innocent might not be confounded with the guilty; or at least that innocence should not be oppressed in order that delinquency might be concealed.

Had Lord Gambier reflected that recrimination is the very worst mode of defence, he would no doubt have blotted out from his memorial, many aspersions that are aimed solely at Lord Cochrane; and which, instead of promoting the proper object of his Lordship's cause, seem directed solely, to the gratification of pique and resentment. "At the time," says his Lordship, "that Lord Cochrane made this *general complaint*, "I had not the smallest suspicion, that there existed in his "mind those sentiments of disapprobation of my conduct, which "by his proceedings, since his return home, I am to suppose he "then entertained. It would in such case have been liberal, "and, I think, also his duty, to have made a communication to "me, to that effect. I should then have been enabled to have "guarded, in some measure, against his attack upon my character, "on his arrival in England." (P. 110.)

The distinct meaning of this passage is, to shew that Lord Cochrane acted illiberally and deceptively: indulging himself in complaining *generally* to Lord Gambier, "against the Officers "commanding the other ships, engaged at the same time with "himself;" but wilfully concealing his disapprobation of Lord Gambier's own conduct. We will, however, examine this appeal to the passions of the Court-Martial; and the result of our enquiries will evidence the reliance that ought to be placed on it. It has already been shewn, that the first part of it is erroneous: as the complaints to which it alludes were never made; and in addition to the facts we have deduced on that head, there is a very strong circumstance, resting indeed upon an inference, to be drawn from the conduct of Lord Gambier on the occasion. It does not any where occur, either in the Defence, or in the course of the Examination of Witnesses, that his Lordship took any steps in consequence of such asserted complaints against those officers: not even by hinting to them that reflections had been made upon their conduct, of a very prejudicial tendency; and to suppose that Lord Gambier having heard such complaints, would suffer them to pass unnoticed, would be derogatory to his situation as Commander in Chief: a slur upon his character as an Officer; and an impeachment of his feeling as a man. And the supposition becomes the more obnoxious, when we view his Lordship through his correspondence with the Secretary of the Admiralty. It cannot be possible that his Lordship, who, in one of the Letters of that correspondence, seems so deeply impressed with those refined notions of professional honour, that to his consideration, "even a doubt is injurious to the reputation of an Officer," (P. 13.) should have allowed direct complaints to be made against the character of Officers, serving under his command, and never once think of them, or of the honour they attacked, until his own conduct had been arraigned, and then only, as appearances would imply, to serve his own interest, by hinting to those Officers, in language not easily to be mistaken, that to maintain the purity of their honour, which had been most unjustly assailed, he was compelled to the measure of demanding a Court-Martial. We must therefore conclude, that in the precipitancy with which he has made his averments and protestations, he has inadvertently said more than he meant. In his censure of Lord Cochrane, for alledged concealment of sentiment, he has spoken *unadvisedly.* Lord Cochrane, it is true, did not, in direct terms, tell him, that he disapproved of his conduct; such proceeding would have been the very height of rudeness and of rashness. Lord Cochrane acted with more delicacy and prudence, and in a way that evidences he was solicitous only for the good of the service: and that the enemies of his country should be destroyed; and that selfishness and envy were alike strangers to his bosom. His Lordship thus ex- " presses himself:—When I arrived at the outer anchorage, I men- " tioned to my Lord Gambier, that as there could be no jealousy " with respect to Admiral Stopford, it would be a matter essential " to the service to send the Admiral in with the frigates or other " vessels, which his Lordship thought best; as his zeal for the " service would accomplish, what I considered yet more credit- " able than any thing that had been done. I apologized for the " freedom that I used with his Lordship, and stated that I took " that liberty as a friend; for it would be impossible, things re- " maining as they were, to prevent a noise being made about it " in England. I said, my Lord, you have desired me before to " speak candidly to you, and I have used that freedom. I have " no wish or desire but for the service of our Country. To " which his Lordship replied, that if I threw blame, it would " appear like arrogantly claiming all the merit to myself."— (P. 61.)

And Lord Gambier, so far from disputing this statement, has actually admitted it, by quoting a part of it relative to the service that had been performed, and which might possibly have been still further attempted towards the destruction of the enemy's ships, in the following words. " Lord Cochrane states a conversation to " have passed between his Lordship and myself, in his return " from Aix Roads, in which he represents me to have said, " that if he threw blame, it would appear like arrogantly claiming " all the merit to himself." (P. 135.)

It is therefore conclusive, that Lord Gambier received from Lord Cochrane *intimation enough* to convince his Lordship, that Lord Cochrane did not approve of his conduct; and that much more might have been effected than had been achieved. Nay, Lord Cochrane pushed the matter much further and in such terms, that on reflection ought to have operated with Lord Gambier, as a stimulus to some further exertions against the enemy; as his Lordship's words conveyed the plain meaning, that Lord Gambier had not duly employed the powers with which he had been invested; and that neglect and delay were too evident to escape the observation of the public. "When," says his Lordship, "I arrived at the outer "anchorage, I mentioned to my Lord Gambier that as there "could be no jealousy with respect to Admiral Stopford, it "would be a matter essential to the service to send the Admiral "in with the frigates, and other vessels. I apologized for the "freedom I used with his Lordship, and stated, that I took that "liberty as a friend; for it would be impossible, things remaining "as they were, to prevent a noise being made about it in "England." (P. 64).

Lord Gambier, therefore, was in full possession of Lord Cochrane's sentiments, and had he acted upon them, he might perhaps, have destroyed an additional number of the enemy's ships, instead of thinking how he might defend his own character: for it is according to the construction of his Lordship's own words, (p. 134,) that any disapprobation of his conduct, which Lord Cochrane could have pronounced, would not have operated a fresh attack upon the enemy; but merely have enabled him to guard in some measure against what is erroneously stated to be Lord Cochrane's attack upon his character.

Having thus followed Lord Gambier through what may be considered the Preface to his written Defence, we arrive "at the "points which appear to his Lordship to be" under the consideration of the Court. With these points we will proceed according to the order in which Lord Gambier has thought proper to arrange them, and first,

Whether the lapse of time between the discovery in the morning of the enemy's ships being on shore, and the attack, was not, under all circumstances, absolutely necessary for the advantageous accomplishment of the intended service? (P. 110.)

"*At* 5. 48. *A. M.*" says his Lordship, "The Imperieuse, "then about three miles from the enemy, and about the same "distance from the Caledonia, made the signal to me by tele-

" graph, that seven of the enemy's ships were on shore, and that " half the fleet could destroy them.

" The actual situation of the French fleet, at that time, was " this: Seven of their ships were on shore on the Palles, two " had escaped towards the Charente, and two lay either at their " original anchorage, or a very little removed from it, *with their* " *broadsides bearing upon any thing that might approach, to* " *attack the ships on shore.*

" I ordered the fleet to be unmoored immediately; the wind " was at N. W. and the tide was then nearly at the last quarter " ebb, and much too far spent to admit of a force being sent " in, so as to effect any thing, with the possibility of returning, " in case of disaster, before the making of the flood, which " would effectually have locked up our ships within the enemy's " confined anchorage, during the whole of that tide. Here " they would have been exposed, not only to the point blank " shot of the batteries, but also to the broadsides of the above-" mentioned two line of battle ships, then lying in Aix Road, " *and which, even without assistance from the batteries, must* " *have entirely crippled every one of our ships in their approach,* " *through so narrow a channel; besides which, some of the* " *grounded ships were sufficiently upright, and so situated as to* " *enable them to bring their guns to bear upon the entrance.*"

" I would here submit to the Court, whether the idea which " appears to have been entertained by Lord Cochrane, that a " force could have been sent in so as to have arrived before low " water in the morning, was not in itself preposterous and im-" practicable.

" Upon the fullest consideration that no possible attempt " could be made until the tide had flowed for some time, un-" less a previous change of wind should take place; all I had to " do, was to make every *preparation* for the attack on the " enemy's grounded ships; accordingly I made the signal for " the fleet to weigh, and the Rear Admiral and Captains being

" assembled on board the Caledonia, I gave orders to the Com-
" mander of the Etna, the only bomb present, *to proceed, as soon*
" *as the tide would permit that vessel to approach near enough,*
" *to bombard the enemy's ships.* I at the same time ordered the
" Insolent, Conflict, and Growler gun-brigs, to accompany her,
" and directed the Captains of the Valiant, Bellona, and Re-
" venge, with the frigates, to take an advanced anchorage, as
" near as possible to the Boyart Shoal, to be in readiness to pro-
" ceed to the attack, as soon as the water had sufficiently flowed
" to enable them to do so. At between nine and ten A. M.
" which was much before the flood was sufficiently made to
" commence effective operations, the fleet ran in, and came to
" an anchor within about three miles distant from the enemy's
" fortress of Aix; the three ships before mentioned, with the
" frigates, anchored about a mile nearer to the Boyart, *but the*
" *bombs and brigs did not come to.*

" As the flood-tide made, three of the seven ships, which had
" grounded on the Pallés Shoal, and were the farthest from us,
" being lightened, succeeded in warping off, and made for the
" Charente.

" The two line-of-battle ships, still at their anchorage in the
" situation before described, took, at the same time, advantage
" of the flood, and proceeded likewise towards that river.—Most,
" if not all these five ships, *now* ran aground at the mouth of
" the Charente, *and were never assailable.*

" These movements of the enemy's ships were not, as I submit
" to the Court, to be prevented by any means that I could
" adopt, with the smallest chance of success, and without his
" Majesty's ships being put to the most unwarrantable peril, and
" when, as Rear Admiral Stopford has, in his evidence on the
" part of the prosecution, most emphatically described, ' Ours
" ' would have been all the loss, and the enemy's all the advan-
" ' tage.'

" The wind blew directly in, so that in the event of our ships
" being crippled, while the flood tide was running, which ap-

D

"peared inevitable, it would have been impossible for them to "have worked out, or to have retreated to an anchorage out of "the reach of the enemy's shot and shells, the consequence of "which could scarcely have been less than their utter destruc-"tion.—These serious impediments induced me to delay the "attack until the latter part of the flood, in order to give any "ships which might be disabled on their approach, a chance of "returning by means of the receding tide.—Had the wind been "favourable for sailing both in and out, or even the latter only, "there could have been no doubt that the sooner the enemy's "ships were attacked the better." (p. 127.)

When the fleet was ordered to unmoor, it seems rather unaccountable that Lord Gambier did not immediately take up the ground on which he afterwards anchored. His Lordship has not explained why he did not, and as there were no shoals, or any danger of shot or shells, nor a want of water, it might have pointed itself out to his Lordship as "a situation best calculated "to watch the motions of the enemy, and give assistance to the "attacking vessels;" without waiting for a signal from the Imperieuse. The truth, however, is, that the fleet did not weigh until eleven o'clock, as appears by the testimony of Lord Cochrane, supported by the circumstance of the Etna bomb, which vessel, although she got under weigh with the fleet and continued her course to the inner roads of Aix, without coming to an anchor, did not pass the Imperieuse until about one o'clock. (p. 127, 39 and 173.) And, therefore, had the fleet sailed at the time marked by Lord Gambier, the Etna bomb, with the wind and tide in her favour, the former blowing very strong, (p. 143), and the latter running upwards of three miles an hour, (p. 146.) must have occupied nearly four hours to perform a distance of about three miles: a thing that carries absurdity upon the face of it. The conclusion, then, is, that his Lordship allowed *five hours*, (p. 35), to elapse between the time that the signal was made by Lord Cochrane and the weighing of the fleet.

It is not here meant to convey an idea, that Lord Gambier did, by such delay manifest any want of that zeal and ardour for the service, which he has so often mentioned; but speaking to the fact, unacquainted as we must be with those matters that might have been passing in his Lordship's mind at the moment, as his Lordship has not thought proper to communicate them, it seems very extraordinary, that "under all the circumstances of the case," when eleven of the enemy's ships of the line and a number of frigates had been attacked on the night of the 11th, by our fire-vessels, and when it was of the greatest importance to the country, that those ships should be destroyed, his Lordship did not move towards the scene of action, even before the period at which the Imperieuse made the signal referred to, (p. 33). The very appearance of the fleet "under sail, and approaching them," would have added to the horror and increased the confusion and panic that had seized them. There were, however, other considerations of equal moment, namely, to succour and assist our own vessels, which had advanced so close towards those of the enemy as to be open to their attacks; so that if the enemy had been so strong in boats of all description (as Lord Gambier would have it believed) or had they not been completely panic struck, as some of the witnesses have stated, they would at least have compelled them to fall back; which would have been a much greater disgrace "to the enterprise and to England," (p. 163), than that which Captain Beresford has noticed in his evidence; but these were considerations that do not appear to have occurred to his Lordship's mind, nor to have roused his zeal into action.

Regardless, however, of such matters, which it is possible, he might have contemplated as trifles, or imagined that they would escape general notice and inquiry, his Lordship endeavours to shew, that when Lord Cochrane made the signal, at 5 hours 48 minutes, *A.M.*, it was impossible for the fleet or any part of it to have proceeded into Aix Roads. "The wind," says his Lordship, "was at N. W. the tide then nearly at the last quarter ebb, "and much too far spent, to admit any force to be sent in, so as "to effect any thing with the possibility of returning in case of "disaster, before the making of the flood, which would effec- "tually have locked up our ships within the enemy's confined "anchorage, during the whole of that tide; here they would "have been exposed not only to the point blank shot of the "batteries, but also to the broadsides of the above mentioned

" line of battle ships, then laying in Aix Roads, and which, with-
" out the assistance of the batteries, must have entirely crippled
" every one of our ships in their approach through so narrow a
" channel, besides which, some of the grounded ships were suf-
" ficiently upright, and so situated as to enable them to bring
" their guns to bear upon the entrance." (p. 125.)

The wind being " at N.W." was the fairest that could blow for carrying ships in, and as to the state of the tide, upon which great stress is laid, in order to shew, as his Lordship has asserted, and on which the principal part of his Defence turns, that there was not any unnecessary delay, we may venture to assert, that it was nearly as favourable as the wind, and that his Lordship might have gone in with about the same degree of safety, as at any other time. The fact is established by several witnesses, amongst whom are Captains Seymour, Malcolm, and Broughton.

The Evidence his Lordship offers in support of his proposition is very far from being satisfactory; and the following facts will probably evince that his Lordship's judgment either misled him, in one instance, or that it was fluctuating in another. The Cæsar and Theseus, ships of the line, although they did not go into the inner Roads of Aix, until it had become dark, were ordered thither about five o'clock in the afternoon, (p. 161), at which time the tide must have been nearly as it was in the morning.

Let any man then, carrying this fact in his mind, and combining it with the reason assigned by the Commander in Chief for delaying to send in ships, at the time the signal was made at day-light, by the Imperieuse, put his hand upon his heart, and say, if he can, that such delay is, or can be, justified. It is not to be supposed, that had a force been sent in, it would have effected any thing in less time than a few hours; but recurring to his Lordship's objection, we cannot refrain from remarking, that if the anticipation of possible danger is to awe a British Fleet, when the enemy is within its reach, and by an effort of no uncommon enterprise might be destroyed, we must take our farewell of those gallant exploits, of those heroic achievements, that have thrown a lustre over the annals of our country, and excited the admiration and envy of the universe. Did the immortal Nelson, at the attack of Copenhagen, consider the Forts and Floating Batteries that were opposed to him: the strong position of the enemy's Fleet, and the Shoals that surrounded it, at the mouths of the Nile; or the state of the winds, when he engaged them off the Coast of Spain? —We are not so rash or unreasonable as to call upon a Commander in Chief to controul the winds and tides, and check the currents, like that Persian prince, who, for disobedience of orders, put Neptune in chains, "*qui vinxerat Ennosigæum;*" but we call on him for that vigilance that instantly, and, as it were, instinctively, seizes on the moment of action and enterprize; and for that prudence and prowess that converts the circumstances of winds and tides and currents to the advantage and the benefit of his country. It is readily granted, that the lives of our brave sailors, and the safety of his Majesty's ships, are not to be wantonly exposed to unnecessary danger. God forbid they should! the one is too precious and the other too valuable; but in those cases, in which necessity demands it, where the interest of the country is deeply engaged and at stake, and its welfare, nay, its very existence requires it; dangers, which lessen as they approach, must be bravely met; and difficulties, that give way to spirit and exertion, must be resolutely encountered.

Lord Gambier, however, in order to give support to his arguments on these points, relies in a great measure upon Mr. Stokes's Chart, which he thus introduces; "I have yet to call "the attention of the Court to the Chart, drawn by Lord Cochrane of the positions of the Enemy's Ships, as they lay aground "on the morning of the 12th of April, and to that position "marked upon the Chart verified by Mr. Stokes; the former "laid down from uncertain data, the latter from angles measured, and other observations made upon the spot;—the difference between the two, is too apparent to escape the notice of "the Court; and the respective merits of these Charts, will not, "I think, admit of a comparison."

But, it here happens that this famous Chart, so exultingly brought forward, is absolutely falsified by Mr. Stokes himself, who is said to have verified it, and who at the same verifies the derided Chart given in by Lord Cochrane.

By Mr. Stokes's Chart the Enemy's ships, at daylight in the morning of the 12th, are placed as follows. The Foudroyant and Cassard nearly South of Aix, and about a mile distant from it. The three decker, Tonnére and others, not named, upon the South East part of the Pallés shoal at the distance of about 2 miles and a quarter. In his Evidence Mr. Stokes says, "At daylight I observed the whole of the Enemy's ships, excepting " two of the line, on shore: four of them lay in a group, or lay " together, on the Western part of the Pallés shoal; the others " on the Eastern side of that shoal. The three decker, was " on the North West edge of the Pallés shoal with her broad- " side flanking the passage, the North West part nearest to the " deep water," (p. 147): which is *precisely as Lord Cochrane has placed them*, as will be seen by an abstract of his Lordship's plan Chart, annexed to that by Mr. Stokes. If, then, any person takes up Mr. Stokes's Chart and Mr. Stokes's Deposition, and compares the one with the other, he will immediately discover the fatal variance between them.

But what will be the feeling of the Public when they perceive a very strong probability, that this very Chart which contains the pretended positions of the Enemy's ships on the 12th, is actually a Chart of the 13th, a fact that is also proved by Mr. Stokes.

President. "I observe in the Chart I had from you, the " situation of the Ocean particularly, is not marked on the 12th; " she is marked on the 13th as advanced up the Charante."

Mr. *Stokes.* "The only ships marked in the Chart, on the " 12th, are those that are destroyed. The reason I marked her " on the 13th is, that a particular attack was made on her by " the Bombs," (p. 147.)

Yet, this Chart was to be a directory to the several witnesses who were examined, to shew, principally, that the ships of the Enemy were not within reach of our shot, on the 12th of April, as insisted on by the Chart delivered by Lord Cochrane!!

Of equal importance is the Testimony of Mr. Stokes, respecting the bearings and state of the Enemy's ships on the 12th, taken in another point of view; for Lord Cochrane's Chart will establish, at least, the prominent and most material features of it.

If, then, the Chart by Mr. Stokes is thus completely invalidated: and that of Lord Cochrane as completely authenticated; "the confined "Anchorage, the point blank shot of the Batteries, and the broad-"sides of the Enemy's ships" will vanish, like dreams that trouble the distempered mind: for it is not Lord Gambier alone, who has pinned his faith upon the credit of this Chart; but many of those Gentlemen who have been produced on his Lordship's Defence! Yet even by this Chart we might venture to say, that, except immediately upon known shoals, there was depth of water enough for the largest three decker in the Navy to have run alongside of the Cassard and Foudroyant, at any time of the tide, even in the situation in which Mr. Stokes, in direct contradiction to his own evidence, has placed them.

To give, however, every possible advantage to Lord Gambier, we will look at the evidence he has introduced upon the subject, and see how far we can cure the infirmity his Lordship has in the first instance introduced into his Chart. Mr. Fairfax, examined by his Lordship, speaks to it as follows:—

"Did you know, previous to the 12th of April, of any "anchorage above the Boyart Shoal, and near the *Pallès* Shoal, "for line of battle ships, out of range of the enemy's shells?"—"I knew of no anchorage."

"Have you acquired a knowledge of any such since?"—"I have not." (P. 142.)

"Is the space for the anchorage for large ships in Aix "Roads much confined, and the water round it shoal?"—"The space is much confined—I have not sounded myself there." (P. 140.)

"Is the navigation of Aix Roads difficult, as far as you "know?"—"Very much so."

"What is the rise and fall of the tide, as far as you know?" —"I should suppose from eighteen to twenty feet."

President. "I should think you should express from what

" *datum* you speak."—" What I speak particularly from *is* " *the night I was in Aix Roads* in the Lyra." (P. 141.)

Here it is to be remarked, that Mr. Fairfax shifted his position, in the Lyra, after the tide had made (P. 142), and weighed from the next anchorage before it had ebbed. Consequently, he was not a whole tide in any one place; and therefore could not have learnt *that night* any thing of the rise and fall he deposes to. To explain the source of his information, relative to the confined state of the anchorage, he says:—" In the first place, I went to the " NNE. of the Isle d'Aix, till I brought the enemy's line touch- " ing the Citadel. I then took the direction that they bore from " that point, and, afterwards, the direction of their line, which " was S by W. by compass. After ascertaining that, I went " towards the Boyart, in such a situation as to bring the Northern " part of the Isle d'Aix to bear East, and the Citadel ESE. by " compass. *Having the distance from the Citadel*, it then be- " came a question in trigonometry, to ascertain the distance " from the ships, and the space which they occupied; which was " three quarters of a mile, the length of the line." (P. 140.)

Here Mr. Fairfax assumes a fact which he could not ascertain, namely, the distance from the Citadel to the spot on which he stood. The current threw his vessel from one point to another, during her progress along the base line, which crossed the mouth of the Harbour of Aix, at a rate so great, as to induce him to believe by *report*, that " no ship could beat out against it:" and on being asked " by *what report?*" he answers, " by what I have " *heard* from Pilots of the *narrowness of the Channel.*" (P. 146.) There were also other requisites not within his power to command; and every nautical man, and every mathematician will say, that without the whole assemblage, it was impossible for him to have drawn his base line with accuracy; and that, if inaccurate, or not drawn with the utmost precision, mistake and confusion would be the only result. If premises be untrue, the conclusions drawn from them must, of consequence, be false; and had it been correct, a knowledge of the length of the enemy's line was no better proof that the anchorage was confined, and the water round it shoal, than the distance found between the extreme ships at Spithead would ascertain the compass of its anchorage. It will be recollected, that Mr. Fairfax evidenced, in the first instance, that he knew nothing of the anchorage, or of the depth of water there, as "he never sounded himself;" (p. 140.) that in the second instance, building the question upon such his professed ignorance of the subject, he was required, in reference to those two points, to state "*so far as he knew:*" so that he could not possibly have committed himself; and his deposition, exempt from all responsibility and liability to punishment, would have the specious appearance of delivering positive testimony in his Lordship's favour.

Here, then, is the sum total of the support that Mr. Fairfax has given to the propositions of Lord Gambier, as raised upon this spurious Chart. He knew of no anchorage, and how should he?—he never searched after it!—he never sounded himself, and yet, which must appear very extraordinary, he took upon himself to depose in the *most positive terms*, that "*the navigation was very difficult,*" (p. 141)—a circumstance that places him in a legal dilemma, of which, in all probability, he was not aware when working towards it. His trigonometrical information, by which he attempted to prove confined anchorage, is not better founded. The distance from the Citadel, which he pretends to have "ascertained," was, as seen in his testimony, a mere matter of conjecture; and the whole must be regarded, only, as the effusion of fancy, or an attempt at delusion.

Admiral Stopford, another of Lord Gambier's witnesses, to the same point, in giving his reason for recalling the Revenge, Valiant, and Theseus, says: "It was the imminent danger to which "the ships were exposed, by a longer continuance in that anchor-"age; also the *certainty* that they could not be employed with "effect in the further destruction of the enemy's ships." (p. 72.) But it is to be observed, that the Admiral went in when it was so very dark, that the enemy did not discover him; (p. 72) and that he came out again before it was light. Consequently, he could not state any facts, of his own knowledge, except that he got on shore somewhere, he did not know where, either upon a continuation of the Boyart, or a bank in the direction of that shoal.

E

(p. 72. a.) He thinks, however, that it was within less than a quarter of a mile of the part which shews itself, or is visible, at near low water. Yet, according to measurement, on Mr. Stokes's Chart, it was neither the one nor the other; but the Boyart itself! The testimony of Admiral Stopford, therefore, is of no more weight than that extracted from Mr. Fairfax; although featured very differently.

It is readily admitted, that many of the witnesses, examined on behalf of Lord Gambier, have spoken of the extreme danger and the probable loss of our ships, in passing the batteries of Aix to attack the dispersed and stranded ships of the enemy; but we venture to assert, that it is mere speculation opposed by facts, and consequently cannot be endured for a moment. Such evidence, however, grows out of, and is in unison with, his Lordship's Defence, which is for the most part mere matter of opinion, and hypothesis, uninformed by experience; and seldom extending to probability—thus—" *If* he had sent in any ships, and they " should have been necessitated to remain a whole tide in the " Roads of Aix: *if* they should have been crippled in going in: " *if* the wind, which was favourable for carrying them in, should " not have shifted, so as to bring them out again, and that even *if* " the wind were fair, and they should lose their foremasts, they " would not have been able to get the ships before the wind;" and such complexioned anticipations of dangers and their concomitant horrors. And if, upon an impartial examination of the Defence and the Evidence brought forward in support of it, the Public should find that this brief synopsis is perfectly correct; we hope and trust, that they will ever keep it in view, whilst perusing the Notes which we now offer to their judgment. It is indispensably necessary to the ends of truth and justice, and to the honour and interest of the Country.

In corroboration of what we have said, we will now shew, by the indisputable testimony of facts, that occurred in an experiment actually made, that the speculations and supposititious cases we have noticed, as put by Lord Gambier, and answered by his witnesses, were totally unfounded, idle, and visionary.

Some short time after two o'clock in the afternoon on the 12th of April, "in consequence of a signal from the Commander in "Chief to assist a ship in distress," (p. 196) the Beagle, then under weigh, stood into Aix Roads; and the Indefatigable got under weigh for the same purpose. (p. 89.) The Revenge sailed about the same time (p. 167), and was followed by the Pallas, (p. 189), and the Valiant (p. 154).—All these vessels necessarily passed the batteries of Aix, and what was the injury they sustained, and the casualties that occurred amongst the people from the point blank shot, and shells?

On board of the Revenge, the bowsprit was severely wounded; great part of the running rigging and sails cut to pieces: five planks in the quarter deck cut through, and a quarter deck beam entirely carried away, (which must have been occasioned by a falling shot) hence it is conclusive, that our vessels were beyond point blank range. A number of shot in different parts of the hull; three men killed and fifteen wounded, two of whom afterwards died, (p. 209.) "A part of the running rigging," however, was cut whilst engaged with the Aquilon and Varsovie; (p. 209) and on board the Indefatigable, "a shot passed through the main topmast, *the hole of which measured seven inches,* and wounded the main topsail yard!" (p. 89).

Lord Gambier has talked much of his zeal, and of his utmost exertions towards promoting the honour and interest of his Country: the public will judge from the Evidence immediately before them, how far the one has been manifested, and the other applied; and, under such circumstances, how far the *delay of eight hours* can possibly be justified!

With such facts before their eyes—facts proved by the testimony of the witnesses, called upon by Lord Gambier to justify his conduct against the charge of the Lords' Commissioners of the Admiralty—how could the Court-Martial listen to the *extreme,* the *terrible* dangers, which his Lordship stated would have befallen his Majesty's ships, and seamen, had he sent them into Aix roads, at the time, *the only time,* in which they could have been eminently serviceable; when the whole of the grounded ships remained in the position in which misfortune had placed them on the preceding evening?

If the vessels we have just named, and indeed all the others, for Lord Gambier says in his Defence, "not even one of the "smallest vessels employed was disabled from proceeding on any "service that might have become necessary," (p. 138,) could so easily, and with so little damage, have passed the *tremendous* batteries of Aix, at 2 o'clock in the afternoon, why could they not have performed the task at six in the morning, when the Imperieuse stated, by signal, the disabled and miserable situation of the Enemy's ships? "When the Ocean was heeling" (p. 209,) and while "the group" lay on the NW. part of the Pallés shoal, "the NW. part nearest to the deep water," (p. 147,) close to the situation in which Mr. Stokes has thought proper, on his Chart, to place the Cassard and Foudroyant, and within a cable's length of the spot on which the British ships afterwards anchored? The delay was giving the enemy so much time to retrieve their errors, and enable them to get out of our reach: nor did they neglect the advantage thus afforded; and their incessant labours, on the occasion, are deserving of the highest praise.

Exclusive, however, of the *dreadful* dangers menaced by the batteries of Aix, Lord Gambier's imagination had collected others not less *tremendous*. Two of the Enemy's line of battle ships were still at anchor, and "must," according to his Lordship's notions, and the expressed opinion of some of his witnesses, "have entirely crippled every one of our ships in their approach "through so narrow a channel;" (p. 125.) although that channel appears, even by Mr. Stokes's Chart, to be considerably more than a mile, between the fort of Aix and the Boyart. Admiral Stopford, whose ship grounded on the opposite side, states it to be a mile and an half wide: (p. 74.) and the *Neptune Françoise* two miles and a half; he, therefore, deferred sending in any force until those vessels should run away, for which purpose they only waited a favourable moment. This soon presented itself: the flood tide made; and our brave tars had the mortification to perceive them gradually gliding out of their reach. So that when our force did go in, the richest part of the spoil, which in the morning they might have secured, had escaped. What was to be apprehended from the broadsides of those ships in their confused and distracted state: with their consorts scattered on the adjacent sands, in various directions: some, to all appearance, irretrievably wrecked: some in the greatest danger of suffering the same fate: others so circumstanced that their fall into our hands was considered as unavoidable; whilst they themselves were oppressed, confused and overpowered by the melancholy prospects before them of inevitable destruction?

Were, then, those two ships, left to themselves, to hurl defiance against the British fleet? Were they thus to stand between the heroes of the ocean, and the spoils that lay at their feet? For we have before demonstrated, that little or nothing could have been done, by the batteries of Aix. Are we to suppose that under the influence of some fatal and superstitious spell, those vessels, constructed like the Trojan horse of old, "*divina Palladis arte,*" contained in their womb all the implements of death and destruction, that could intimidate and terrify men, accustomed to brave every danger on their native element, and far greater than that which haunted the imagination of the Commander in Chief.

But even if the broadsides of the *two vessels* were so formidable to the apprehension of an over-strained prudence, that they could not be attacked in the mode proposed, some other mode might have been adopted. In war much depends upon the resources of a man's own mind, and these he employs, when the pressure of the moment demands them. If then, passing through the Roads of Aix, within the range of its batteries, and of the broadsides of those ships, was a measure pregnant with too much of risque, and therefore rather too rash for execution; might not an expedient have been resorted to, that would have given abundant facilities to the undertaking, and disarmed fear of its mighty powers? To this end let us refer to the Chart, even as it has been fashioned by Mr. Stokes, and see what water is marked on the coast of Aix. We shall find, that within half point blank shot of the Citadel, there is not less than thirty feet, at dead ebb. If then, some part of our fleet had been advanced, for the purpose of battering that fortification, is it to be supposed, that so circumstanced, it would have much annoyed our vessels, had any been directed to pass it? And what would have been the opposing power, or rather, the opposing disposition of the two ships at anchor? On this point, we have the Evidence of Captain Malcolm, who was examined by the President.

Q. "You have stated, in the answer to the preceding question, " that any ships sent in, previous to the removal of the French " ships, that got off, would be liable to considerable *annoyance* " from them, as well as the Isle d'Aix:—would you then, have " sent ships in before the two ships were removed, and the *three* " *decker got off?*" (p. 210.)—*A.* "Had it appeared to me that " there was no other chance of destroying those ships, *but by* " *such an attack, I certainly think it ought to have been* " *made,*" (p. 211.)

Captain Broughton's Evidence goes more directly and decidedly to it, and will clear up every doubt that can be entertained.—Having spoken of the two French ships at anchor, and of the superior advantage that would have resulted, had two line of battle ships been sent into Aix, between 11 and 12 o'clock, instead of the time they actually did go in, he is asked, "Would not " the two ships sent in have been exposed to the fire of the two " ships that remained at anchor, the French Admiral's ship, and " the batteries of the Isle of Aix, at the same time?"—He answers, "Certainly; but I conceived they were partly *panic*-struck; " and on the appearance of a force, coming in, might have been " induced to cut their cables, and try to make their escape up " the River. (p. 221.)

Q. "In the event of their proving not to have been panic-" struck, and of their having defended themselves, aided by " the batteries on shore, are you of opinion that the British ships " must have suffered greatly on the occasion?"—*A.* "I think " they might have suffered; but that *a ship or two* might have " been placed, in my opinion, *against the Batteries on the* " *Southern part of the Isle of Aix*, so as to take off their fire, " and silence them. I mentioned to Sir Harry Neale, on board " the Caledonia, when the signal was made for all Captains in

" the morning, that I thought they were attackable: speaking " of the confused state in which the French ships appeared to " be at the time," (p. 221.)

Here, then, is a complete answer to Lord Gambier's fears and alarms: and a mode suggested which, in adoption, would have given into our possession, perhaps, the whole of the Enemy's ships; and rendered the enterprize as glorious, as the wishes of the patriot, and the enthusiasm of the public, sought for.

As Sir Harry Neale was made acquainted with Captain Broughton's sentiments, he would, of course, have communicated them to the Commander in Chief. It is strange then, that this suggestion was not attended to, the more particularly, as it must have been known, both to Lord Gambier and Sir Harry Neale, that Captain Broughton was an officer of experience; and that he possessed local knowledge of the roads and fortifications of Aix, which will be well illustrated by giving his own words in the course of his Examination.

Q. by the President. " In your services in Basque Roads, " had you any opportunity of making observations upon the " state of the enemy's fortifications on the Isle d'Aix?"—*A.* " Yes, I had.

Q. " Narrate what were those observations?—*A.* " I was on " board the Amelia when she was ordered to dislodge the ene- " my from the Boyart shoal, and being nearly within gun shot " of the Isle d'Aix, I observed the fortifications: they appeared " to me to be in a very different state to what I observed them " when serving, two or three years before, nnder Sir Richard " Keates: I thought they were repairing the works, from the " *quantity of rubbish* that was thrown up, and I counted on a " semi-circular battery, which commanded the roadsted, where " the enemy lay, between fourteen and twenty guns: I am not " positive as to the exact number—There was a small battery " lower down, nearer the sea—I do not know the exact number " of guns; there might be six or nine I suppose. What I had " before taken to be a block-house, above the semi-circular bat- " tery, seemed to have *no guns whatever*—there appeared to be " loop-holes, in the upper part, for musquetry, I suppose: it ap-

"peared to be a barrack for containing the guard. I thought, "from this observation, that the fortifications of the island, at "least in that part, were not so strong as we supposed; and I "*reported my opinion, to that effect, to Lord Gambier.*" (p. 218.)

We say that Lord Gambier must have known those facts; as we should otherwise suppose him to have been extremely deficient, "under all the circumstances of the case," in a very essential part of his duty. He had not any knowledge of the place himself: the Pilots of the whole Fleet were, almost, equally uninformed: and Admiral Stopford complains that they were extremely ignorant (p. 78,); consequently, his Lordship should have searched for information amongst the officers of the Fleet. Sir Harry Neale, however, was not permitted, when giving his Evidence, to speak to this point: and we are, therefore, left in darkness, as to the opinion he formed, or the steps he took in consequence of the conversation he held with Captain Broughton; or in relation to other matters, that came within his observation, of essential importance to the points in issue, Lord Gambier having interrupted the Court, when he was upon his examination, upon grounds, which we shall state by and by, when we come to Sir Harry Neale's testimony, that ought to have been reprobated, but in which the Court concurred.

Having spoken to two of the greater obstacles that were capable of giving the alarm to Lord Gambier's mind, and which certainly operated most powerfully with him, to forego any attempt upon the enemy's ships, on the morning of the 12th of April, we come to the lesser and last of the group. "Some of the "grounded ships were sufficiently upright, and so situated as to enable them to bring their guns to bear upon the entrance." (p. 125.)

Captain Malcolm, in answer to questions proposed by the President, relative to the three decker, says, "till noon she was "heeling considerably, and appeared to be throwing her guns "overboard; when she righted, she could have annoyed our "ships coming in." "He could not speak exactly, when she "removed from her situation, but supposed about 2 o'clock." (p. 209.) And so says Mr. Hockings, (p. 202.) Captain Malcolm does not speak of *some* of the enemy's ships; his testimony, as well as that of Mr. Stokes, is confined to *one* of them, so that Lord Gambier's fears must have deceived him, and by their multiplying powers produced many dangers from one, and to lessen that danger, we learn from Capt. Malcolm the enemy were so extremely anxious to get away, that in order to lighten their ship sufficiently for the purpose, they were busily engaged in throwing her guns overboard, and that it was only when she righted, that, " she could have *annoyed* ships coming in." And, is it reconcileable with common sense, that so circumstanced, as she is thus represented to have been, she would have been competent, or had it in her power to "annoy" any of our ships that might have moved towards her, with the very few guns she preserved, and which, according to the account given by Admiral Stopford, amounted to between twenty-six and thirty, (p. 204.)

Hence we may safely say, that she was not an object to create terror or spread alarm: and at one time she must have appeared altogether insignificant, even to his Lordship, who says, " I gave " Orders to the Etna, the only bomb present, to proceed, as " soon as the tide would permit that vessel to approach near " enough to bombard the enemy's ships.* I, at the same time, " ordered the Insolent, Conflict, and Growler gun brigs to ac- " company her." (p. 126.)

This was, according to his Lordship's statement, between nine and ten o'clock in the morning, and his Lordship shews, that the Etna passed the Imperieuse about one, and " began the attack, " some time before the Imperieuse arrived up," (p. 127.) an occurrence which, as Mr. Hockings and Mr. Stokes speak of, took place during the time that the Cassard and Foudroyant were yet at anchor, and a considerable time before the three decker got off; so that this little bomb, and her three associates smaller than her-

* We cannot imagine the object his Lordship could have had in view, in venturing to state an absurdity so manifest and glaring. The Etna drew at the very utmost no more than twelve feet, and yet Lord Gambier was obliged to defer sending her in, until there was sufficient depth of water. Had she sunk in any part of the passage, her mast heads, so deep was the water, would scarcely have been perceptible; and this fact is proved even by Mr. Stokes's chart.

F

self, had to encounter the combined destructive powers of the "point blank shot of the batteries,"—" the broadsides of the "two line of battle ships, then lying in Aix Roads," and "some "of the grounded ships, that were sufficiently upright, and so "situated, as to enable them to bring their guns to bear upon "the entrance of the inner Road of Aix." (p. 127.)

This circumstance absolutely turns the whole of his Lordship's combination of dangers into ridicule and contempt: exposed to such tremendous engines, as Lord Gambier has described them, and so terrific in aspect, as to paralize his Lordship's purpose, and hold the operations of the Fleet in check, one might have expected to learn that these devoted little vessels had been torn to atoms, and never more heard of; yet such conclusion would have proved fallacious. Captain Godfrey, who commanded the Etna, does not state, that either the Etna or her companions received any damage. He *thinks* only, that some of the enemy's shot went over them, (p. 173) and, on being asked whether they "were annoyed by shells," he says, "the shells went far over "us:" but not a mast yard, or even a rope yarn, appears to have been touched. The Imperieuse immediately followed those vessels; her injury was very trifling, and that not from the batteries; but in consequence of her engagement with the ships of the enemy, that were afterwards captured. Here, then, is the fable of the Mountain in Labour verified, and here is exhibited all the shadows of those shades of danger, that excited the dread "of the batteries of Aix, the two line of battle ships at "anchor, and some of the grounded ships, which would bring "their guns to bear on the entrance of the passage." Such are the facts of the case, and the public will judge whether every proposition, contained in the passage immediately under discussion, be not fully and completely refuted, and proved to be wholly and totally groundless.

If further demonstration were wanting, it could be found in that part of his Lordship's own Defence, in which he says: "three out of seven of the enemy's ships aground, on the Pallés, "were from their first being on shore, totally out of reach of "the guns of any ships of the Fleet, that might have been sent "in:" and, "that the other four of the eleven ships, of which

" the enemy's fleet consisted, were never in a situation to be as-" sailed." (p. 137.) Whence his Lordship would indubitably have it understood, that in delaying, from six o'clock in the morning, until past two in the afternoon, to send a proper force into Aix Roads for attacking the enemy, he could not, in the nature of things, have lost any advantage, or committed a breach of duty; and that had such force been sent in early in the morning, or even when the fleet got under weigh, no more of the enemy's ships could have been captured, than those which were afterwards actually destroyed. Yet his Lordship has an observation, in another part of his Defence, of a very different complexion; having given a state of the wind, and supposing calamities that would, in their occurrence, have prevented a retreat, out of the range of the enemy's shot and shells, he says, " Had the wind " been favourable for sailing both in and out, or even the latter, " there could have been no doubt, that the sooner the enemy's " ships were attacked the better." (p. 127.) From this observation we must conclude, that it was not the apprehension of danger from the point blank shot from the batteries: or the broadsides of the two line of battle ships at anchor: or from the guns of some of the grounded ships, (p. 134,) that terrified his Lordship's apprehensions, and over-powered all his energies; but merely the unfavourable state of the wind, which, though fair for going in, was foul for returning; and, therefore, in the event of the ships being crippled, the consequence, according to his Lordship's declared opinion, " could scarcely have been less than their utter " destruction." (p. 127.) And Admiral Stopford tells us, that he witnessed his Lordship's " impatience and disappointment, at circum-" stances not allowing him immediately to go in with the fleet." (p. 78.) All this certainly manifests much prudence and spirit; but it is unfortunately at variance with the other constituent parts of his Lordship's Defence, and with the fact, which we will demonstrate at a proper time. For the present, therefore, we shall only remark, that, accustomed as we have been, to contemplate the splendid narrations, of the daring intrepidity of our enterprising Naval Commanders, we are greatly surprised to find, that one of them could, for a moment, hesitate to attack his enemy with wind and tide, in his favour, upon the suggestion of an apprehension, that it might *possibly* be attended with great danger: because it might so happen, that his ships might be crippled; and because, in that event, they might not have a fair wind to bring them out again.

Lord Gambier submits to the Court, "Whether the idea, that "appears to have been entertained by Lord Cochrane, that a "force could have been sent in, so as to have arrived at low "water in the morning, was not in itself preposterous and im- "practicable?" (p. 125.) How far Lord Cochrane's idea was, or was not preposterous, is a point on which we will not waste an argument; but of the practicability of the measure, to which it pointed, we have undeniable proof. The Cæsar, of 80 guns, and drawing more water than any ship of the fleet, and the Theseus, of 74 guns, weighed, with nearly a corresponding tide, and sailed for the Roads of Aix. (p. 171.) It is true they both grounded: but they were got off again when the flood made; and if the Cæsar had not hugged the Boyart too close on board, to avoid the shot of the batteries, she might have continued her course in perfect safety, and anchored within a cable's length of the Pallés Shoal; that part of it described by Mr. Stokes, "the "NW. part nearest to the deep water, on which the three- "decker had by that person been grouped with other ships," (p. 147) and on the spot, whence by his chart, the Cassard and Foudroyant escaped.

To carry the matter a little further, we have, in full support of Lord Cochrane's opinion, the depositions of Captains Seymour, Newcomb, Malcolm, and Broughton, who speak in the spirit of regret, that the measure proposed by Lord Cochrane had not been adopted: although they judged the best time for the purpose would have been between 11 and 12 o'clock in the morning; instead of between five and six. (pp. 194, 200, 211, 215, and 224.)

Lord Gambier, pursuing his subject, shews, that as the flood tide made, some of the stranded vessels of the enemy, succeeded in warping off; and that the line of battle ships which were at anchor quitted their station, and sailed towards the mouth of the Charante (p. 126,), and submits to the Court, that "those "movements of the enemy were not to be prevented by any means "that he could adopt with the smallest chance of success, and "without his Majesty's ships being put to the most unwarrantable "peril;" quoting the following "emphatic" words used by Admiral Stopford: "Ours would have been all the loss, and the enemy's "all the advantage." (p. 126.)

That the movements of the enemy's ships could not have been prevented by any means that his Lordship did adopt, is lamentably evident; but that they might have been prevented, by means within his power, is equally evident. Captain Broughton, in the course of his Examination, being asked by the President: "Whether every thing was done, that could be done to effect the "destruction of the enemy's ships?" says, "I think it would "have been more advantageous, if the line of battle ships, fri- "gates, and small vessels had gone in at half flood; which I "take to be about eleven o'clock, or between eleven and twelve." (p. 220.) Captains Seymour and Malcolm express similar opinions; and Captain Newcomb coincides with both.

At the time to which Captain Broughton refers, it is in evidence that the enemy's ships, to which Lord Gambier had reference, had not moved, and were consequently assailable, if ships had been sent against them. (pp. 144, 145, 149, 150, 152, &c.) But if amidst the hypothetical confusion of "*ifs*" and "*buts*," and the calculation of *possible risk* and *conjectural disasters*, the objects of our hopes be allowed to escape, then, indeed, our means become extremely contracted, and our expectations must be at an end.

Lord Gambier knew that, during the ebb and rising tide, those ships of the enemy, that were on shore, were making exertions to warp off, with the flood; and that those which were at anchor would be prepared to cut or slip, that they might run for the mouth of the Charante. He was therefore to resolve on an immediate attack upon them, in their miserably helpless state; or give up all hope of effecting any important purpose against them. (p. 220.)

When the Fleet moved to its second position, the terror of the enemy must have been in the extreme; and their confusion, in all probability, inextricable. Had the ships, therefore, which Captain Broughton speaks of, been sent in, even at the time he has mentioned: and a demonstration made of others ready to follow them, the business would have been done, and the glory of the day rendered complete. Nor is this reasoning mentioned unadvisedly; it arises out of the evidence delivered (p. 50) by Captain Malcolm and others, who say the Ocean was heeling till about noon; and that the crew appeared to be throwing her guns overboard. (p. 209.) Lord Cochrane says, the Ocean and two other ships, seemed to have their yards locked together. Mr. Fairfax, to every intent and purpose, supports his Lordship, although evidently contrary to his disposition. (p. 144.) Mr. Stokes says, that "four of the enemy were lying in a groupe, or "lay together;" (p. 147) and Captain Broughton notices the two ships at anchor (and which were assuredly much better situated than their consorts on shore, as they had not received any manner of damage) as having been partly panic struck. We have also Mr. Stokes's famous Chart: and if we consider the situation of the enemy's ships, scattered on the sands in various directions, and given up to dismay, horror, and despair, could any man, witnessing such a scene, have required further or other demonstration to convince him of their utter incapability, in every respect, to defend themselves against an adversary, flushed with the havoc he had made, and the consternation he had spread: fresh in vigour, and in powers: resolutely determined on their annihilation; and with ample facilities to insure success.

But if a people, so deplorably circumstanced, do not perceive any preparations making by their adversary, to take an advantage of their situation, they will naturally imagine that he is embarrassed also, and from some unknown cause controlled and restrained in his operations; they will of course dismiss their alarms and apprehensions as groundless, and strain every nerve to recover, as far as possible, from their disaster and disgrace.

We will examine how far the delay, permitted by Lord Gambier, proves the truth of our reasoning. Several of the crew of the stranded vessels finding, contrary to their expectation, that the blow they had received was not promptly followed up: roused themselves from the panic into which they had sunk; and having a little recovered their senses, called in every resource to their aid that their situation required, and ultimately succeeded in warping their ships into deep water. And thus all was lost!

That Lord Gambier had a right to consult his own judgment, and act as it might dictate, is readily granted; but here are facts, under his own eye, that spoke to his judgment in the strongest and most favourable terms, and demanded, not the forebodings of ills, that were as likely never to exist, as ever to be realized: not when the wind which blew towards the object, would also blow from it; but the most zealous exertions of all his powers; and his language on the occasion should have been—"There is "the enemy, and we must destroy them: this your King and "your own honour require; and England expects that every "man will do his duty." If our gallant Tars could have required a stimulus, such language, applied upon an occasion so urgent, would have been more than sufficient; but they require no spur to exertion—let them but behold their enemy, and the genuine ardour of their character, at once, bursts forth; and, regardless of dangers but to despise them, they rush forward with an impetuosity not to be resisted, and with a firmness not to be shaken! Such their towering spirit, their prowess and determined bravery, Lord Cochrane knows how to value, and revere; and therefore, when the Vote of Thanks was proposed, he objected only "so far as it should apply to the Commander in Chief." His feelings revolted at the idea of bestowing that honourable reward upon others, which was due only to distinguished and exalted merit; and which ceases to be a proud mark of the highest distinction, the moment it is indiscriminately conferred. Policy, sinister policy, which in States, when it wants to make the crooked paths of honour straight, generally addresses men on the side of their virtues (that side, on which weak men are mostly ruined), here calls in to its aid our Sons of the Ocean, and makes them believe, that their fame was equally depreciated with that of the Commander in Chief; and that, consequently, they were in honour bound to give to him every support. To this stratagem may be assigned his Lordship's expression, "I had to adopt this mea-

"sure, or, by a tacit concurrence in the insinuations thrown out "against me by Lord Cochrane, have compromised, not only "my own honour; but also that of the brave Officers and Men "serving under my command." (p. 106.)

His Lordship has often spoken of "insinuation:" this passage is the best definition of the word, and embraces all its illiberality. It represents a Sailor to his brethren in arms, in the odious and equally false colourings of having endeavoured, by whispers, to detract from their merits, and under-rate their services to the Country: that "like a worm in the bud," he had secretly preyed upon their worth; and that his object was, by such means, to deprive them of those rising honours which their Country was ready to confer upon them.

Lord Gambier has so many obstacles and dangers in his vision, that if one had the appearance of not being sufficiently strong to justify the delay, he allowed to take place, between the morning when, it is stated, the ships ought to have gone into the inner road of Aix, and the afternoon, when some of them did proceed thither; that in shewing the errors of his Lordship's imagination, it is difficult to avoid confusion, whilst endeavouring to observe the necessary perspicuity in arranging them. His Lordship says, "Had I acted upon Lord Cochrane's signal, and sent in at that "time half the Fleet, he calculated upon the loss of three or "four of his Majesty's line of battle ships; and that, if in de-"fiance of the obstruction of the other ships of the enemy, I "had sent in a force before *the three ships* had warped off the "Pallés Shoal, it is a positive fact, that it would not have ad-"vanced to the attack of those ships, on account of the shoal "water." (p. 127.)

If Lord Cochrane really made the declaration here given to him, it is totally impossible to connect it with any motive whatever; and as his Lordship does not appear to act, at any time without a motive, there is certainly something of context wanting to entitle it to any degree of credit. Perhaps, this something might have been forgotten in the hurried conversation in which the declaration was made, that is, if it ever was made. Every one, acquainted with the affairs of life and in the habit of mixing in society, is well aware, that misconception of expressions frequently occurs; and that memory is very unfaithful in a variety of instances: —that taking the text without the context, produces a meaning never intended to be conveyed: making that which was altogether inoffensive, appear to be highly blameable, nay, absolutely criminal both in its nature and tendency; and that we should, therefore, not deal either candidly or fairly towards Lord Cochrane, were we to receive this detached sentence, as it stands, without knowing what preceded or followed it.

Mr. Wilkinson, Lord Gambier's Secretary, who seems to have been with his Lordship at those times, when Lord Cochrane held any conversation with him, does not appear to have heard a syllable on the subject: and Sir Harry Neale, the Captain of the fleet, and first Captain of the Caledonia, Lord Gambier's own ship, was not even asked a question, that at all connected with it; and as these, or one of these gentlemen, must have known or heard of it, had it taken place, we are inclined to imagine that his Lordship may have been mistaken. But, in whatever way Lord Cochrane might have delivered an opinion to Lord Gambier, it cannot be brought forward to support errors, or oppose established facts; and notwithstanding his Lordship's assertion to the contrary, we have the sanction of Evidence, submitted to the Court, by an Officer of acknowledged merit, who was upon the spot, and who possessed a previous and tolerably intimate acquaintance with it, that a force might not only have been sent in, so as to have advanced to the attack of the enemy's ships; but that even such force ought to have been sent in for that purpose. Captain Broughton, asked by Lord Gambier, "Whether every thing was not "done, that could be done, to effect the destruction of the "enemy?" answers, "I think it would have been more advan-"tageous, if the line of battle ships, frigates, and small vessels "had gone in at half flood, which I take to have been about "11 o'clock." "There were nine sail on shore with the frigates; "the Rear Admiral and Commodore remained at their ancho-"rage." (P. 220.) And Captain Malcolm, after a very extraordinary Examination, such as, perhaps, never appeared in the proceedings of any Court, and such as we sincerely hope and trust we shall never again witness, says, "Had it appeared to me, that "there was no other chance of destroying those, but by such "an attack; I certainly think it ought to have been made." (P. 221). Again, upon the following Question being proposed to him, and which, when the Answer he had just given be considered, must appear rather more than extraordinary, he strengthens and confirms that opinion.

Q. "Upon the whole, are you of opinion, that the French "ships, which got ashore on the Pallés, on the night of the 11th "April, any more of them could have been destroyed, than were "destroyed, had the ships been earlier sent in, on the 12th of "April, to attack them?"—*A.* "Had they been attacked by the "British ships, in my opinion, they could not have been warped "off from the shore, as it was necessary so to do, to lay out "anchors to heave them off." (P. 211).

Much has been said of the two ships, that were at anchor. Upon that head, Captain Malcolm is interrogated at considerable length, and shews, that if our ships had not been sent earlier, they, certainly, should have gone in, as soon as those ships quitted their position. "The moment that those two ships quitted "their defensive position, the risk was then small, of sending "ships; and, of course, I would have sent them in instantly." (P. 212). Now, according to Mr. Stokes and Mr. Hockings, who noted the time by their watches, the one of those ships made sail at 10 o'clock, and the other at 20 minutes past one. Let us, then, examine what steps were taken upon the spur of the important moment; Did Lord Gambier, in his ardour for the service, immediately dispatch a force to attack the fugitives, and the ships that remained ashore? Did he give any proof of that zeal and exertion, of which he boasts so loudly and so repeatedly? Did he, in any way, establish those merits, which were, according to his account, to have been honoured with "the Thanks of both Houses of Parliament," and which, with more of rancour than propriety, he alludes to in his petulant Letter to Mr. Wellesley Pole? (P. 13).

Captain Rodd says, "The signal was made, by the Com- "mander in Chief, about two," (p. 89), and others state it to have been at a later period, to weigh; that he weighed shortly afterwards; that he anchored, about half an hour after three o'clock, within the distance of conversation with the Imperieuse, and commenced a fire upon the Calcutta, (p. 89). Captain Bligh weighed, at half past two, in company with the Revenge, (p. 154), at which time, the Imperieuse, even by Lord Gambier's own account, had actually commenced action with the enemy, at a distance (as may be seen, by looking into Mr. Stokes's Chart) of, not less than five miles from both the Valiant and Revenge.

Hence we have it manifested to us, that his Lordship allowed an hour and a half to elapse, after the Cassard and Foudroyant sailed, without a single step, or the least exertion, to enter the inner Roads, by any of our ships; although every moment was precious, and required the most prompt attention. Such is the evidence of the merits, he has so frequently spoken of, in the course of the Minutes of his Court Martial: and of the zeal, judgment, ability, and anxious attention to the welfare of his Majesty's service, for which that Court have honoured him with the highest encomiums; and upon which, in fact, they acquitted him!

The facts adduced, and there are others yet stronger and, perhaps, still more in point, prove the fallacy of his Lordship's plea of Shoal Water; nay, the Chart, upon which his Lordship has so much relied, shows a channel a mile in width, with from thirty to seventy feet water at dead ebb: without a single shoal to interrupt any ships, that might have been sent in, until they should have ranged alongside of the two ships, that remained at anchor, and within two cables length of the three decker and the groupe, where they would have had sufficient water, and been in a great measure, secure from the shot of Aix. The batteries would scarcely have ever fired at our ships, through the certainty of frequently striking their own; and ours might have fired upon the ships aground, which they would have captured or destroyed.

We would earnestly press a mature deliberation, and the fullest consideration of the several points we have embraced, and then let the judgment decide; whether Lord Gambier was only deterred, as he has declared, by the dangers he apprehended, from sending in a proper force, against the enemy; or whether, upon observing the first signal, made by Lord Cochrane, on the morning of the 12th, he did not disapprove of the measure, to which it called his attention, and determine never to adopt it. Indeed, we will prove the latter to have been the correct proposition: that Lord Gambier never intended to send any force into the inner Roads; and that, on being informed that several of the enemy's ships were on shore, he expressed himself satisfied, that the fleet, under his command, had done all that he wished: all that he could possibly have required; and much more than could have been expected.

We will also prove, from something more than the best circumstantial Evidence, that had not Lord Cochrane acted upon an extreme extension of the spirit of his orders, even after the departure of the Cassard, Foudroyant, and Ocean; the ships that were ordered, at two o'clock, and subsequently, to go in to the attack, the prostrate enemy, would not have proceeded. Lord Cochrane saw several of the enemy's line of battle ships warping off, and others making every preparation to follow them. He contemplated the scene, with the utmost distress, as appears from the account he gives, in the Evidence he has delivered; and, as there was not any movement, in our fleet, to indicate any intention of an adequate force being sent in, to oppose their progress, he imagined all the hopes he had raised of honourable and glorious achievement were about to be blasted; and, animated, in common with others of his profession, by that irresistible impulse which leads to arduous enterprise, rushed forward to the attack. What will the friends of Lord Gambier say, to this assemblage of circumstances, that bears so severely upon his conduct: and what will be the sentiments of the public? Will they deem such conduct deserving of the high applause, expressed of it, by his Lordship's Court Martial: who have decided upon that conduct, and proclaimed it to the world, as worthy the adoption of others: a pole star, a land-mark, for future Commanders in Chief to steer by; a monitor to direct and govern their actions! With such proofs against him, what will they think of his Lordship's attempt at extenuating these omissions, by calling their attention to trifles.

Of what consequence is it to the public, whether the Imperieuse did, or did not, go in with the Etna bomb, to the attack of the enemy; and, if strictly correct, in point of fact, whether it was before, or, half an hour after the Etna had proceeded, that the Imperieuse and Beagle went in? It is proved, that the Imperieuse did go in, and had begun the attack, some time before Lord Gambier ordered in the force, which afterwards joined in the attack, and which ought to have been dispatched, many hours earlier. Of as little consequence is the time, when Captain Bligh received his Lordship's directions, to proceed into the inner Roads of Aix, as that officer did not carry those directions into effect until past two o'clock; and it was then, and not till then, that the signal was made, by the Caledonia, for the Valiant to go in; and not, even then, to attack the enemy; but to assist a ship in distress, (Lord Cochrane having made a signal, that the enemy was superior to the chase), although, from the confusion, with which the circumstance is entangled, it might be imagined, that these directions were given, long before they were executed. Every man in the fleet was, beyond any doubt, anxious enough to proceed against the enemy; they lamented only, that they were not permitted to do so. Obedience would have joined hand in hand, with any orders to that end; there would have been no occasion for repeating them.

Lord Gambier, speaking of the three of the enemy's ships, that were destroyed by ours, about five o'clock in the afternoon, says, "a short time after the Tonnére was set on fire by the "enemy." (P. 5). "This ship is admitted, by the Evidence of "Lord Cochrane, to have been out of reach of our fire; and it is "a notorious fact, that the three decker and the other two ships "that got afloat, had been aground at some distance beyond "the Tonnére," (p. 128). Which, taking the whole as correct in all its parts, merely shews what might have been performed, by what had actually been accomplished; and the burning of the Tonnére, by the enemy is the very strongest evidence of the despair, distraction and horror, into which they had been plunged, on seeing, that something, in the shape of a serious attack upon them, was at last commenced. It is at the same time a death blow, to the justification of the delay, which Lord Gambier acknowledges to have taken place. (P. 106).

Such are the advantages that his Lordship derives, from the introduction, of such occurrences, into his Defence. Nor is his Lordship's exultation, on Lord Cochrane's statement, relative to the position of the Tonnére, more happily conceived; as it is a notorious fact: "that although the three decker, and the other two "ships, that got afloat, had again grounded, at some distance, be-"yond the Tonnére; yet they would all have been within reach "of our ships, had they been sent in, between eleven and twelve "o'clock, in the forenoon."

Captains Seymour, Malcolm, Broughton, and Newcomb have distinctly deposed, and Lord Gambier has stated himself, that some of the grounded ships would have annoyed our ships, had they been sent in; particularly the Ocean, which lay with her broadside flanking the passage, and, according to Mr. Stokes, in a groupe with others, precisely in the same situation, as laid down in Lord Cochrane's Chart, delivered to the Court-Martial. "At day light," says Mr. Stokes, "I perceived the whole "of the Enemy's ships, excepting two of the line, on shore; some "of them lay in a groupe, or lay together, on the Western part "of the Pallés shoal. The three decker was on the North West "edge of the Pallés shoal, with her broadside flanking the pas-"sage; the North West part, nearest the deep water," (p. 147.) And, by a reference to the Chart, it will be perceived, that the Western part of the Pallés shoal, and the NW. edge of it, "flanking the passage and nearest to the deep water," is within a cable's length of the ground, that our ships afterwards took up.

Lord Gambier must have conceived, that whenever he could state a plausible argument to justify delay; the precise point of time, with which it connected, would not be thought of; and, therefore, in one part of his Defence, to justify delay, he stated the Ocean, and other ships aground, as sufficiently upright, and so situated, as to enable them to bring their guns to bear on the entrance, (p. 125. 134.) In another part of it, when desirous of shewing, that no material consequence could have resulted from that delay, he attempts to shew, that had our ships been sent in earlier, than they were; those of the Enemy were not within our reach (pp. 128. 137,): carefully keeping out of sight the fact, that those ships had moved from the position, in which they were completely assailable; and that they reached the distance, in which they were no longer so fully within our power, in consequence of the delay, on the part of his Lordship, which the circumstance of that distance has been brought forward to justify, or palliate.

Hence it is also conclusive, that the four ships destroyed, were not, as Lord Gambier has asserted, "the only ships assailable "at the time the signal was made," if his Lordship means the signal from the Imperieuse, at between 5 and 6 o'clock, in the morning: but if he alludes to the signal for assistance he may be nearer accuracy, though, even then, far from being correct; and he will, even then, have to assign some other reasons, than those which he has advanced, for permitting those ships to remove so far from his reach; possessing, as he certainly did, the most ample means for preventing it.

With all these facts and circumstances, pressing upon his conviction, how could his Lordship venture to assert, so positively, in the face of his country and the world, that "the destruction of "the Calcutta, the Ville de Varsovie, and the Aquilon, would "not have been effected, if he had not delayed the attack, until "the time he did," (128.) Such an assertion is more bold than prudent, and argues more of authority and power than fortitude and innocence. Language more mild, and less declamatory, would have been better adapted to the situation, in which he stood.

To proceed; if four, out of seven, of the Enemy's ships, had been destroyed, and the other three of the seven, first on shore, were never in a situation to be assailed, a circumstance offered by his Lordship in two different parts of the Defence, (pp. 125. 137): where was the object, that could have induced him to send in "Rear Admiral Stopford, in the Cæsar with the Theseus?" How was the success, that was acquired, to have been followed up? Against what object was the attack to be directed? Did the shoals vanish: the water become deeper; and the batteries, of Aix, lose all their powers between 5—48 in the morning, and six o'clock in the afternoon of the 12th? If those ships, and some others, had been sent in, even at the time pointed to by Captains Seymour, Malcolm, Broughton, and Newcomb: that is, between eleven and twelve o'clock, in the morning: and if the frigates, which were ordered, at between two and three o'clock, had been sent in at that time; a brilliant advantage might indeed have been obtained, that would have enriched the page of our Naval History. But sending them in, when the enemy had, according to his Lordship's own declarations, fled beyond our reach, was sending them in to be exposed to the remarks of the garrison of Aix; and it is natural to suppose, those would not be of the mildest, or most liberal description. We will leave them with a single observation, that it was sending them in, not to follow up our successes, but to acquire disgrace, and become objects of sarcasm, and contempt.

It might appear extraordinary, that Lord Gambier should have introduced the story, of the Rear Admiral's expedition; but his Lordship was consistent with himself, and imagined it would, in the way he should manage it, work wonders in his favour. In describing the consequences that followed, he says, "scarcely had "the Cæsar reached Aix roads, before she grounded, and lay in "a perilous situation, exposed also to the point blank shot of the "batteries," (p. 128.) His Lordship's object, then, is here explained. It was to prove, that his hypothesis, of shoals and point blank shot, was tolerably well founded; but its error has already been detected, when we shewed, that at the time the two line of battle ships went in, a most improper time in the evening, when it was dark: (p. 81,) with a pilot ignorant of the navigation; and when the state of the tide, if that was of any consequence, was nearly low water: that the Rear Admiral edged too closely upon the Boyart: that he was not within point blank shot: (p. 74), on the contrary, he was scarcely within the range of random; and, that the only shot, which reached him, must have been totally spent, as the following examination proves.

Q. "Did the shot pass far?"—*A.* "The shot from the Isle of Aix passed over the ship, not FAR."

Those who have been amongst point blank shot, must know, that they will fly, as great a distance beyond that range, as they make in reaching it. The Rear Admiral says, it did not pass far over the ship, and as this was in the dark, it must, indeed, have fallen very close, for him to have seen it. It was fortunate, for Lord Gambier, that the Rear Admiral happened to be on the watch, at the lucky moment, or he would not have had it in his power to say, whether the spot, on which he somehow grounded, was at all within the reach of the batteries of Aix, by any kind of range; as he says, only one shot passed in that direction.

Small, as is the praise due to Lord Gambier, for his zeal in sending in the Cæsar and Theseus, at night "to follow up our success," when, as he himself has insisted, there was not an object within their reach, that little will become still less, when it shall be proved, that his Lordship, did not order those ships in, to the intent that he has asserted; that he did not send them in with a view to follow up our successes; but with a view totally different.

Captain Beresford, who commanded the Theseus, the only witness examined to the point, says: "The Theseus's signal was " made, about five o'clock, to proceed into Aix Roads, and assist " ships in distress; on which we instantly sailed;" (p. 161) and Captain Beresford is supported, by the testimony of Captain Rodd, and by Captain Newcomb (p. 196). This was following up the signal, made by the Imperieuse!! (p. 196). Yet, though late, it was a proper measure; but it certainly had no reference to any new enterprise, against the enemy, or, in his Lordship's words, " to follow up our success, by an attack upon the *five* ships that " had escaped," which, in another part of his Defence, his Lordship has declared " were never within reach of the guns, of " any ships of the Fleet;" and " were never in a situation to be " assailed, after the fire-ships had failed, in their main object." (P. 137.) In this way, his Lordship has constantly attempted to defend himself, in the expectation, that all his statements would be received, as he ventured them, without investigation: that plausibilities would be accepted, as indisputable facts; and that sophistry would supply the place of candid reasoning and solid

H

argument. And thus has his Lordship, constantly laid himself open to detection and refutation.

Why Admiral Stopford should have retreated, so precipitately, as he did: or how he merited the compliment bestowed upon him, on the occasion, by his Lordship, who says, "He very judi-"ciously, before day-light, on the 13th, availed himself of a "providential shift of wind?" is a question with which we shall not interfere. He went in, when it was so dark, that the enemy could not see him, and returned again, to the Fleet, about four o'clock in the morning, before it was day-light: carrying with him, not only the ships of the line, but all the frigates also, that saw, or understood his night-signals. It was a singular mode of making discoveries, as to the state and situation of the enemy; a very singular mode of following up our successes; and the whole constituted very singular merit, to challenge unqualified praise!

Having followed his Lordship, through some of the mazes of that part of his Defence, which was to prove his four propositions, we come to a passage, which his Lordship calls, an addition to such proof. "In addition," says his Lordship, "to the in-"contestible proofs, already advanced, of the impracticability of "effecting, any farther destruction of the enemy's fleet, I will "advert to the high professional character of Rear Admiral "Stopford, and Captains Beresford, Bligh, and Kerr, who can-"not, for an instant, be supposed likely to omit any circumstance, "likely to effect the object, for which they were sent, by me, into "Aix Roads; and I am morally certain that they did not with-"draw their ships, until it was wholly impracticable to annoy the "enemy farther." (P. 129.)

His Lordship could not have appealed to better authority, than to men, of high professional character, to extricate him from the difficulties, in which, he must have been sensible, he had entangled himself. Unfortunately, however, Admiral Stopford and Captain Beresford, could not have known any more on the subject of Aix, than his Lordship had acquired, on board the Caledonia; they lay in these Roads, about eight or nine hours of darkness, and, therefore, whatever might have been his object, or what the objects were, that surrounded him, he could neither understand nor discern. In illustration of this fact, we have his own words: " Before I went in, and in going in, I observed the enemy's ships " that had not struck, had gone so near to the batteries, of the " Isle d'Aix, that, both with respect to the navigation, and the " exposure from the batteries, the ships could not have been " employed, with effect, without imminent risk of their safety." (P. 72.)

The truth is, that no such ships, of the enemy were, at the time, to which the Rear Admiral refers, or at any other, in the situation he mentions. He saw them, as they must have appeared, when viewed from the Fleet, over the Island of Aix. At that time, every one of them had advanced, from the batteries of Aix, towards the Charante.—Such was the confused appearance of things, to the mind of the Rear Admiral; and, of course, he was ill calculated to report, whether the enemy could, or could not, have been any further annoyed.

The other two had certainly a more favourable opportunity; they went in, about three o'clock, and had the advantage, of a few hours, of day-light; but then, they were, as they have shewn, in their depositions, too busily occupied, in the management of their own ships, to have much time, for observing distant objects. Captain Bligh, indeed, shews, that at five o'clock, in the evening, the Ocean and Foudroyant were both "annoyable," as he was preparing to attack them (p. 155) by fire-ships; but that they could not be got ready, until half past eleven o'clock: when it was discovered, that two lines of the enemy's boats, were moored across the stern of the Ocean; and that there were, likewise, boats in advance. It is rather surprising, that Captain Bligh is the only witness, who speaks to that point.

Captain Kerr says, that "three of the enemy's ships, that were " on shore, and afterwards got off, were not in a situation, at any " time, to be attacked by us;" (p. 167) and " that no more of " the enemy's ships could have been destroyed." (p. 168.) These gentlemen are, certainly, at variance with each other; but

Captain Kerr has said, that his mind was too much occupied with other subjects. On being asked, "Did you observe the "state of the fortifications of Aix?" he answers, "No, I did "not; the situation of the Revenge was so critical, that I was "otherwise taken up." (p. 169) And if he could not disengage his mind from his own ship, so as to observe the state of those fortifications, that were pouring their fire upon him: as he was placed, according to Captain Bligh, between the fortifications and our frigates, "and appeared to him, to draw off their fire to "himself;" (p. 156.) it is to be presumed, that he could not make those remarks, that were necessary to inform his judgment, upon the state of the enemy, and whether they were, or were not, assailable; or whether an attack on them, would, or would not, be attended with great, or any, risk. Of Captain Beresford's testimony, nothing can be said; because he has not said any thing himself, to the point before us.

Such is the feeble support, Lord Gambier has derived, in this instance, from the high professional characters, to which he has appealed. The only one of the party, that gives any thing like a professional reason, for withdrawing our ships, on the "moral certainty," that it was wholly impracticable, to annoy the enemy any farther, is Captain Bligh; and the reason he gives is a very curious one. "As the wind continued to blow, directly out, at four "o'clock in the morning, I judged the farther attempt impracticable; and, *at day-light*, I weighed, in obedience of a signal "from Admiral Stopford," (which was a night signal,) "and proceeded to Basque Roads." (p. 155.) How far common sense will endure such a reason, or how the Court could have received it, as such, are questions, which we shall not take upon ourselves to solve. The wind seems to have been a grand auxiliary: called in to the aid of all parties, and by all parties abused; but, in the present case, it seems to have been an ill-wind—in the strictest sense of the old proverb.

To prop up this miserable fabric, as if aware of its rotten foundation, Lord Gambier directs his attention towards Lord Cochrane, and hopes to derive some assistance from his Lordship's conduct; but he proceeds, not in an "open" and "direct" manner, but by suggestions and insinuations. He says, "Lord "Cochrane *remained* in the Road of Aix, during the 13th and "14th, accompanied by the Pallas, sloops, and gun-brigs; but "nothing was attempted by those two frigates." (p. 129.) The fairness of the comparison, between the force that remained, under Lord Cochrane, and that which was with Admiral Stopford, the former consisting of two frigates and a few small vessels, and the latter, had embracing those, also two ships of the line, and half a dozen of frigates, will not be much to Lord Gambier's credit, even had the Imperieuse not been occupied, as she really was, during the whole of the 13th, in repairing the damages received, (Ap. 1, 2, 3.) we leave to the judgment of those, who weigh every thing candidly, and decide impartially. If, however, any conclusion should appear, deducible from such premises, to furnish something like the shadow of evidence, in favour of Lord Gambier's assertion, as to the impracticability of annoying the enemy any further, provided a proper force had been applied, and the necessary orders issued for the purpose, his Lordship's public Letter, to the Admiralty, would demonstrate its futility. "On the following day, the "13th, the Rear Admiral perceiving, that nothing could be further effected, by the line of battle ships: and being satisfied, "that the remaining part of the service, could be performed only, "by frigates and smaller vessels; he, *most wisely*, took the advantage of a providential shift of wind, and returned, with the "line of battle ships, to Basque Roads." (p. 10.) Lord Gambier should also have stated, as the fact really was, that the Rear Admiral, not only carried out the line of battle ships, but the frigates also (p. 106), except the Imperieuse and Pallas. Again, "On the 14th, at day-light in the morning, I observed three or "four, of the enemy's ships, still apparently aground, at the mouth "of the river; I ordered Captain Woolf, of the Eagle, to relieve Lord Cochrane, in command of the smaller vessels, advanced; and endeavour to destroy any of the enemy's ships "which were assailable." (p. 10, a.)—It is worthy of notice, that this passage is contained in his Lordship's letter, of the 10th May, after his arrival in town, when his Lordship, doubtlessly, obtained privately, the information, he soon afterwards received publicly—that Lord Cochrane had determined to oppose the Vote of Thanks, intended to be brought forward in Parliament, so far as it should apply to the Commander in Chief; but, in Lord Gambier's former letter, on the 14th, when every hope was on the wing, no mention, whatever, is made of those four of the enemy's ships, or of Captain Woolfe's having been, in consequence, sent in to relieve Lord Cochrane, but in the postscript to that letter is the following notification: " P. S. This morning, three of the enemy's line of battle ships, are observed to be still on shore, under " Fourras." There is here, certainly, a confusion of dates, and if the letter addressed, by his Lordship, to Lord Cochrane, be referred to, on the subject of Captain Woolfe's being sent in, to relieve his Lordship (p. 54), and the deposition of Mr. Hockings (p. 175), and of Sir Harry Neale (p. 185), upon the same subject, be also considered, the confusion will be increased, each differing with the other, on the same substantive fact.

To continue the course of evidence, in refutation of Lord Gambier's statement, it will appear, from his Lordship's words, that one of the enemy's ships, and that the only one, that remained still on shore, was assailable, even at a distance of nine days afterwards. " I gave," he says, " directions to Captain " Woolfe, to put two of the Aigle's 18 pound-long guns, into " each of the four gun-brigs; and use every means in his power, " to drive the enemy out of the ship, near Fourras, and attempt " to set her on fire."

Lord Gambier has to reconcile such contradictions, inconsistencies, and absurdities, into which he has, perhaps, been led by his too eager advisers, in their zeal to criminate a character, which malice prompted them to persecute; and to panegyrise others, whom policy instructed them to draw to their interest. They should have known, that their first object, was to arrange and marshal facts, and to produce such evidence, in support of them, as could justify a conduct, that had been impeached, not by any individual, but by a body of men, composing a part of his Majesty's Government; for it is idle to insinuate, as Lord Gambier has frequently done, that the charge preferred against him, was at the instance of Lord Cochrane solely, because, as a Member of Parliament, he had signified an intention of objecting to the Thanks of Parliament, so far as they should apply to Lord Gambier.

Lord Gambier, however, insists, that Lord Cochrane went further, on that point, and absolutely supplied their Lordships with materials for the Charge, that had been exhibited against him, in a letter, which Lord Cochrane, afterwards, addressed to the Lords Commissioners of the Admiralty: but this insinuation, is as unfounded, as many others; and this we shall endeavour to substantiate, by the following statement of facts.

Upon an application made to Lord Cochrane, by their Lordships, through their Secretary, for "the grounds, upon which his "Lordship objected to the Vote of Thanks," he answered, that, "the Log, and Signal Log-books, of the Fleet, at the period "alluded to, contained the particulars of the late service, in "Basque Roads, and furnished premises, whence accurate con-"clusions might be drawn." (p. 12.) And if the whole of his letter be perused by any one, who is not obstinately pre-determined, to affix a construction upon it, contrary to its true import; it will appear to be a determined evasion of the question put to him, and a disposition to evidence aversion, in any way whatever, to interfere with Lord Gambier, unless forced to the measure, by an attempt, in the House of Commons, to obtain a Vote of Thanks, to his Lordship; and, in the course of his examination, adverting to the letter from the Lords of the Admiralty, he says, "I considered the affair in Basque Roads, in every respect, "as passed; and, whatever my opinion might have been, inca-"pable of a remedy." (p. 56.) But what does the Charge itself say; does it appear, from that document, that Lord Cochrane had been, in any way, instrumental in bringing it forward, or furnishing materials for forming it? No; it speaks distinctly, to the understanding of the world, that the Lords Commissioners, having been applied to, by Lord Gambier, for an enquiry into his Conduct, as Commander in Chief of the Channel Fleet, in Basque Roads: had, in compliance with their Lordship's request, considered it their duty, to make some enquiries, respecting that conduct; and the result, of such enquiry stands, upon the face of the charge, thus: "And whereas, by the Log book and Minutes of "Signals, of the Caledonia, Imperieuse, and other ships, em-"ployed on that service, it appears to us, that the said Admiral "Lord Gambier, on the 12th of the said month, of April, the "enemy's ships being then on shore, and the signal having been "made. that they could be destroyed, did, for a considerable "time, neglect, or delay, taking effectual means, for destroying "them." (p. 2.)

In further illustration of Lord Cochrane's sentiments, respecting the manner, in which the First Lord of the Admiralty had acted upon the expression, that had fallen from him, when speaking in the language, of a Member of Parliament, upon a parliamentary subject, and that he had not the most distant intention of pressing any Charge against Lord Gambier, or giving any grounds, on which to rest any such Charge, we will turn to his Lordship's Examination. In order to assist his memory, he had recourse to some memoranda, which he held in his hand; these were objected to, and Admiral Young commented upon them, with severity, in consequence of the correspondence, that had taken place between his Lordship, and the Lords of the Admiralty, a copy of which correspondence, although not connected with the Charge, had been laid before the Court, by Lord Gambier, who had received it from their Lordships. Admiral Young was followed by Admiral Stanhope, who observed, "that Lord Coch-"rane, in answer to their Lordships' Letter, did nothing, but "refer them, to the Log books of the Fleet; and that, after-"wards, his Lordship, having noticed, that a Court-Martial was "to take place, judged proper to commit to paper, such things as "he thought right to state, and wished to have them introduced; "which appeared to him, under any circumstances, improper; but, "more especially when coupled with that Letter." Lord Coch-rane replied: "The Lords of the Admiralty did, what I consi-"dered, a very improper thing: they questioned me, as to my "conduct in Parliament; and I thought that Letter, a very proper "answer, to their Letter, on the subject," (p. 41.) which must be perfectly satisfactory to any unprejudiced man, that, so far from intending to make any accusation against Lord Gambier, he manifested, even a degree of honest indignation in his answer, to the Letter, of the Lords of the Admiralty, which in appearance sought to obtain it.

The impression made upon Admiral Young, and Admiral Stanhope's mind, by this correspondence, does not admit of a doubt; and the effect it produced on the mind of others, is equally clear. The introduction of it, therefore, is matter of regret; and it is to be hoped that such proceedings will not occur a second time. If such extraneous matters were to influence the opinion of the Judges, on the trial of any cause that might come before them, a colouring might be given to it, not exactly compatible with the strict principles of that equity and justice, which alone should govern their proceedings.

Possibly, the Lords of the Admiralty were justified, in making Lord Gambier acquainted with a Correspondence, which they had commenced, and were carrying on with Lord Cochrane, in reference to a point of, no trivial, national importance, without giving to his Lordship the least intimation, that they were so doing: whilst calling upon him, by Letter, for a full statement of the grounds, on which he had objected to the Vote of Thanks, (p. 11.) stating to Lord Gambier the substance of that Letter; and, at the same time, promising him a copy of it, together with the answer of Lord Cochrane, without delay. If, when the cause be considered, the Lords of the Admiralty were actually justified in the measure, and in the full extent to which they pursued it, of which the public will judge; still we must be of opinion, that it ought not to have made a part of the Minutes of the Court-Martial, where it could tend only, to create an unmerited prejudice against Lord Cochrane, over whom Lord Gambier had all the advantage, he could possibly have wished, and we have seen how he employed it.

Passing over those parts of Lord Gambier's Defence, which, however much they may speak, of the trust reposed in him, by the Lords Commissioners, and the manner in which he discharged it, have no relation with the operations in Basque Roads, we come to that part, in which his Lordship says, " By the foregoing nar- " rative, as well as by the Log, and Signal books, of the Cale-

I

" donia, it will, I conceive, be seen, that I fully met the charge, " which has been preferred against me; and if the impression, aris- " ing out of the enquiry, should prove less favourable to Lord " Cochrane, than that which may have been produced, by my " Letter, to the Lords Commissioners of the Admiralty; his " Lordship must be sensible, that as the instigator of this Court- " Martial, he will himself, have been the cause, of this change of " sentiment." (p. 131.)

On the subject of the Narrative, to which Lord Gambier alludes, we have endeavoured to shew, that his Lordship had no great claim for extraordinary credit: we have opposed his Lordship's assertions by facts established, or by arguments grounded on the Evidence, contained in the Minutes of the Court Martial; and we presume that we have, by such means, refuted every point, of any importance, which that narrative embraces. And had his Lordship extended the Appendix, to the printed Minutes, by a copy of "the Log, and Signal books of the Caledonia," and by copies of every other Log of the Fleet, we might, possibly, have had it in our power to notice some errors in "the Log and " Signal books of the Caledonia." At all events, they ought to have been given, that the public might have had an opportunity of exercising their judgment upon them; or the Logs, written by Lord Cochrane, and that kept by the Master of the Imperieuse, should not have appeared. To give those to the public, and argue upon their defects and errors, and, at the same time, speak an eulogium upon the perfection and accuracy of others, without producing them, is an *ex parte* proceeding, and, in our humble opinion, neither fair nor just.

If all these Logs, and Minutes of Signals, that have been kept from the public inspection, correspond so exactly, with each other, and are so unanimous, in favour of Lord Gambier's conduct, as to have contributed largely towards the most honourable acquittal, that has been pronounced upon it, by the Court Martial; what will be the opinion formed, by many, of the Lords' Commissioners, who had all those Logs before them, when they framed their Charge against his Lordship, and which they, professedly, founded upon "the Log book, and Minutes of Signals of the Caledonia, Imperieuse and other ships?" Certainly not much for their deliberate consideration. But the public at large, reflecting upon the suppression of those Documents, and somewhat influenced by the wisdom, that informs the judgment, and marks the decisions of their Lordships, will probably entertain very different sentiments. And if his Lordship should find nothing to distress his mind, when throwing his eye over the "foregoing narrative," which speaks an opinion, as to the way in which his Lordship has met, and defended the Charge, preferred against him; we think Lord Cochrane, who, after what has appeared, cannot be considered "the instigator of the Court Martial," will not experience any uneasiness, in consequence of the enquiry, that has taken place; so far as it may relate to any change of sentiment, towards him, in any quarter. Should his Lordship be capable of giving his thoughts to such trifles, or regarding them, otherwise than, as he would, the fleeting vision of a dream: and if he did not sacrifice every thing, of individual consideration, to the sacred duties he owes to his King, and Country; he would not be the person that we have supposed him; nor one, for whom we should have interested ourselves. We have looked on his Lordship as a Briton, in the martial acceptation of the word; and as a man, in the best sense of it.

Whether Lord Gambier be right, in his conception of the effects, produced by the fire ships, upon the enemy's fleet, on the night of the 11th of April; or whether the effect, to which he alludes, was not produced by the explosion vessels, those terrible engines, as the Moniteur designates them, is a point of little account. In reasoning upon the subject, his Lordship says, "the "blast of the explosion vessels, under Lord Cochrane's immediate "direction, did not take place, so near the enemy's ships, as his "Lordship had intended." (p. 136). That might have been the case, and yet the failure not chargeable to his Lordship. But it is admitted, that it did take place, and near to the enemy's ships; and a rapid survey of the scene, as it passed, will be sufficient, we conceive, to do away any doubt, if any can possibly exist, as to the effect it produced, on the mind of the enemy. The night was extremely dark and cloudy, with strong gales; so that, according to his Lordship's own remarks, the enemy did not think the protection, they had previously resorted to, necessary to shield them against an attack. (p. 122.) The Imperieuse, followed by other frigates, about five o'clock in the evening, passed to the inner Roads, close to the Boyart, and within shot of the Isle of Aix. Lord Cochrane and Lieutenant Bissell, then proceeded in one of the explosion vessels, and having placed her in a proper direction, at the hour of eight o'clock, his Lordship, with his own hand, set fire to the fuse, and, of course, instantly quitted her. But, such was the violence of the opposing wind and tide, that, with every exertion they could make, they were scarcely beyond the range of her shells, when she exploded; and she exploded considerably nearer the enemy than the fire ships were, at the time, and before they had been kindled. The explosion of some hundred barrels of gunpowder, and several thousand shells and granades, must have been terrific, in its appearance: displaying an instantaneous and a vastly extended blaze, whilst the shells were flying in the air, and spreading, as they flew, in all directions; striking the mind with astonishment and dismay. When all this shall have been considered, and that the fire ships were, as Mr. Fairfax says, to windward of the Lyra, which vessel was, as that gentleman states, half a mile further from the enemy, than the explosion vessel, (p. 177); we should presume, that it will be unnecessary to pause in deciding, whether it were the fire ships, or the explosion vessels, that gave the first cause of alarm, and occasioned that consternation, that immediately prevailed in the enemy's fleet, and led on to the confusion which followed.

In concluding the passage, in which he endeavours to give to the fire ships, the merit of driving the enemy from their anchorage, Lord Gambier insinuates, that some circumstances, in Lord Cochrane's conduct, "were not altogether satisfactory to him:" (p. 131), which is a proceeding, that does not carry with it much of the features, that distinguish candour or liberality; and not very consistent, with the tenor of his public Letter, to the Lords of the Admiralty; in which he gives, to Lord Cochrane, unqualified praise, for that conduct which he now arraigns, nor with the Letter which he addressed to Lord Cochrane, dated the 13th of April, in which he thus expresses himself. "My dear Lord:—

"You have done your part so admirably, that I will not suffer "you to tarnish it, by attempting impossibilities." (p. 53). If his Lordship observed the conduct of Lord Cochrane, to have been blemished, by the undefined circumstances, to which the present insinuation points, he ought to have noticed it earlier, and in such a way, that Lord Cochrane might have had an opportunity, to explain and defend himself; and not waited, till he came upon his defence. Upon the whole, Lord Gambier has placed himself in the predicament, that we must believe either his Letter to the Admiralty was incorrect: or that his present insinuation is unfounded, and that his Letter to Lord Cochrane contained his real sentiments; or that his language and his feelings, were in opposition to each other.

In the appeal, which Lord Gambier makes, to the evidence of the second in command, and to that given by Captain Rodd, (when in consequence of a very extraordinary proceeding, they were required to give evidence upon, "what may be called," the prosecution,) as distinctly denying any neglect, or deficiency, on any part of his Lordship's conduct, and the conviction, he himself expresses, that "had the prosecution, called all the other "witnesses, summoned upon the Trial, a corresponding testi- "mony would have been given:" (p. 131), his Lordship seems to have been proudly conscious of his innocence; and that it was unimpeachable. But subsequent occurrences proved, those assertions and conclusions, alike erroneous: Captains Seymour, Malcolm, Broughton and Newcomb, have proved the truth; and actually maintained the Charge, by pointing out, in their Evidence, the instances, in which it appeared to them, that neglect, or delay was evinced, on the part of his Lordship. (pp. 220, 211, 200, 193, &c.).

We are at some loss to understand, whom it is Lord Gambier means, by "the Prosecutor" in a course of proceeding, that had no definite designation, by which it could be distinguished: a kind of non-descript, that required a name to be given to it, but which even the President of the Court-Martial, himself, could not assign; and, therefore, thus speaks of it, "what is *called* the

" Prosecution," (p. 69,) and " what may be termed the Prose-
" cution."

And we feel, almost as much difficulty, to account for his Lordship's meaning, in speaking of the Evidence, given by Admiral Stopford, and Captains Rodd and Woolf, as " having distinctly " denied the Charge." Admiral Stopford, interrogated to this point, says; " I do not *think*, there was any delay, or deficiency, on the part of the Commander in Chief, in executing the service, entrusted to his Lordship's care." (p. 70.) And does such Evidence amount to a " distinct denial?" Admiral Stopford *thinks* so only: he does not even venture his belief, which would, still, have been merely a comparative, not a conclusive term. Captain Rodd stated, that he *knew* of *no* delay," (p. 88.) that " it did not *appear* to him, that any blame was imputable to " Lord Gambier;" (p. 88.) and that " he believed, that every " thing was done, that could have been done, to effect the de- " struction of the Enemy's ships, with safety to his Majesty's " ships." (p. 88,)—An assertion, that any man could have made, in every action that is fought. Every enterprize, that is undertaken, must place his Majesty's ships, employed on such occasions, in danger: that danger, however trifling in its degree, they would have encountered, had they gone into Aix; consequently, to keep them in safety, was to keep them at anchor, in the outer Road, where the Enemy's shot could not reach them. Captain Rodd, however, in answer to a leading question, from the Court, shews his meaning of the expression, that " they would have been exposed " to more danger, than circumstances would justify;" and which circumstances he thus explains—" I thought, if they had gone up " FURTHER, every ship would have been lost;" that is, had they gone upon the Pallés shoal, on which the Enemy's ships were aground, there indeed destruction would have been inevitable; and such would be the fate of any one, who, knowing the situation of a shoal, still, obstinately and foolishly, persisted in running upon it. And does such testimony, which is evidently confined to the transactions of a few hours, that took place in the inner Roads of Aix, specify A DISTINCT DENIAL of the Charge, which embraces a period of several days?

Captain Woolf, the last of the gentlemen, whom his Lordship has named, as having defended him so decidedly, is examined by Mr. Bicknel: and considering Mr. Bicknel, as a Lawyer and Solicitor to the Admiralty: and as the conductor of that part of the proceeding, which "may be termed, or called, the Prosecu-" tion," his mode of Examination is singular enough.

Q. "Did it appear to you, that any blame was imputable to " my Lord Gambier, for any part of his conduct, or proceedings, " as Commander in Chief, of the Channel Fleet, employed in " Basque Roads between the 17th of March, and the 29th of " April last?"—*A.* "I have no recollection, of any thing of the " kind." (p. 87.)

Such is the boasted "distinct denial" of the Charge, on which his Lordship, so confidently, plumes himself: and if to be ambiguous is to be perspicuous: if to be indefinite is to be conclusive; if to be confused is to be distinct, his Lordship is certainly in the right.

Satisfied, in his own mind, that his former statement had administered conviction to the Court, his Lordship says, "I have " next, to refer to the Evidence of the Log, and Signal Books of " the Fleet, on which the Charges purport to be founded." But instead of a mass of such documentary Evidence, which we, by his Lordship's prefatory proposition, were taught to expect, and which, as we have before suggested, would have been highly gratifying, both to the public and to individuals, he once more enters into a long story, relative to the Master's Log of the Imperieuse, which he contrasts, with two Logs, written by Lord Cochrane. He talks much of the difference between them, and on that account stigmatizes the whole.

It is, however, somewhat strange, that his Lordship did not point out the material difference, between the Logs delivered in by the Master and by Lord Cochrane; for there does not appear any other difference, than would most commonly occur, where two people, without constant communication with each other, making observations upon occurrences, that are connected with the common object of both: and demonstrates, in the strongest possible way, that Lord Cochrane, and his Master did not compare Notes, to make a compilation, that was to answer a particular purpose, as Lord Gambier and others would insinuate; and, therefore, if any errors are to be traced, in those Logs, they must be the errors of controuling circumstances, and not of intention. But, that any material error ever was discoverable, upon the face of those documents, we have some tolerable good grounds for denying. We have had sufficient experience to know, that when any thing, like error, makes its appearance, or any thing, that had a tendency to be reduced to a tangible shape, Lord Gambier did not allow it to escape him, nor any unnecessary delay, to intervene, in bringing it forward, to the notice of the Court; as the following passage, from his Lordship's Defence, testifies; "I must, however, remark," says his Lordship, "that "amongst the deviations, in these papers, from the ships original "Log, the Signal immediately in question, which is recorded in "the latter, to have been for half the Fleet, stands in both these "compilations, as having been made for *part* of the Fleet only." And where is the great deviation? Is not half a part of the whole? The half indeed is definite, but a part may mean either the half or five, or it may extend to six out of eight. But were it otherwise the consequence would have been still the same; or rather there would have been no consequence at all. In Lord Cochrane's subordinate situation, the making of a Signal, was the mere notification of a fact, upon which the Commander in Chief might, or might not, act. To use the sentiments of Admiral Stopford, upon another occasion, "the Commander in Chief had the free exercise of "that discretion, which every Commander in Chief must possess, "in the execution of those measures, for which he is, alone responsible." What danger, then, could there have arisen in any signal, that Lord Cochrane might have made; whether it expressed a part, an half, or the whole of the Fleet? Had Lord Gambier been disposed to think the information, so conveyed, of importance, and that it was necessary to follow it up, by sending in a part of his Fleet, or standing in with the whole, he would, it is to be presumed, have first gone in himself and reconnoitered the ground, and the position of the Enemy, so as to be enabled to form his own opinions, upon a point of so much moment.

But his Lordship, without examination or enquiry, without taking the trouble to ascertain, whether Lord Cochrane had, or had not, formed a distinct and correct judgment, on the state of the Enemy, and of the means, by which they might have been annihilated, treated the Signal with silent contempt; and instead of sending in half the Fleet, he did not venture a single ship, and for this very good reason—they might have been "annoyed by the "batteries and ships of the Enemy"—a circumstance, that would have been in the very teeth, of that part of his duty, which dictates a careful provision, for the safety of his Majesty's line of battle ships; and, as his Lordship was desirous of discharging that duty literally, he wisely determined on keeping the whole at anchor with himself, where they would, most assuredly, be out of the reach of shot and shell, until the danger, in the inner Roads, was reduced to a trifle, by the removal of the two ships, that were at anchor, and the warping off of those on shore, that were capable of giving annoyance: although he well knew, that there would then be no object worth a moment's attention, or that could call for, or deserve, the slightest exertion; but in his Lordship's calculation, and "under all circumstances of the case," that was not a matter to be lamented. It may, however, be a subject of regret to those, who think and feel with his Lordship, that there are few in the Navy, that sphere of real action, that theatre of great achievement, who seeing the Enemy, in a situation to be assailed, and a prospect of effecting their destruction, would act with the same cold caution and stoical forbearance. They would not waste their time in fruitlessly conjecturing, whether they ought, or ought not, to be attacked; but employ it, in devising the best possible mode, by which the attack should be directed, to insure the more complete success. They would not burthen their deliberation with what might be the melancholy consequence, if, in the meditated engagement, they should lose a mast, or have their rigging cut: but, animated by the prospect before them, and glowing with enthusiastic ardour, press every sail, and, trusting to that good fortune, which never forsakes the brave; rush forward to the combat: grapple with the foe: and nobly exerting every effort; challenge the palm of victory. Not insensible, however, to danger, they would adopt every measure, that well-tempered prudence should suggest: nor regardless of their ships and men, they would

K

not expose them wantonly, nor unprofitably:—yet to vanquish the enemies of their country, and draw towards it the respect and admiration of the world, would, in their estimation, be a duty paramount to every other consideration.—Such men! would, in a burst of true British valour, exclaim, We can always find ships, our ports are full of them: but we cannot always find the enemy; they elude our pursuit, flying as we approach them.—Such men! fired by those generous sentiments, and acting upon those patriotic feelings, would not think the loss of a ship of the line, " a disgrace to their enterprise, and to England." An idea so chilling and discordant, would never enter their reflection: Should, however, the misfortune occur, they would regret it, as men should do; but would not mourn over it, as an event that would tarnish their acts with ignominy.

If, then, the Signals made by Lord Cochrane, on the morning of the 12th of April, should appear in the light, in which Lord Gambier has placed them, that is, should they be regarded " as " unprecedented and improper," (p. 133) let the peculiar situation in which Lord Cochrane was placed, and the circumstances it connected, be taken into consideration; and then let the unbiassed judgment decide. His Lordship was entrusted with the conduct of the most important service, that could fall to the lot of an Officer, so young, and one of the most important, that the public ever witnessed—the destruction of a Fleet of the enemy, intended to pour vast supplies into the stores of their exhausted garrisons, in their distant colonies; and produce incalculable evils in our own. It is true, that service had been performed, as far as it depended upon his Lordship, on the preceding night: and, so successfully, as to call forth the unqualified praise of Lord Gambier; but when, on the next morning, he beheld the consequence:—the ships of the enemy, lying on the shore, incapable of moving, yet with every hope of being enabled to warp off, if not timely prevented, as soon as the tide would be in a state to serve them: and fully satisfied, that from their helpless condition, they could be totally destroyed, with the greatest ease; he made the signal, which his judgment and sense of duty, at the moment, deemed necessary and proper (p. 33, 44). The Fleet weighed in consequence (p. 5), although some hours after his Lordship's signal had been answered: and he was encouraged to look forward for the fulfilment of his expectations, and the gratification of his wishes; but it again anchored midway, between its first position, and the Fort of Aix; and he experienced all the distress of the most painful disappointment: yet he fancied, that something, preparatory to action, had induced Lord Gambier to the measure, and that the delay, therefore, would be but temporary. "Twelve o'clock arrived, and no signal to weigh: half "past twelve, still no signal." (p. 47.) About one o'clock, the Etna bomb passed the Imperieuse, and Captain Godfrey, who commanded her, on being asked by Lord Cochrane, what was the plan of attack? informed his Lordship, that it was to bombard the enemy. The Calcutta, Varsovie, and most of the other ships, were then pressing sail, to force themselves towards the Charante; and the three-decker was swinging to her hawsers. (p. 49.)

The workings of Lord Cochrane's mind, whilst occupied in contemplating these circumstances, cannot easily be conceived. In the course of his evidence, his Lordship has, himself, attempted to describe them, in the following words: "I had the charge of "the fire-ships; they had failed of their expected purpose: I "knew what the tongue of slander was capable of: and although "I admit that the feelings of my Lord Gambier, for the honour "and interest of his Country, were and are, as strong as my "own; yet personal considerations were enough. The expecta-"tions of my Country, the hopes of the Admiralty, and my "own prospects, were about to vanish." (p. 40.) If, therefore, his Lordship, with such feelings, from such impressions: with a mind perplexed, and almost distracted—his strength nearly exhausted, by excessive exertions, and a total privation of rest, should have made any signal, that was not strictly conformable to the practice of the Navy, but which was, notwithstanding, intended to serve his Country; the man of candour and spirit will not be hasty in censuring it.

Such are the minutiæ, to which Lord Gambier stoops, to detect errors, and depreciate the conduct of others, without clearing, or in anywise benefitting, his own, by their introduction; and such is the general fate of his Lordship's exertions. The shaft he throws recoils, and wounds, only, himself.

Having in this manner, with more of the rancour of resentment than the spirit of candour, commented upon the conduct of Lord Cochrane, and the Master of the Imperieuse, he suddenly breaks off, to signify, to the Court, that he must call the signal Lieutenant of the Caledonia, to shew, that the signal of recall, on the 13th of April, said to have been observed by the Imperieuse, never was made by the Caledonia; and that the signal, of the 14th, recorded in the Caledonia's Log, as made by the Imperieuse, "if permitted to remain, can destroy the enemy," was denied by Lord Cochrane. (p. 133.) In this extraordinary manner, has his Lordship evaded his own proposition, of referring to the Log, and Signal Log Books of the Fleet; as if he meant, merely, to amuse the Court, and lead their mind from its proper object; or, by heaping confusion on intricacy, deprive them of the means of exercising their judgment, so as to arrive at a correct decision.

It was not the Logs of the Imperieuse and the Caledonia only; but the Logs, and Signal Books of every Ship in the Fleet, on which the Charge purports to be founded. And of this his Lordship appears to have been fully assured, when he said, "I "have next to refer to the Log, and Signal Log Books of the "Fleet." He should therefore have made that general reference as ample and complete, as was within his compass; it was due to his own honour, and to the Country; and justice demanded it. Had the Minutes of the Court Martial remained, in the situation in which they originated, all might have passed in silence: but, when his Lordship, on suggestions best known to himself, drew them, from their depositary, for the purpose of submitting them to the consideration of the public, he was bound, in fairness and common justice, to have given the whole of those Documents, or none at all; acting, as he has done, he has rendered those Minutes a garbled compilation. It was making a case for himself, and then soliciting for it, the implicit confidence of the Country, at the expence of justice, and to the wrong and injury of individuals. Previous to the appearance of these "Minutes," in an authenticated form, the public were favourably disposed to be silent, upon the subject of the Court Martial. They are now forced to animadvert upon them, and must observe, that Lord Gambier has not refuted the Charge brought against him; on the contrary, that it has been established by some of his own Witnesses; and if, to use his Lordship's own words, as addressed to Lord Cochrane, "the impression arising out of this inquiry "should prove less favourable," than it formerly was, "his Lord-"ship must be sensible, that his own measures will have worked "this change of sentiment," (p. 131.)

Whether the signal of recall, on the 13th, which is denied by Lord Gambier, was or was not made, must be left to the judgment of the public, upon the proofs that will be laid before them:—In the first place, we have the following words, inserted in the Log of the 13th, delivered into the Court, by the Master of the Imperieuse, and is annexed to "the Minutes:"—"Answered recall from the Caledonia—made telegraph to ditto;" and Lord Cochrane says, "the signal of recall was reported to "me, to have been made by the Caledonia. I answered, by "signal, that the enemy could be destroyed." Mr. Bicknel remarked that, that was another day; Lord Cochrane said, he was clear with respect to the date.—Here Lord Gambier interfered, and observed, "this was on the 13th, that Mr. Bicknel asked to." Lord Cochrane replied, "I am deposing to the 13th; and I am "further confirmed in this opinion, by a demi-official letter, "which I hold in my hand, addressed to me, by Lord Gambier." His Lordship then produced the Letter, together with his Answer to it (p. 53): and these taken separately or together, support the purpose of his Lordship's reference to them, and which purpose requires no trifling aid, from the evident anxiety, that seems to have possessed Lord Gambier's mind, during this part of Lord Cochrane's examination: it for a moment superseded his prudence; and he forgot, that he interrupted the examination, whilst attempting to divert his Lordship from the line he was pursuing.

It might have been imagined, that with such testimony; with Lord Gambier's own testimony, under his hand, to give it force;

together with the agitation manifested by his Lordship, in the course of delivering it; both his Lordship and the Court would have desisted from pressing further a point, that, taken with all the advantage it could render, was not worth a moment's contention. But the fact is otherwise; "The question," observed the President, "is, whether the signal was made on the 13th."— This question, in the shape of a remark, is the more extraordinary, on the part of the President, as Lord Cochrane had, only a moment before, deposed, that on the 13th the signal of recall had been reported to him, to have been made by the Caledonia; and that he had answered it, by signal, that the enemy could be destroyed (p. 52), and which answering signal, is admitted to have been entered, in the Caledonia Signal Log, on the 13th; although the mandatory signal to the Imperieuse, does not appear to have been inserted.

To the remark of the President, Lord Cochrane answered: "I positively swear, that, to the best of my belief, it was made;" and, after stating a variety of circumstances on the subject, in order to illustrate and strengthen his averment, his Lordship concluded, by producing a second Letter, addressed to him by Lord Gambier, also dated on the 13th, which not only speaks of having recalled him; but to make that recall certain, tells him, that he had ordered in Captain Woolfe, to relieve him. (p. 54.) Still Lord Cochrane did not obtain the desired credit; and his own deposition, and the documents, bearing the signature of Lord Gambier, uniting with it, appear to have been considered, as of little note. Lord Gambier proceeded to examine witnesses with the view of refuting Lord Cochrane, and, to that end, called Lieutenant Hockings.

Q. "Was the signal of recall made to the Imperieuse, on the "13th of April?"—*A.* "No, *not that I recollect.*"

This answer appears to have been considered too complex, even by Lord Gambier, and, therefore, he endeavours to bolster it up, by another.

Q. "*Must you have known it*, had there been a signal, to that "effect?"—*A.* "Certainly." (p. 175.)

And with this answer Lord Gambier seems to have been perfectly satisfied, as he did not further question Mr. Hockings. But he should have considered, that this last answer was absolutely dependant upon the first, which speaks Mr. Hockings's want of recollection upon the subject, to which he was interrogated: and the whole resolves itself into this proposition, that no such signal could have been made, *without his knowledge;* but whether it was, or was not, made "*he could not recollect!*" Yet he was the Signal Lieutenant, under whose inspection the Caledonia's Signal Log was written; and we are taught, by Lord Gambier, to believe, that both Mr. Hockings and the Log, are to be relied on, for their accuracy.

To another point, Mr. Hockings speaks more positively, still, however, without committing himself, as he deposes, only, from appearance, not of his own knowledge.

Q. "Did you observe a telegraphic signal, made by the Impe-
"rieuse, on the 14th of April: 'If permitted to remain, can de-
"'stroy the enemy?' and at what time of the day?"—*A.*
"Yes, I recollect *that* signal; I believe it was *just after the re-*
"*call made, on the 14th* April, about *forty minutes* after nine,
"A. M. *It is on the Signal Log.*"

The vivacity with which he recollects one signal, and the uncertain manner in which he flounders, respecting the other, cannot fail to make a deep impression upon the thinking mind. The concluding sentence, however, indicates, that he must have had the Signal Log in his hand, whilst giving his evidence; or, that he had it perfectly on his recollection, as he says "that *is on the* "*Signal Log.*" (p. 175.) If the former was the case, he might have answered, with the same readiness, in the one instance, as in the other; if the latter, it is extraordinary, that he should, in one instance, have answered so decidedly: not only as to the fact itself, but to the time also, marking not only the hour, but the number of minutes, in which it occurred; and that, to the other, he should speak, in all the embarrassment of uncertainty, and all the confusion of total ignorance: as if he had been employed in the general duty of the ship; and had no manner of acquaintance, with either Log or Signals.

Had the Court thought proper, to have put two or three questions to Mr. Hockings, the fact would have been cleared up; he would have informed them, whether the signal, of the 13th, was, or was not, made, or whether he was, or was, not some time below, or otherwise absent from the deck, leaving the signals to some other officer; and that, therefore, the signal might have been made, during such absence, which rendered him, at any rate, incapable of deposing to it.

Indeed, it does appear, that Lieutenant Hockings, was not constantly even on board the Caledonia: that, on one occasion at least, he was on board the Imperieuse; and, therefore, could not depose to a signal on the 12th of April, as will be seen by the following examination, by Admiral Young.

Q. "You are Signal Lieutenant of the Caledonia?"—*A.* "Yes."

Q. "Then you will be able to speak to ALL THE SIGNALS, "that were made, by the Imperieuse, on the 12th of April?"—*A.* "YES, I CAN."

Q. "Can you say positively, that the telegraphic communica-"tion, mentioned, was '*half the Fleet* is sufficient to destroy the "'enemy?' I *particularly mean* to press the word *half*, upon "your mind?"—*A.* "I CANNOT answer to that Signal; because "I was coming on board the Caledonia, from the Imperieuse."

Without stopping to remark, at large, upon the direct and positive contradiction between, YES I CAN, and NO I CANNOT; we shall go on to notice, that, to supply this deficiency, Mr. Sparshot, the signal mate of the Caledonia, was called in, and spoke to the question, promptly and perspicuously. *But he was not questioned*, touching the Signal of recall, *on the 13th*, nor was any other of the Signal mates called on, to depose to that point: notwithstanding, it is a known fact, that whilst the Signal Lieutenant may be engaged below, or out of the ship, on duty or pleasure, one of the mates must be always upon deck, nor can he remove from it on any plea or occasion, until first regularly relieved. Nor was Sir Harry Neale, the Captain of the Fleet, and first Captain of the Caledonia, who was afterwards called upon, respecting the Signal of the 14th, questioned to the Signal in reference. Circumstances, that wear an extraordinary, and rather a suspicious aspect; and the more so, as Lord Cochrane had not only stated, that that Signal had been made; but had also corroborated that statement by the circumstantial Evidence, that he himself directed the answer, which was given to it.

Lord Gambier's own Letters, likewise, are closely in point; and the Master's Log, of the Imperieuse, is further in proof of the fact. Indeed, Lord Gambier, during the Examination of Sir Harry Neale, furnishes further collateral and very strong evidence, as he admits, that Lord Cochrane did, on the 13th, express by Signal, "Can destroy the enemy," (p 187.) But, then, his Lordship would shew, that, that Signal was made upon another occasion; and that the Signal of recall was thrown out, in consequence of inactivity, on the part of Lord Cochrane, "who remained in the "Road of Aix, during the 13th and 14th," (p. 129.) without attempting any thing, with the frigates under his command.

But Lord Gambier has not said, either in his written Defence, or in his comments afterwards, or by his witnesses, what Signal, from the Caledonia, could have led to the answering Signal, "*If permitted to remain*, can destroy the enemy." Will common sense endure the idea, that Lord Cochrane, whose business it was, to have destroyed the enemy, and who has given ample proof, that his disposition rather outstript the purposes of his duty, should have been guilty, of not only, the unnecessary, but altogether absurd act, of making the Signal, "Can destroy the "enemy?" And it would have been an equally glaring absurdity, had Lord Cochrane stated, "*if permitted to remain* can destroy the enemy;" unless the Signal of recall had actually been made. It would have been asking, that which was already in his possession. To offer further argument, on this head, would be altogether superfluous, and when Lord Cochrane's own Evidence, and that afforded by the Letters of Lord Gambier: the admission of his Lordship, of the Signal of the 13th, and the Log of the Imperieuse, be taken together: and when due consideration

L

be given, to the very extraordinary manner, in which Mr. Hockings delivered his Testimony; a doubt surely cannot remain, that the Signal of recall was made, not only on the 14th of April, but on the 13th also.

Thus has Lord Gambier, after having brought the Log of the Caledonia into discussion, and fixed upon a particular feature of it, as a specimen of its accuracy; and after having insinuated, that the statement of Lord Cochrane, in reference to it, was unfounded, left the whole in a state, as helpless, as was that of the French Fleet, on the morning of the 12th of April. He did not think proper to bring forward, any other than one, self-confessed incompetent witness, to support a miserable negative, which sinks into something, worse than nothing, when opposed to the commanding position, that is taken by an affirmative. What faith can be given to a document, that has been so disgraced, even by those who were so loud, in proclaiming its certainty, and truth? Had that document been laid before the Public, as it ought to have been, together with every Log in the fleet, or the Log of the Imperieuse, and those kept by Lord Cochrane, should have been withheld, we have some reason to imagine, that it would have been found to contain more of error, than already traced. We will state one, that Mr. Hockings carelessly allowed to fall from him. Asked on what day the Regulus got off, and went up the Charante? He answered, " I *think* it was daylight, in the morning of the " 29th. I can only speak *from the Log—it was noted on the* " *Log*. " It appears on the Log, that at daylight, on the 29th, " an enemy's two decked ship, got off, and moved to the WEST-" WARD; *it ought to have been* EASTWARD," (p. 184.) In pointing out this error, we become furnished with some other traits of Mr. Hockings' incompetency, to speak to the accuracy of the Log of the Caledonia. Like Mr. Wilkinson, who, because one vessel was spoken of, conceived that all vessels, of her description, must have been meant: he believes, that because the Regulus was a two decked ship, and a two decked ship had got off; " *it must have been that ship.*"

Beaten from the field, on one ground, his Lordship rallies upon another; advised, perhaps, by his friends, that although worsted in his attempts to establish a negative proposition, he might be more fortunate in his endeavours to secure one, that rested on the affirmative; Mr. Hockings is called upon to support the Signal said to have been made on the 14th; and to this end, he says, he believes it occurred, just after the Signal of recall was made (p. 175) so that the existence of the telegraphic Signal, said to have been made by the Imperieuse, on the 14th, depends upon the signal, made on the 13th, as we have fully established the fact to have been, by the best evidence; and therefore, the testimony of Mr. Hockings, on this, as on a former occasion, is nugatory.

Sir Harry Neale, to the same fact, says, "I was walking upon "the poop, when I directed, by the Commander in Chief's orders, "the signal of recal to be made; the Imperieuse replied "*if permitted to wait, can destroy enemy.*"—"*It was reported to* "*me,*" "and that in consequence Captain Woolf, of the Aigle, "was directed to proceed, and take the command of the in-"shore squadron" (p. 185). Here, it is to be remarked, that Sir Harry Neale does not mention any particular day, on which this transaction took place; and, therefore, he has merely shewn, that such a signal was made; and stated, that such a consequence followed.

On the other hand, there are, independent of the testimony we quoted, when discussing the signal of the 13th, two Letters, written by Lord Gambier, and addressed to Lord Cochrane, both bearing the same date, namely, the 13th of April—The former of these, hints at the signal of recal, having been then previously made, and the answer, "if permitted to remain, can "destroy the enemy," or it means nothing. These are Lord Gambier's words: "You have done your part so admirably, "that I will not suffer you to tarnish it, by attempting impossi-"bilities. You must, therefore, join, as soon as you can, with "the bombs, &c." (p. 53); and the latter, which is of more importance, as it shews his Lordship's *ostensible* reasons for recalling him, observes "It is necessary, I should have *some communication* "*with you, before I close my dispatches to the Admiralty,* I have "THEREFORE ordered Captain Woolfe to relieve you;" which proves, beyond all manner of dispute, (if these Letters, bearing the signature, and admitted to have been written by Lord Gambier, are to be believed) that Captain Woolfe, was not directed to take the command of the in-shore squadron, " in consequence of the signal " made by Lord Cochrane," " if permitted to remain, can " destroy the enemy," nor in consequence of Lord Cochrane's " having remained, in the Roads of Aix, during the thirteenth " and fourteenth, without attempting any thing with the frigates." (p. 129). But in consequence of Lord Gambier's desire, to have some communication with his Lordship, and that his Lordship " might convey Sir Harry Neale to England, or *return to* " *carry on the service*," Lord Gambier signifying, to his Lordship, by way of consolation, that " he expected two bombs, to " arrive every moment; and that they would be very useful in " it." But why was not Sir Harry Neale asked a question, in allusion to the signal, asserted by Lord Cochrane, as above mentioned, to have been made on the 13th? The reason is tolerably obvious, and, to those who throw their eyes over the contrasted testimony of Sir Harry Neale, as we have given it, in another part of these Notes, it will be evident; that Sir Harry was not to be interrogated to any other point, than such as Lord Gambier should think proper, and in consequence, his Lordship checked the Court when, he imagined, they were proceeding too far with him.

Lord Gambier appeared, in the former part of his Defence, and, until Captain Malcolm gave his Evidence, to triumph over the Charge exhibited against him, by the Lords of the Admiralty On one occasion, he took upon him to dictate, even to the Court, respecting the examination of a witness, whilst delivering his Evidence; and on another, he expressed his full persuasion, that he should receive, at their hands, " ample retribution for the " aspersions," (as he was pleased to denominate the solemn Charge against him " on his character." (p. 204.) Yet there are few instances, in which a man, similarly circumstanced, has been more unfortunate, in the means adopted towards the end proposed, than Lord Gambier: every position he lays down, as a ground, on which to defend himself, turns out to be utterly untenable.

Had his Lordship been wisely advised, he would have confined himself to a more contracted range, and directed his attentions entirely, to the justification of his own acts; instead of pointing them. towards those of others, whom his imagination had converted into enemies. He ought to have recollected how unequal he was to the task, of defending himself, before he resolved, on any attempt, to depreciate Lord Cochrane's abilities, and establish the fallacy of his judgment, during the period, in which he served, under his Lordship, in Basque Roads.

Lord Gambier says, "I have yet to call the attention of the "Court, to the plans drawn by Lord Cochrane, of the position "of the enemy's ships, as they lay aground, on the morning of "the 12th of April, and to that position, marked upon the "Chart, verified by Mr. Stokes; the former laid down from "uncertain data; the latter from *angles measured,* and other ob-"servations *made on the spot.* The difference between the two, "is too apparent, to escape the notice of the Court; and the re-"spective merits of these Charts, will not, I think, admit of a "comparison." (p. 133).

Mr. Edward Fairfax, the Master of the Fleet, called upon to shew, from the soundings he had made, whether the Charts, in the Neptune François, were correct, says, "the variation is pour-"trayed in the Chart, produced by Mr. Stokes; I gave Mr. "Stokes the marks, and I have all the different angles *in my* "*pocket.*" (p. 140). This will account for Mr. Fairfax's name being affixed to those Charts, instead of Mr. Stokes's. Questioned, as to the situation of the enemy's fleet, at day light, on the 12th of April, (p. 143), he referred to a Chart, that he had previously produced, which he asserted was correct, (p. 141), and stated, that he had therein described that situation. (p. 143). "He "could not point out their situation at noon; because, having "met with a contusion, he went below at eleven, and did not "return to the deck until two;" but observed that the enemy's ships "were then in nearly the same situation, as the Chart "expressed." (p. 143).

Mr. Stokes, on the contrary, shows they had considerably and materially altered their situation. "The Cassard, bearing the "Commodore's broad pendant, slipt or cut, and made sail for "the Charante, at eleven minutes past one; and the Foudroyant, "bearing the Rear Admiral's flag, made sail for the Charante at "twenty minutes past one." (p. 160).

So much for the accuracy of Mr. Fairfax's eye sight, and the correctness of his judgment; and "if they were so far defective," as to render him incapable of distinguishing ships under sail, from ships at anchor, what must we think of the service they rendered him, in ascertaining the distance of the enemy's ships; and the space which they occupied, when he measured, as he pretends, the anchorage of Aix? We answer, without hesitation; they led him into deception on the one hand; and involved him in wretched solutions on the other. Possibly, Mr. Fairfax had become somewhat confused, in consequence of the pain he speaks of, as resulting from the contusion he received, in the night of the 11th of April, and in that case, we should certainly commiserate him, though we may be permitted to mark the fallacy it originated, in his depositions. Mr. Fairfax, however, has himself alone, to blame, for the misfortune he met. He should have reflected, that a man advanced in years, cannot make those leaps, with impunity, that youth may safely venture on. He has, however, as we are informed, obtained a very snug and lucrative situation, as a reward for his good services; and an healing salve from Lloyd's benevolent dispensary. We therefore trust, that his *wound*, and the deck, against which he received it, will no longer be thought of.

Captain Bligh, "thinks the enemy's ships were, as represented "on the Chart." (p. 153). Captain Kerr is of the same opinion, and adds, "I recollect the situation of the enemy's fleet on "shore, perfectly: seven sail of the line on shore: two sail of "the line afloat; and one line of battle ship advanced some distance up the river." (p. 166). Captain Douglas says, "to "the best of his recollection, two sail of the line were afloat," and only "the three decker, and three other ships of the line on "shore." (p. 171). Mr. Stokes demonstrates that, those gentlemen, and others who have deposed to the same point, in nearly the same manner, were egregiously mistaken, with respect to the Chart. He says, the only ships, marked in the "Chart, *on the "morning of the 12th, were those that were destroyed,"* (p. 147), so, that in fact, those gentlemen, by some unaccountable inadvertency, had deposed to a Chart, of the positions of the enemy, that was intended for the 13th instead of the 12th of April. And this will be evident, by comparing it with the testimony of those gentlemen, and that of Mr. Stokes's, just quoted. By such comparison, the Chart will be found to contain other ships of the enemies, than those which were destroyed; and consequently could not have been the Chart of the 12th, as "the only ships "marked thereon, were those that were destroyed," namely, the Ville de Varsovie, Aquilon, and Calcutta, together with the Tonnere, which was destroyed by the enemy. Mr. Stokes, in giving the bearings of the ships that were on shore, goes diametrically in opposition to his own Chart, and at the same time, as we have already remarked, confirms the Chart delivered by Lord Cochrane.

Whilst we are on the subject of Charts, we may notice, that there is, on this head, a strange jumble, partaking of mystery and confusion, not to be penetrated. At one time, Mr. Fairfax produces a Chart, on which was sketched the position of the enemy's fleet in Aix Roads, on the 11th and 12th of April, and of some of our fire ships, before they were kindled, and of the explosion vessel, conducted by Lord Cochrane and Lieutenant Bissell. (p. 141). To this Chart, he afterwards refers, as having the Lyra marked on it. (p. 177), and tells the Court, that "the "variation in the Neptune François, was pourtrayed in the "Chart, produced by Mr. Stokes, whom he had furnished with "the marks, having all the different angles and soundings, in his "own pocket." (p. 140). At another time, we find Mr. Stokes in answer to a question from the President, speaking to a Chart, but not producing it: yet Captains Bligh, (p. 153); Beresford, (p. 162); Kerr, (p. 166); Raven, Master of the Cæsar, (p. 169); Godfrey, (p. 175); and others, depose to Mr. Stokes's Chart. Again, all the Charts, published with the Minutes, have the name of Fairfax! But in what part of the Proceedings can we find precision? Had the most consummate art been employed, to render those fabrications, and the points connected with them, intricate, indefinite, and confused; it could not have been more successful than the mode that has been adopted.

Instead of pursuing a regular chain of examination, we behold, both the Court and Lord Gambier, flying from subject to subject, forwards and backwards; and equally as fluctuating in principle as in form. Sometimes the doctrine of evidence flows one way; sometimes it takes an opposite course. It enforces rules with rigid exactitude, when Lord Cochrane is giving his testimony; but relaxes on other occasions.

On this very important point, important because interfering with justice, and violating the established law of the land, we shall, before we close our labours, take the liberty to ask a few questions of the impartial President, some of the Members, and the learned Judge Advocate. Although the former is a casual office, and Sir Roger Curtis may, probably, never again act in it: yet, that future Courts Martial may be benefited, by precedent; and that the incautious may not err under the sanctions of example, a few words may be necessary. The Judge Advocate is differently circumstanced: his office is permanent, and he officiates at every trial; and as the person, who is to advise the Court, in matters of doubt or difficulty, is the proper subject for the severest censure, whenever he deviates, either from usage or the law. How far a ministerial officer, who, in a situation of high trust, swerves from his duty, and, "knowing the right still "the wrong pursues," is worthy of continuing in that trust, which gives him an opportunity of trifiing with the feelings: sporting with the honour, and damning for ever the fairest characters in his Majesty's service; is a matter on which the superior judgments of the public will decide. In our humble opinion, it is question of the highest importance, and, we doubt not, will receive all the attention, that is due to it.

In returning to the subject of the Chart, we have to remark, that its invalidity has been proved, and its deception detected. Thus has the star, which was to have illumined the path of truth, turned out to be a mere *ignis fatuus*, that has led us astray, and for a time, left us in all the wanderings of uncertainty, in all the mists of confusion. Thus has the master-piece of skill, and ingenuity, of Messrs. Fairfax and Stokes, been rendered abortive; and thus it ever will be with men, who suffer their prejudices to supersede their reason. They will unavoidably receive objects through improper mediums, and the angles of the sight, and the workings of the mind must, in their consequences, lead only to deception and injustice. Is it for a moment to be endured, that the Master of the Caledonia, and the Master of the Fleet, whose occupations, as they have themselves represented, were multifarious, did, or could, at such a time as they have stated, actually measure and work angles, to ascertain at *a future period* "by trigonometrical cal- "culations," the distance and bearings of the stranded ships from each other. And is it to be endured, that those persons, so occupied and circumstanced, were enabled to make observations, equally accurate with those made by Lord Cochrane, whose unremitting attentions were directed towards the situation of the enemy's fleet, and every thing of moment that belonged to it? Mr. Fairfax, on the other hand, left it so early in the morning, (pp. 145, 146.) that owing to the darkness of the hour, it was totally impossible for him to have distinguished the position of vessels, several miles distant from him, and which distance he was constantly increasing, as "he worked out, towards our own "Fleet." Indeed, such was the confused state of his mind, at one part of the time, possibly, as we have before remarked, from pain, occasioned by the accident he met with, and partly from other circumstances, that he did not know *whether it was light or dark*, (p. 145.) Of Mr. Stokes' knowledge we have the best information: he derives it from the observations he made in the mizen top of the Caledonia, which lay three miles and an half from the batteries of Aix; and, according to his own Chart, the grounded ships were still two miles further off. He has however signified, that he was assisted, in those observations, by somebody, whom he does not name; in some way that he has not explained. (p. 149.)

Such were the heads, and such is the substance of Lord Gambier's chapter, upon those infallible Charts: and such is the complexion of his Chart-makers opposed to Lord Cochrane, who, not only drove the enemy's ships in question, on shore, but remained near to them, from that period until the afternoon of the 12th; at which time he greatly assisted, in destroying three of them.

It may be true, that Lord Cochrane did, as Lord Gambier asserts, give an opinion, that the French Charts, on which his Lord-

M

ship relied, and of the accuracy of which he had spoken in strong terms, were, in some points, not exactly what they expressed, and if such were the fact, we should congratulate Lord Gambier on the occasion, and sincerely wish, for his sake, that such occasion had oftener occurred; instead of being, as it thus would be, a solitary instance of his Lordship's correct recollection. Unfortunately, for his Lordship, the fact is, notwithstanding its appearance, rather hostile to his purposes. Sir Harry Neale, deposing to the point, as arising out of a conversation, between him and Lord Cochrane, thus expressed himself: "His Lordship "said, that the French were in the habit of giving a *smaller space* "upon their Charts than was true: that he had an instance of it, "upon a former occasion: when standing into the Pertuis Breton "he expected to have found, by the Chart, that the space was "*smaller*; but he found it near five or six miles broad." (p. 186.) And thence we may infer, that the anchorage and Roads of the Isle of Aix, were more extensive than the French wished them to appear. These Charts, therefore, were guides, that might have been safely relied upon, as they professed less than they gave; which, in Charts, is not considered an error; or if an error, it must assuredly be on the safe side. Every person, in reading what Lord Gambier has written upon the subject, would of course suppose, that these Charts marked five fathom, when there were only two; two where there were five, and so on. We have however, shewn the error to be of a totally different nature, and that the French Charts are marked by caution, in aid of humanity. Lord Cochrane had proved their worth by his own experience: he gave to them his confidence; and they never disappointed him.

Drawing towards the conclusion of his written Defence, Lord Gambier proceeds to examine in what manner Lord Cochrane had attempted, by what Lord Gambier denominates "an unsup-"ported opinion, to maintain the Charge." (p. 183). "In the "course of his Evidence," says Lord Gambier, "Lord Cochrane, "in allusion to the danger which would attend his going without "encouragement, to the attack of the ships, at the mouth of the "Charante, says, (speaking of himself,) 'a heavy, very heavy "'responsibility would lie upon my shoulders, in case of disasters,

" 'which, in military operations, are sometimes unavoidable; if I " 'had, had my cables shot away, for instance, I might have been " 'sunk.' Yet, whilst on the one hand, his Lordship seems " to have been so sensible of the weight of responsibility im- " posed upon himself, by the command of a frigate and a few " small vessels, he appears on the other, to have been unmindful " of the far heavier degree of responsibility, attached to my com- " mand, during so complicated an undertaking; in alluding to " the dangers of which, I must take this opportunity to mention, " five furnaces for heating shot, which Lord Cochrane reported " to me, to have himself discovered, when he went in to recon- " noitre, previous to the attack." (p. 134.)

Lord Gambier should have considered the difference, that marked their respective situations: placed in the command of the Fleet, with the injunctions of his superiors, to use his utmost endeavours to destroy the enemy, satisfied of course in their own minds, that the achievement was practicable. And if, under such sanction, he had, in the strenuous exertion of his endeavours, encountered misfortune, "which in military operations is some- " times unavoidable," (p. 56.) the public would have past it by unnoticed, anxious only, to pay a just tribute to the zeal, in which it originated. Had Admiral Byng, impelled by that noble ardour which animates the hero, engaged the French Fleet and lost half of his own in the contest, he would not have been condemned to that death which he suffered.

The public, ever generous in their sentiments, and liberal in their constructions, cheerfully make every allowance for the disasters, that will sometimes attend the best arranged plans; and kindly hail the merit on which fortune had frowned. Lord Cochrane was, on the 14th, so peculiarly circumstanced, that had he attempted any enterprize of any kind, it would have argued the extreme of rashness. He was not prepared, or even in a situation, to enter upon any enterprize; until the evening of the 13th; until that time he was repairing the damage that had been received by his ship from the enemy. His Lordship's own words will best illustrate the fact: " I wish also, to call the attention " of the Court, to my reason, after the Imperieuse was refitted,

" on the evening of the 13th, and after the receipt of the Letter " (marked A.), during the evening of that day, or on the morn- " ing following, previous to the second signal of recall being " made, for not having, with that ship and the Pallas, attacked " the enemy: that I felt, after the Letter above alluded to, ex- " pressing the opinions of my Lord Gambier, and of the cap- " tains who had come from the inner anchorage, that without " any subsequent encouragement, a heavy, a very heavy re- " sponsibility, would lie upon my shoulders, in case of any dis- " aster, which in military operations, is sometimes unavoidable. " If I had, had my cables shot away, for instance, I might have " been sunk: all these things are possible; though not at all pro- " bable." (p. 56.)

What then, is become of the comparative responsibility that Lord Gambier has drawn, between Lord Cochrane and himself; or whence the advantage, his Lordship flattered himself he should derive from it? His Lordship was a free agent to act as he might think proper, and had every encouraging stimulus to action. Lord Cochrane, had not only received a Letter of recall to all intents and purposes; but it conveyed the opinion of Lord Gambier against any further proceedings, as visionary. " You " have done," says his Lordship in that Letter, " your part so " admirably, that I will not suffer you to tarnish it, by attempting " impossibilities." (p. 55.) It is also to be remarked, that about forty minutes after nine o'clock, in the morning of the 14th, Lord Cochrane was recalled by signal; (p. 175.) and soon afterwards actually relieved by Captain Woolf. (p. 185.) His Lordship had once taken responsibility upon himself. Seeing the enemy's ships moving away, and no prospect of a force being sent in against them, he sailed, *without orders*, to attack them: and it was to that risk, and it was a bold one, that we are, in all probability, indebted for the destruction of the four ships, on the 12th of April: all the merit of which, however, Lord Gambier has very generously taken to himself; as he asserts positively, that " it was entirely owing to his delay in sending in ships, that, " that destruction took place." (p. 128.) It is also, to be remarked, that Lord Cochrane was deprived of the force, that had been sent in to his assistance; as Admiral Stopford had taken upon himself, in a manner that has not been satisfactorily explained, to order the whole to join the Fleet.

In refutation of Lord Cochrane's statement, in his deposition, that a seventy-four gun ship might go into the inner anchorage, between the Boyart shoal and the Palles, at any time of the tide, Lord Gambier has recourse to the Charts of the two Masters, Fairfax and Stokes, and then reasons upon the rise and fall of the tide, concluding with these words: "even if I had previously "known as much of the inner anchorage, as I do now, I would "not, as the wind was at the time, have done otherwise than I "did; and if Lord Cochrane really knew, what he has now pro-"fessed to have known, when he was in Aix Roads, it was a "duty incumbent upon him, to have communicated that inform-"ation, on the afternoon of the 12th, to the Captains of the "line of battle ships, which he saw in so perilous a situation, "aground within point blank range of the batteries." (p. 134).

To the first part, it would be a sufficient answer to say, that the Charts, abandoned by Mr. Fairfax, have been proved by Mr. Stokes himself, to be totally incorrect and erroneous. (pp. 147, 149). But it appears, by testimony which his Lordship cannot dispute, because brought forward by himself, and is in corroboration of the Evidence given by Lord Cochrane, that there is a sufficiently capacious and good anchorage, out of the range of Aix, for six sail of the line. This is the substance of the concurrent testimony of Captains Seymour, Malcolm, Woolfe, Godfrey, Broughton, and others. Lord Cochrane, indeed, is rather more particular: asked, if he had any authenticated Chart or Evidence to shew, that there was a sufficient depth of water? his Lordship says: "It was actually from soundings we had in "going in. I studied this Chart some days before. The tide "appears, by the French Chart, to flow at three hours and "twenty minutes full moon. The rise and fall of the tide is, I "understand, from ten to twelve feet, it is so mentioned in the "French Chart; I have no other means of judging." (p. 35).

President. "You say, that there was room enough for six "sail of the line, to be without range of shot and shells; Do you

" mean that, at any time of the tide?"—*A.* " It was the heighth " of the springs, and at the tide of ebb; there was five and a " quarter fathoms, under our bottom." (p. 35).

Mr. Spurling, Master of the Imperieuse, speaks of " a good " anchorage, for three or four sail of the line in five and an half, " or six fathoms, dead low water." The marks of that anchorage were taken by himself; and he says, " that he obtained his " knowledge, by his own observation—he was in the first instance " acquainted with the fact, only from the French Chart; but not " choosing to trust to that, he proved it of himself," (p. 83). Questioned by Lord Gambier. " Whether any person, whatever, had communicated to him, before he surveyed it, the anchorage for three or four sail of the line," he answers, " I discovered it myself, " being ordered to sound round the ship at some distance; as I " expressed, in answer to a question before asked."

Q. " Was it known before the Imperieuse went in, that there " was such anchorage?—*A.* Only by a view of the French " Chart, as we had no French pilot on board, or ever took any." (p. 85).

Asked, Admiral Stopford, if there was anchorage, within the Road of Aix, capable of holding six sail of the line, out of the reach of shot and shells, from any of the enemy's batteries? says, " I have understood, it never contained more than four ships in " five fathoms at LOW water, " out of the range of shot or shells." p. 72).

Captain Woolfe speaks of an anchorage as secure; for, says he, " if the ships had remained there," (meaning the ground on which the enemy's ships had lain, that were destroyed) " without " removing to the second anchorage, they must all have been " destroyed." (p. 85); and he afterwards explains, that this second anchorage, was where the Imperieuse and the other ships lay. (p. 86).

Q. " What do you mean by this second anchorage? that we " may have a just comprehension. The first was on the tail of

" the Palles?—*A.* Yes; the second anchorage I call, where the " squadron remained till they were withdrawn.

Q. " Where the Imperieuse and other ships remained?—*A.* " Yes.

Q. " That was further to the southward, than where you were " before?—*A.* Yes, east from the first anchorage, at the distance " of a mile or so; in the second anchorage, (having been there, " fifteen days after the enemy's ships were burnt) I think four or " five sail of the line, might have lain clear of the enemy's bat- " teries; but they must have been moored very short and very " close, with other small vessels to fill up the intervals. I lay " there with the Pallés, and fifteen or sixteen brigs, gun brigs, " cutters and schooners. I was sent in on the 13th. I call the " anchorage of the Isle d'Aix, where the enemy lay; but this is " a different anchorage, of which we knew nothing before." (p. 86). This anchorage was delineated on the French Chart, as deposed to by Mr. Spurling, Captain Broughton, (p. 222), and Captain Newcomb, (198), and the excellence, therefore, of that Chart is thus clearly and decidedly established. The examination that follows the part quoted, of Captain Woolfe's deposition, is very curious. The President is desirous of ascertaining something of a " supposed shoal," between the Boyart and the Pallés, which is introduced by Mr. Stokes, in his Chart, to shew the impossibility of getting into, what he himself has set down as deep water; as if it had been necessary to pass this shoal, in order to get at the French ships, thus interrogated.

Q. " Would the casting your eye upon this Chart give you a " clearer comprehension?"—*A.* " No—I have it all in my mind " —I received orders to assist Mr. Stokes, on a survey."

Q. " What was their report of the depth of water, at any par- " ticular time; of the tide, in the situation I have pointed out, be- " tween the Pallés and the Boyart, if you can recollect it?"— *A.* " I do not recollect any particular remark of Mr. Stokes, or " our Master, except Mr. Stokes having said, he had found *deeper " water and a little more room further to the Southward.*"

The President then framed a question in a way, certainly not very conformable to the practice of any Court whatever; and again endeavoured to press Mr. Stokes's Chart into the service.

Q. "I believe what you are stating applies more to the an-
"chorage, than to that which I am inquiring about. It appears
"by this Chart as if there was a shoal between the Road of Aix,
"and this other situation (pointing it out): what I wish to know
"is, what water there was upon *this bar or bank*, (pointing to
"the Chart)?" (p. 86.)—*A.* "That does not come within my
"knowledge, in the particular part to which the President alludes,
"with the exception of the Cæsar having grounded, much about
"the spot pointed out in the Chart, shewn me by the President.
"I will not take upon me to say, the exact situation of the Cæsar
"grounding." (p. 86.)

The mode here shewn to have been adopted by the President, assuming the fact, that there was a shoal, by inquiring what depth of water was upon it: instead of first investigating, whether such a shoal actually existed: and the means he used to assist the comprehension of the Witness, by endeavouring to fix his attention upon a Chart, of the authenticity of which he had himself no information, must, even to the dullest mind, appear very extraordinary; and every man, of understanding, will immediately conceive its tendency, and the effect it was capable of producing.

Captain Rodd, the next Witness to the same point, says: "He never knew, that line of battle ships could be within the Isle of Aix, *until he saw the frigates, after the action, move to the anchorage they took up.*" (p. 87.) The President immediately observed, "that seeing the frigates there, could be no proof, that the line of battle ships could lie there." This observation led Captain Rodd to a correction of his Evidence, which he did in the following manner: "I never knew that line of battle ships could lie there, for I do not know the depth of water!! I did not know, that the frigates could lie there, out of shot and shells, until that time." (p. 88).

Mr. Fairfax says, the space of anchorage, for large ships, was much confined, and, immediately afterwards, shews that he was ignorant of the fact, for that "he had not sounded there him-"self." (p. 140.)

Mr. Stokes says, that "to the southward of the Pallés shoal, "there was a place in five fathom at low water; but that it was "necessary, in order to get there, to pass a bank, with from 12 "to 16 feet only upon it, which could only be done at nearly "two thirds flood." (p. 148). But he afterwards shews that he, like his brother officer Fairfax, was ignorant of the fact to which he thus positively deposed; as will be seen from the answer to the following question:

Q. "Is the account which you gave of sixteen and twelve feet "water, at low water, between these shoals, derived from the "information of your own soundings, which you have just men-"tioned?"—*A.* "Not entirely from my own soundings; but "from the soundings taken by the Master of the Dotterel, whom "I sent for that purpose, and who reported to me, in writing, to "have found those soundings." (p. 150.) Deposing as truth to that, which depended on the veracity of others.

Lord Gambier admits, in his written Defence, that Mr. Stokes found on this bar or bank, between the Boyart and Pallés, "from "14 to 19 feet." (p. 134.) The Neptune Francois gives from 20 to 30 feet: but Mr. Stokes marks on his Chart, only from 12 to 16 feet, in the deepest part. He also deposes to these soundings "*having been reported to him to have been found.*" (p. 150.) Here it might have been expected, that the learned and impartial Judge Advocate, as in the case of Lord Cochrane's Minutes, (p. 41,) would have said: *but are these soundings put down in the place in which they were actually found;* "if not, they are "still objectionable."

It is a pity, that this favourite object, on which the President laboured so much, and on which so much of the time, of the Court had been exhausted, should have been defeated in a breath; but truth will, occasionally, support its own rights, and triumph over blunders and bad memories. Captain Newcomb

N

says, "he had been furnished with a French Chart, by Lord "Cochrane, and considered it a good one." (p. 199.) Captain Malcolm states, that "if ships had been disabled, with the wind, as "it was, they could not have come out; but must have gone "to the mouth of the Mamuson Passage, for anchorage." (p. 210.) This is another attack upon Mr. Stokes's Shoal; as the anchorage Captain Malcolm refers to, is situated between the Pallés and the Boyart, as we learn from the following.—*President:* "That is a passage between the Pallés and the Boyart?" —"Yes, which was ill understood, but where I had been led to "believe, there was anchorage for a few large ships." (p. 210.) And Captain Broughton says: "I think as the wind was North "Westerly and Northerly, they (alluding to the crippled ships) "might have found a safe anchorage and protection, in what is "called, in the French Chart, which I had on board, La Grand "Trousse, particularly where the Aigle afterwards lay; where "there is thirty or forty feet water, out of range of shot, and "shells in any direction." (p. 221.) Asked, "If on the 12th of "April he knew of such safe anchorage?" he answered, "only "by the *French Charts*, and which, from *having been long ac-* "*customed to use*, I imagined *were correct.*"

Q. by the President. "Do you know, from the anchorage in "Aix Road, to the anchorage you have just now described, there "is any shoaler water, between the Boyart and the Pallés Shoal; "I mean in the entrance of this anchorage, that there is a bar "goes across?"—*A.* "No; I do not know any thing of it. I "sounded from the wreck of the Varsovie, to that anchorage, "and found no shoal there."

President. "That is not the place; it is marked in some of "the Charts, that between the Boyart and the tail of the Pallés "there is a bar?" (p. 223.)—*A.* "I sounded, as I came in from "the fleet; but I did not find out any bar."

This alone, proves the falsity of that part of Mr. Stokes's Chart, which has been so much contended for, and which he himself had laid down, not from his own knowledge (p. 150,)—a circumstance, which, of itself, ought to have sufficiently operated with the Court, to refuse it admittance upon the Minutes. Yet the Chart, so founded, was not only considered, by the Court, as evidence, but, by the confidence with which they produced it, the Witnesses appeared to have regarded it, as indisputable. When the public reflect on this, and on the powerful influence such proceeding was calculated to produce, on the minds of junior officers, whilst giving their testimony, they will, in their wisdom, decide, whether justice has been duly administered, and whether there has been any cause to complain of a course having been pursued, which tended to defeat her of her best objects.

We have now adduced sufficient proof, conformably to the idea we have embraced, of the points we have gone over, to demonstrate, that there is not such a bank, in existence, as that insisted on by Lord Gambier: that the Master of the Fleet never sounded upon such a bank; and that the Charts, on which pretended soundings are traced, are worthless in the extreme.

Under these circumstances, Lord Cochrane, in spight of Lord Gambier's forebodings, of dreadful disasters accruing to his Majesty's ships, stands justified in his statement, that "a 74 gun-" ship might have gone into the inner anchorage, between the "Boyart Shoal, and Pallés, at any time of the tide;" and all Lord Gambier's adverse reasonings upon the subject, falls to the ground. His Lordship's ideas, as connected with them, however, is another consideration; and we allow his Lordship, all the credit due to the assertion: that "if he had, even previously, known, "as much of the inner anchorage, as he then did; he would "not, as the wind was at the time, have done otherwise than he "did." (p. 134.) We the more readily believe his Lordship, upon this occasion, because it is in unison with his former declarations to Lord Cochrane, in answer to the Charge, which he had, by inference, brought against him, and which we shall now bring forward. "If Lord Cochrane really knew, what he has now "professed to have known, when he was in Aix Road, it was a "duty, imperiously incumbent upon him, to have communicated "that information, upon the afternoon of the 12th, to the Cap-" tains of the line of battle ships, which he saw in so perilous a "situation." We will take Lord Cochrane's own words, upon his Examination by the *President*.

" I beg permission of the Court to ask one or two questions. " When did your Lordship first discover, that, in the inner road " of Aix, or Basque, there was anchorage, sufficiently capacious, " to contain six sail of the line to ride, without being in range of " shot or shell?"—*A.* "I had been in possession of the French " Charts, which I have not found to be defective, in any mate- " rial point, for a period of years; and from those Charts I had, " at all times, drawn my conclusions, with respect to the depth of " the water, or other circumstances, which relate to the naviga- " tion upon the enemy's coast." (p. 57.)

President. " That coast of the enemy, I suppose you mean." —*A.* " I refer to the French coast. The Spanish Charts also " are exceedingly good; I always go by them, and on them, as in " this case, and in all others, I placed my dependance. I went " in—on my way, I found them correct: I knew by the Chart, " that, when in pursuit of the Calcutta, I was to find a Bank: I " found it, and anchored upon it; and this I did, knowing what " I was about."

Admiral *Young.* " Was the bank the anchorage?"—*A.* " I " could not get so close, as I was desirous of going."

Q. " When did you discover that there was this anchorage, in " deep water?"—*A.* " I have said, that in going in, I found the " soundings correct, in my track close by the Boyart; and that, in " fact, I had that confidence in the Chart, that I had said to " Admiral Keates, when we were off there, and to Admiral " Thornborough, that there could be no difficulty, in going in " there, and destroying the enemy's fleet; and I took the Chart " on board Admiral Thornborough's ship. It was at that time, " that the plan went to the Admiralty, for destroying the French " fleet. I will only say, by what has long appeared to me, " that this anchorage might, if any object was in view, be " taken."

President. "In the Chart, that your Lordship consulted, upon " this occasion, are the soundings so marked, as to afford a space " sufficient for six sail of the line, not within range of shot or

" shell?"--*A.* "That conviction was upon my mind, and is " upon my mind: but by refering to the Chart, which is exactly " the same as others, that have been in my possession, those " soundings are marked; the Court can, by referring thereto, de-" cide the question."

Q. "When you found, by experience, upon going into Aix Roads, " that the soundings were correctly laid down, in the Chart you " made use of, in which you state you placed great confidence, " and from whence you drew a conclusion, that there was safe " anchorage for six sail of the line—Did you make any commu-" nication, of that important fact, to the Commander in Chief?"—*A.* " The Commander in Chief had the same Charts, I believe, " as I was in possession of; upon which, as I have already stated, " I formed my conclusions, with respect to the anchorage above " alluded to. He had also French pilots on board, upon whose " reports, from previous experience, I knew the Commander in " Chief to rely, above all other authority. In reconnoitring the " fleet, the first day, when so near as to induce the enemy to open " a fire, from almost his whole line, I reported to the Comman-" der in Chief the ruinous state of the Isle d'Aix, it having the " inner fortifications completely blown up and destroyed: which " I not only ascertained from the deck, with perfect preci-" sion, as to the side towards us; but also, as to the opposite side, " from one of the tops of the ship—There were only thirteen " guns mounted." (p. 58).

Admiral *Young.* " Will you consider, my Lord Cochrane, be-" fore you go on, how far this is relevant?"

Lord *Cochrane.* " I am only going to say, the impression, which " I knew, was upon his Lordship's mind, notwithstanding I vouch-" ed for these facts with my own eyes, and notwithstanding these " French pilots had not been there for several years; there " were only thirteen guns mounted on that side, on which I " had formerly seen, to the best of my recollection, about fifty. " In making these observations to his Lordship for his informa-" tion, he stated his perfect reliance upon the opinion of the " pilots, and assured me, that the Isle d'Aix was exceedingly " strong; and that (I think) it had three tier of guns mounted to-" wards the shipping. I then observed to his Lordship, that the

" circumstances I had related, fell within my own observation; " which did not alter his Lordship's opinion. I noticed also, the " little confidence which was to be placed in these pilots; and " said to his Lordship, as well as to Sir Harry Neale, that I never, " yet, had a pilot."

Judge Advocate. " Can this relate to the question, which is " asked?"

Lord *Cochrane.* " Yes; I conceive so: as my reason for not " communicating to his Lordship."

President. " Lord Cochrane states this, as his reason for not " taking a particular line of conduct?"

Lord *Cochrane.* " I have felt, that if I had answered, Yes or " No, to all the questions, which have been put to me, I ought " to be hung; and that if a Court Martial was held upon me, " and only the answers, *Yes* or *No*, appeared to these questions, I " should be hung for them."

Judge Advocate. " I believe nobody has desired your Lord- " ship to answer merely, Yes or No."

Lord *Cochrane.* " I answered, that I never yet knew a pilot, " particularly a French pilot, who did not find a Shoal wherever " there was a gun; and his Lordship, on the day of my leav- " ing Basque Roads, which was on the 16th or the 15th, still " continued of the same opinion, with respect to the Isle d'Aix: " notwithstanding my assurances then, when I had had full time " to make my observations, upon every part of it; and as the " whole of the frigates, with the exception of the Pallas, had " been withdrawn; and as it was evident, to the knowledge of his " Lordship, as well as to the knowledge of every one of those " Officers, that those frigates might have continued, where the " Imperieuse and Pallas then were; I held their being placed in " that situation, a matter for his Lordship's decision. I naturally " conceived, that as, even these were ordered to return, (I con- " ceived, in my own mind, for I did not express it to any body); " that, as those were not ordered back again, his Lordship did " not require any information, of which he was not possess- " ed." (p. 59.)

If, then, the Commander in Chief, would treat the informa- tion, offered to him by an Officer, who spoke as much from his own experience, as from the Charts, which he recommended, with so much indifference: if his Lordship with that "heavy de- "gree of responsibility, attached to his command, and of so much "complicated undertaking," as was in prospect before him, could turn his back upon information, that was essential to the success of any operations, he should determine on: if he, on whom it was a duty, imperiously incumbent, to make every diligent enquiry, relative to the situation, in which the enemy of his country lay, ready for attack, should reject it, when offered to him, with an indifference, bordering upon contempt; what could Lord Cochrane have expected, from the Captains of the line of battle ships, had he obtruded his opinions upon them—men who were his seniors, and who possessed the very same sources of information, as himself? They would have considered it, as carrying with it, something of arrogance; and possibly, as an insult to their understanding.

Lord Gambier did not judge of general feelings, by his own; or he would never have suggested, that communication to others, which he had, himself, treated so very rudely, as to give the preference, even to consummate ignorance, by stating his perfect reliance upon the opinion of "the pilots," who, Admiral Stopford, says, "were sometimes extremely ignorant," (p. 78.) When the Court so rigidly examined Lord Cochrane, upon this head, it might have been presumed they were fully impressed with the conviction, that had Lord Cochrane, made Lord Gambier acquainted with the knowledge he possessed, of an anchorage, in the inner Road of Aix, and of the accuracy of the French Chart: his Lordship would not have regarded, "the batteries of Aix: the broadsides "of the two ships, that remained on float: nor of those ships on "shore, that were sufficiently upright to have brought their guns "to bear on the entrance," (p. 125); but knowing there was good anchorage, in the vicinity of such terrific dangers, and out of the reach both of shot and shells, he would have rushed forward, with part of his fleet, and, employing two or three of them upon the batteries, attacked the enemy's ships with the remainder. When, however, his Lordship came upon his Defence, and candidly told them, "that had he even known such an anchorage," so perfectly safe, and secure, "was to have been met with, he "would with the wind, as it was, still have acted as he did;" (p. 134,) in other words (and we are warranted in using them, from the tenor of his Defence) his Lordship would not have acted at all; at least, not until the enemy had made their escape; (pp. 125. 128,)—it is most wonderful that the Court should have provoked the investigation any further; such conduct, on the part of his Lordship, was not to be done away, nor explained!

We shall state the fact as it occurred: Captain Malcolm, having spoken in favour of the French Charts, and of the anchorage, in reference; and that there was not any obstacles to prevent the small ships, frigates, and some ships of the line, (p. 214,) from going into Aix Road, he is questioned by the President: "As "you were on board the Caledonia, did you make this known to "the Commander in Chief, that you were of opinion, that by "keeping close to the Boyart Shoal, the ships might have gone, "provided they had thrown ALL *the stores and provisions over-* "*board?*"—*A.* "I do not know that I mentioned this to the "Commander in Chief. *The Charts shewed it,*" (p. 214.) And this, he justly conceived, was a sufficient reason, for not mentioning to the Commander in Chief a matter, which he naturally concluded, must, of course, be already known to him.

The Court had, no doubt, a motive for thus interrogating Captain Malcolm, and by common attention to the whole of Captain Malcolm's examination, and the evidence in general, some clue to it may be discovered. On our part, we shall only remark, that, whatever the motive might have been, the course to which it led, seems to have been a guide, to the steps, taken by his Lordship, who, as a winding up of Captain Kerr's deposition, asks "Did "Lord Cochrane, send to inform you, that there was a safe an- "chorage to the Southward?" and Captain Kerr, answered, "*No,*" (p. 209.)

It may at this time be a subject of deep regret, to Lord Gambier, that he did not think more becomingly, upon his own case; and defend himself, in a manner, more consistently with the circumstances it embraced; instead of distracting his ideas, by endeavouring to injure the reputation of another. His Lordship should have shewn, if within his power, some act, by which the public might have been enabled to judge of that zeal, of which he has made so many professions: and some measure that would have convinced them, that his Lordship did really possess, the judgment and ability, and that ardour and energy, of which he has spoken, and for which the Court have given him their warmest praise. The "impatience and anxiety" which Admiral Stopford mentions to have perceived in his Lordship, argues nothing in his Lordship's favour; but, on the contrary, is incompatible with his dignity as Commander in Chief, if we are correct in our notions; having always understood, that the most essential qualities in a Commander in Chief, are coolness of judgment, in those trying moments, and a fortitude and calmness, not to be shaken by surrounding dangers.

Having admitted the charge preferred against him, by the Lords Commissioners of the Admiralty, namely; "that from "the time of his observing, on the morning of the 12th, the "situation of the enemy, communicated also by Signal from the "Imperieuse, some time did elapse, before the enemy's ships "were attacked," it was a duty, imperiously incumbent upon Lord Gambier, to have brought forward those proofs, that were requisite to satisfy, not only the Court Martial, but the public, also, that such delay was produced by circumstances, that were totally beyond his means of controul, and by the occurrence of difficulties and dangers, that could neither have been foreseen nor prevented; that the best plans within the compass of his judgment to devise, were brought forward, and every expedient used to carry them into execution; and that the disappointment of the hopes and wishes he had raised on them, originated in powers superior to his own, and with which it was utterly impossible to contend.

Instead of this line of proceeding, the greatest exertion seems to have been made, with the view of gratifying his resentments, and exciting the strongest prejudices against Lord Cochrane, whose only crime, was a steady adherence to that integrity, which has marked his Lordship's conduct through life. He had wit-

O

nessed Lord Gambier's measures; and in his own mind condemned them. He saw the enemy at Lord Gambier's mercy; and experienced the utmost affliction at the supineness, which allowed them to escape: as a man, ardent in the interest of his country, and tenacious of his honour, he expressed his sentiments to Lord Gambier, on the occasion, with that freedom which characterizes such sensibility, presenting at the same time, that respectful demeanor, which, he very properly considered, was due to the high station in which Lord Gambier was placed. " When " I arrived at the outer anchorage," says Lord Cochrane, " I " mentioned to my Lord Gambier, that as there could be no " jealousy with respect to Admiral Stopford, it would be a " matter essential to the service, to send the Admiral in with the " frigates and other vessels, which his Lordship thought best, as " his zeal for the service would accomplish, what I considered " yet more creditable, than any thing that had been done. I " apologized for the freedom I used with his Lordship, and " stated, that I took that liberty, as a friend, for it would be im- " possible, things remaining as they were, to prevent a noise " being made about it, in England. I said; My Lord, you have " before desired me to speak candidly to you, and I have used " that freedom; I have no wish or desire, but for the service of " our country. To which his Lordship replied, that if I threw " blame, it would appear like arrogantly claiming all the merit " to myself. I assured his Lordship, I had no such intention, " and mentioned to him, at the same time, that it was not my " desire to carry the dispatches; or to go to London with Sir " Harry Neale, on the occasion. His Lordship, immediately after, " delivered to me an order directing the above. When I weighed " I had the satisfaction to have it reported to me, (I do not re- " member positively whether I saw it or not) that the signal " had been made for Admiral Stopford, which I concluded, to be " for the purpose of going in with the frigates. (p. 64).

Had Lord Gambier reflected, but one moment only, on the warmth and liberal effusion, which gave utterance to those sentiments, he certainly would not have insinuated, that Lord Cochrane had in it an intention, " to exalt his own reputation at the " expence of his Lordship's. (p. 108.) Lord Gambier would have been too thoroughly convinced, that such an idea was abhorrent to Lord Cochrane's conception of the fitness of things, and which would, most naturally, have pointed out to him, that the only way to exalt his character, was to preserve his own honour and independence. He never could have considered Lord Gambier's reputation, as a foundation upon which to exalt his own; and as vanity is a passion, with which he is not, nor ever was, on very intimate terms of acquaintance; he cannot feel much mortification, when he finds Lord Gambier refusing "to reduce his "experience and judgment, to a comparison with those possessed "by his Lordship, whose extent of responsibility," Lord Gambier remarks in derision, "has perhaps never exceeded the charge "of a single ship, while, from his situation, he was responsible "for every act of a Fleet." (p. 109.) We accord with his Lordship in the comparison he draws, between Lord Cochrane and himself, on the score of responsibility; but then we must be allowed the observation, that the officer who commands "a single ship," prosecutes an eager pursuit of the enemy, and vigorously attacks him, deserves, infinitely more of his country, than he who, groaning under the weight of responsibility, which attaches to "the command of a Fleet," is constantly vacillating between doubt and despair; between the possibility of encountering one danger, and the impossibility of escaping another. Were maxims, of such prudence, to prevail with the Commanders of our fleets and ships, the naval glory of Great Britain would soon sink into obscurity; and instead of being the envy and admiration, would become the derision and contempt of mankind. It is that enterprising genius, which directs to arduous achievements: it is that intrepid bravery, which despises all dangers, and that enthusiastic ardour and generous patriotism, which rise superior to every opposition, that have enabled us to contend, successfully, with the combined powers of the surrounding nations; to secure the best of sovereigns in the undisturbed possession of his throne; and our country from those calamities, that have depopulated every other state of Europe, and bent them beneath the yoke of despotism. If then, Lord Cochrane's responsibility never exceeded the command of a single vessel, it cannot be pretended, that he suffered that vessel, at any time, to remain idle, whenever an object presented itself, that was worthy of her exertions; or that he ever remained an indifferent spectator of the enemy's endeavours to elude his attack.

But what was his Lordship's responsibility, on the night of the 11th, when the execution of a very important measure, was entrusted to his discretion? And what was the responsibility incurred by his Lordship, when, in the afternoon, he took upon himself to attack the enemy, without orders; forcing the Commander in Chief, by the signals he made, to send him the assistance, that was necessary to effect the destruction of two ships of the line, and a fifty gun ship; all which he engaged for some time with no other aid, than a distant bombardment, by the Etna, could render him. It was, at that time, that he made the signal, that the enemy was superior to the chase; which signal is blended with that of distress; it was in consequence of that signal, that the signal was thrown out, on board the Caledonia, " to assist the ship making signals of distress." (pp. 196, 161.) It was then, that Captain Newcomb, whom we shall again have occasion to mention, being under weigh, appears to have displayed the true character of naval worth; and without any directions, pushed forward to her assistance. What was the responsibility which Lord Cochrane, in company with the Pallas, took upon himself, when he continued in the inner roads of Aix, after Adm. Stopford had quitted them, and had ordered, by signal, every other ship to follow him? (p. 90.) And after the letter of Lord Gambier, " directing him to join the fleet, with the bomb, " &c. and to desist from 'attempting impossibilities'?" (p. 53.) Were not such proceedings, on the part of Lord Cochrane, connected with as much comparative responsibility, as belonged to the Commander in Chief: although there was certainly a very distinguishing difference, in the use that was made of it; and that difference, is so very obvious, that we shall leave it without further notice.

We repeat, that Lord Cochrane never accused Lord Gambier; and that he never did instigate the Court Martial, as is most erroneously stated. In this assertion, we are borne out completely, by the Minutes of the Court Martial before us; and by the solemn declaration of Lord Cochrane, who considered the affair of

Basque Roads in every respect "as passed, and incapable of all "remedy." (p. 56.) But when it was represented to him, by the First Lord of the Admiralty, that it was the intention of his Majesty's Government, to move the Thanks of Parliament to the Commander in Chief, he considered, that were he to concur in the measure, he would be accessary to the prostitution of the proudest honour, that could be conferred, and to which the highly meritorious alone could aspire: and therefore immediately avowed his determined resolution to oppose it; and that he should feel himself bound by his public duty so to do. A proof, at once, of the honesty of his mind, and the independence of his spirit. As an officer, he had discharged his duty to his King and Country, and he felt, that it was equally incumbent on him to perform, that which was yet due from him, as a Member of Parliament, to both. If the Vote of Parliament had not been introduced to his notice, and pressed upon his attention: it is apparent that he would never have spoken of "the affair in Basque "Roads;" and that Lord Gambier would have been left to his tranquil meditations upon the additional honours that he had acquired in that station, honours, that, whatever might have been their standard, were, at least, equal in estimation with those that he had reaped in the affair of Copenhagen. Possibly his Lordship might have anticipated the latter part of our consideration of this subject, and settled in his own mind, that he was, in course, entitled to another step in another situation; in which, we have no hesitation to say, his Lordship would have met many, with whom he might safely compare merits, without any risk of losing by the comparison. If such was the opinion, that floated upon his fancy, he, no doubt, conceived that the Thanks of Parliament would open the door to the object of his ambition; and, if we are correct in our conjecture, we shall, then, have no difficulty in carrying the rancour, which his Lordship has manifested towards Lord Cochrane, to its proper account. What does his Lordship himself say to this point? "Whether Lord Cochrane supposed "he might with impunity endeavour to lower me in the opinion "of my Country, and of my Sovereign, signal marks of whose fa- "vour had, at this instant, been exclusively conferred upon him; I "know not." (p. 108.) We might hence conclude, without much violence on the matter of fact, that his Lordship had made a "comparison," in his own mind, and held, that if Lord Cochrane, "an officer under his command," had received the honour of the Red Ribbon, he, as the Commander in Chief, had an indisputable claim to the further advancement, on the Peerage: and having been created a Baron, for the affair of Copenhagen; he ought to be made a Viscount for that of Basque Roads. And really, the conclusion followed very naturally. In the Basque Roads affair, he had his "impatience, anxiety, solicitude, and "alarms;" but in the affair of Copenhagen, there was no manner of cause, that could possibly have called forth, either the one or the other.

Returning to his Lordship's evidence, upon the subject that seems to have so much annoyed him, we shall gain a considerable increase of strength, by his Letter to the Secretary of the Admiralty. In that Letter his Lordship says: "I had flattered "myself, that I should have received some signification of an "approbation of my conduct, and have had the gratifying task "of conveying to the officers and men, under my command, the "estimation in which the gallantry and discipline, displayed by "them, upon that occasion, were held by his Majesty and their "Country. Understanding, however, that there are some "doubts, whether the Fleet is to be so honoured: and feeling "that even a doubt, upon such a subject, cannot be entertained, "consistently with my reputation, as Commander in Chief, I "request, that you will be pleased to move the Lords Commis-"sioners of the Admiralty, to direct a Court Martial to be as-"sembled." (p. 13.)

This Letter was written, as may be presumed, in consequence of one received by his Lordship, from the First Lord of the Admiralty, announcing Lord Cochrane's intimation, relative to the Vote of Thanks, and concluding with the following words: "I "have felt it due to your Lordship, to give you the earliest in-"formation of the state of things, and acquaint you that a let-"ter will, this day, be written to Captain Lord Cochrane, in con-"formity to the above resolution of the Board of Admiralty, a "copy of which, together with Lord Cochrane's answer, will, "without delay, be communicated to your Lordship." Here, then, is the developement of the secret; and we learn from it, at once, the sentiment in which the requisition of a Court Martial originated, and the angry passions that operated so much against Lord Cochrane.

Quitting this, the superfluous part of Lord Gambier's Defence, which he seems to have allotted to the gratification of his passions: we shall now enter upon the investigation of some statements, and assertions, which his Lordship offers, in the conviction, no doubt, that they form a principal part of his Defence; and such might have been the case, had they been established by the irrefragable testimony of witnesses.

" Lord Cochrane has expressed an opinion, that two or three " sail of the line sent in, on the morning of the 12th, might, by " running up on the verge of the Boyart Shoal, have passed to " leeward of the two French ships, remaining at anchor. This I " declare to have been absolutely impracticable, as well from the " raking fire of the two ships afloat, *of the upright ones on* " *shore*, in our approach, and the fire of the batteries; as from " the shoal water close under their lee. The testimony of Cap- " tain Rodd, the only witness examined on this point, on the " part of the prosecution, corroborates my opinion, which, I " have no doubt, will be further supported by the evidence of " other competent witnesses, whom I propose calling." (p. 134.)

Turning to the Evidence of Captain Rodd, we cannot perceive that he makes any, the least mention, of passing to the leeward of the French ships, that remained at anchor until between one and two o'clock of the 12th, which was nearly about the time, that he was ordered into the inner roads of Aix; and this very naturally accounts for his silence on the subject. Had he spoken of them, it could not have been much to the point, as any observation he could have stated, must have been made at the distance of four or five miles—too great a distance for him to have been capable of stating, whether these ships could, or could not, have been rounded, so as to get to leeward of them. But although Captain Rodd does not say a word, and is not asked a question, relative to the particular of getting to leeward of the two ships that remained at anchor, yet he says, generally, that they could not have been attacked.

Q. "Did you observe the position of the enemy's line of battle
"ships, that were longest afloat, near the Isle of Aix, on the
"morning of the 12th?"—*A.* "There were two afloat."

Q. "Did you observe their position?"—*A.* "I do not know
"exactly, their bearings to the island; they were lying there, and
"got under weigh, or slipt, and ran up."

Q. "Were they in a situation, that line of battle ships, with-
"out being endangered, and the risk of being aground and lost,
"or being within range to be essentially injured by the batteries
"of the Isle of Aix, could have attacked them?"—*A.* "I do
"not know that they would have grounded; but they must
"have been wholly disabled by the batteries, and two line of
"battle ships, in coming in; I counted *thirteen* guns, as we
"passed, on the battery."

We will now see, how this corresponds with the other part of Captain Rodd's Evidence. Questioned to the defences of the Island of Aix, he says, that "the works were evidently under "repair," (p. 90) "and the enemy shifted their guns from "one part to the other." (p. 89) Which shews, that their means were circumscribed; that they were not capable of that destruction, which Captain Rodd supposed; and amounts to conviction, that his imagination ran away with his reason and judgment.

So much for theoretical danger, or dangers by surmise. We will now oppose them by practical experience. Captain Rodd carried his ship into this scene of horror; and what was the damage he sustained, from the batteries of Aix? "A shot, from the "Isle of Aix, passed through the main-topmast of the Indefati-"gable, the hole of which measured seven inches!!" (p. 90.) And in what space of time did this mighty damage occur? Between three o'clock in the afternoon of the 12th, and half past four o'clock in the morning of the 13th, the period in which the Indefatigable lay at anchor. During the passage in and out, there is not any notice taken of a shot having been, even fired at her; not even whilst Captain Rodd was counting the "*thirteen* "guns as he passed on the batteries."

But there seems to have been a general confusion of ideas, throughout the whole fleet, both as to circumstances and time; and Captain Rodd is not an exception. Speaking to the depth of water, when his ship grounded, he says, in one part of his deposition, "I could not find more than five and an half, or a quar-"ter less six fathoms; it was then about half ebb:" (p. 88) and in another part, "I had, only between four and an half, and five "fathoms, nearly at the top of high water;" which shews, that the higher the water rose, the less was its depth, which is a paradox we cannot solve.

Captain Rodd, however, does not stop here: as he says, "that, "although he lay in between four and an half, or five fathoms; "yet his anchor, at no more than half a cable's length from the "ship, was nearly in *seven* fathom." Hence it is conclusive, that line of battle ships would have had water enough, at, only half a cable's length from the situation, which was conceived, by Captain Rodd, "as good a one, as could have been chosen, for "the destruction of the enemy;" (p. 89,) even, if the fall of the tide had been as great, as Mr. Fairfax says, he *ascertained it to be*, during the night he was in Aix Roads, in the Lyra. (p. 141.)

It therefore remains only, to ascertain the actual state of the "two line of battle ships," which gave them the power "wholly "to disable our ships." Captain Beresford is asked, Whether any line of battle ship, could have run to leeward of the ships at anchor? and he answers, "I certainly should not like to have "risked it myself; there was scarcely room enough for a friend "to have passed, between them and the shoal." (p. 162.)

When Captain Beresford formed his opinion, upon the point, it is to be remembered, that he was, at least, three miles from the outside, of Isle D'Aix; that those ships, according to Mr. Stokes's Chart, besides the length of the island, were a mile beyond it, which makes four miles and an half remote from the

P

objects to which he speaks; and every body knows, particularly every one who has been at sea, or even visited its coast, that being at the distance of four or five miles from vessels, with the land near to them, and viewing the whole in an oblique direction, how totally impossible it is, to say from appearance, whether such ships and the land, be five hundred yards, or a mile from each other. How much more difficult then, must it have been for Captain Beresford to ascertain the fact, when the shoal, to which he alludes, was actually covered with from 9 to 13 feet of water.

Captain Beresford, therefore, spoke only from appearances; and certainly imagined, as he has expressed himself, that there was scarcely room for a friend to pass between the French ships at anchor, and the shoal; and that "the smoke alone, beside "their being crippled, would have caused them to be entan-"gled;" (p. 162,) but such evidence amounts to nothing: it is vague, uncertain, and nugatory; and in that way the Court must have regarded it; or, it is presumable, they would have cross-examined him, in the same rigid manner, as they did Lord Cochrane, and Captains Seymour, Malcolm, and Broughton.

Captain Beresford, speaking to the consequences, had any of our ships been crippled, by the batteries, says: "If they could "not have returned, and he thought they could not, the conse-"quence must, in his mind, have been very serious." (p. 162.) How would it have been serious? They might, as Captain Malcolm says, have remained until slack tide, and continued the action; which, as Captain Broughton very well observes, was not to be supposed would be over in a moment, and then have gone to the mouth of Marmuson Passage, which Captain Broughton says, they might have effected, "even in a crippled state." (p. 222.) But Captain Beresford did not consider, that there was safe and secure anchorage near at hand, for our ships to have retired to, although "every one knew there was such an anchorage;" (p. 222) or, it is probable, his opinion would have been differently constructed. This omission, however, of a very important fact, will shew, that Captain Beresford, in framing his sentiments, did not embrace every combination, that was requisite, to render them correct.

Such is the result of our search, amidst the jumble of discord and testimony, that has been adduced, in Lord Gambier's attempts to prove the destructive powers of the two ships, that remained at anchor. We have not been able to discover a single trace of such powers; on the contrary, it has been tolerably well made out, that those ships were in a state, which, so far from rendering them capable of crippling, or in any way disabling our ships, they were unable to defend themselves; and, therefore, were intent only, upon that flight, which they afterwards effected, and, which they *previously attempted*, about *three o'clock* in the morning—a fact which Mr. Fairfax states, and, as he believes, was known only to himself, he says, "before day-light, they loosed their "sails; shortly afterwards, they got their heads to the Eastward, "and seemed to recede from me—seemed to increase their dis-"tance—their sails were taken in, immediately." (p. 143).

This is abundantly demonstrative of their extreme anxiety to seek safety, even by braving the greatest dangers, and the only probable reason, for furling their sails again, was, that *the ebb had then made;* and that the *night was too dark, to discover the necessary marks,* for their guidance to the Channel up the Charante, before the water had fallen too much. Had Lord Gambier exercised that judgment and ability, for which the Court Martial have given him so much credit: he would have been most thoroughly convinced of such, their enfeebled and deplorable state; and his own reason, if he had reasoned at all on the subject, and his own incomparable "experience," would have impressed it upon his mind. Of all the other ships, that were lying at anchor, on the evening of the 11th, only one escaped; the others had got on shore, (p. 33,) in the morning of the 12th, and every exertion was making to lighten them, so as to warp them off; (p. 211. 233,) in order to push for the Charante, the channel to which is so very shoal, that, according to Mr. Fairfax's Chart, before us, that it does not, at low water, afford more than from 4 to 5 feet. Of this, the French Rear Admiral, and Commodore, were as well informed, as they were of the melancholy consequences, immediately within their view, of attempting it, in that state of the tide: the whole of their consorts, line of battle ships, and frigates stranded, with very little probability of ever getting off again. It therefore, followed, of course, that those Commanders would devise every possible means, to get away from our fleet, and avoid the misfortune that had attended their companions. To this end, the first and chief considerations were, to lighten their ships to the very utmost of their power: and for that purpose, as we have before noticed, when speaking of the ships that were on shore, the guns and shot, as the heaviest and, at the same time, the most convenient articles for removal, would be the first thrown overboard: and, as it was to be supposed, they would take the opportunity of the first flood tide, to carry their plans into execution; they would, of necessity, have disposed of both guns and shot, some time before the flood began to make, if they had not done so at an earlier period—which, in their anxiety to effect their escape, it is very probable they had, (p. 204.) If, then, this reasoning be correct, and the extremely critical situation of those ships, the purposes they had determined: and the immense risks they had to encounter in accomplishing it, be taken into consideration; it must appear to rest upon the strongest probability, that those ships, during the flowing tide, would have been as much divested of all power of resistance, " as if the tide, had then " ebbed, and the ships were fast on the ground, with *their sterns* " *to the westward*, incapable to bring *any* guns to bear on the " ships that attached them," a circumstance, to which Mr. Stokes boldly " ascribes our whole success," (p. 151).

This was perceptible to Lord Cochrane, in the early part of the morning of the 12th; he, therefore, made the signal which has been so much discussed, in the sanguine hopes, that the Commander in Chief, who was moored at the distance of six or seven miles, from any one of the enemy's ships, would have taken the steps that were necessary to secure the whole. " I did " expect," says Lord Cochrane, " that an endeavour would " have been made to dislodge these two ships from their situa- " tion, by an attack, by two or three sail of the line, which were " quite sufficient for the purpose." " Passing over to the " Boyart, and putting their helms a lee, their fore top sail being " to the mast, would have brought their heads towards the " North East, which would have enabled them, at a distance, at " which the shot of Aix would have been of little effect, to have

" brought all their guns to bear upon the enemy's two ships:— " or, until so far down to leeward, that they would have been " enabled, by putting their helms up, to run under their stern, " between them and the ships on shore: and thereby capture " them, or force them to cut and run aground likewise; and " then effect both their destruction, and the destruction of the " other vessels, that were ashore," " at any period, previous to " half past 11 o'clock; and, by the frigates alone, before one " o'clock, when the French three decker swung to her hawsers; " and when the last of their ships began to float." (p. 45).

This testimony, delivered by Lord Cochrane, (and his Lordship's situation afforded him the best means of forming the opinion it offers) goes far to overturn the assertion of Lord Gambier, " that the attack of those two ships were, by the means Lord " Cochrane had pointed out, absolutely impracticable." Nor does Lord Cochrane stand alone, as to the period when the attack ought to have been made; Captain Broughton says, " it " would have been more advantageous, if the line of battle ships, " frigates, and small vessels, had gone in at half flood, between " 11 and 12 o'clock." (p. 220).

Question by the President. " Would not the ships, so sent in, " have been exposed to the fire of the two ships, that remained " at anchor: the French Admiral's ship, and the batteries, of the " Isle d'Aix, at the same time?—*A.* Certainly; but I conceived " they were *partly panic struck*; and, on the appearance of a " force coming in, might have been induced to cut their cables, " and try to make their escape up the river.

Q. " In the event of their proving not to have been so panic " struck, and of their having defended themselves, aided by the " batteries on shore, are you of opinion, that the British ships " must have suffered greatly, on the occasion? —*A.* I think they " would have suffered; but, that a ship or two, might have been " placed, in my opinion, against the batteries, on the Southern " part of Isle d'Aix, so as to take off their fire, and silence them. " I mentioned to Sir Harry Neale, on board the Caledonia, when " the signal was made for all Captains, in the morning, that I " thought they were attackable—speaking of the confused state,

" in which the French ships appeared to be, at the time." (p. 221).

Captain Broughton further says, after having been tortured by the most extraordinary questions, that, perhaps, were ever proposed to a witness, as to the enemy's disabling our ships, and taking and wounding our men, in the event of an attack having been made upon the plan he had proposed, " I conjecture, that " the *discomfited* French squadron would have made little re- " sistance." " It is impossible to foresee what might have hap- " pened; but, from the situation in which the enemy were, *not* " *having recovered their fright* of the night before, I think the " loss would have been very little; *as few of their ships were* " *in a situation to fight their guns.*" (p. 224).

Captain Malcolm, who was interrogated, as to the *multiplied dangers* that would have awaited our ships, had they gone in, while the French Rear Admiral and Commodore were afloat, admits, that, sending them in, whilst the enemy remained upon the defensive, would have been attended with very considerable risk, and his reason is remarkable; " because, had they been " disabled, they could not have come out, but must have gone " to the Marmuson passage for anchorage," (p. 210), which is an anchorage, without the range of shot and shells.

Such was the risk that operated to prevent an attack upon the enemy's ships, that lay in the most wretched state of weakness, within our very grasp, and while fortune, hovering over our heads, invited us to the glorious opportunity of " sinking, burn- " ing, and destroying" them,—Words that, in the instructions given to every Commander in the Navy, are mandatory; but, it seems, they were not of sufficient force to compel Lord Gambier to a risk, in encountering which, he might have rendered a most essential service to his Country:—a risk, very far short of the grand object, for which it was to have been ran; a risk, that, at the most, would only have detained some of our ships, from the fleet eight and forty hours, that is, in the event of their having been so far disabled, as to be compelled to seek protection somewhere, whilst they were repairing their damages; and a safe anchorage was within a few hundred yards of them, very well adapted for the purpose. When the public shall have reflected upon these facts, they will not have any difficulty in coming to a decision upon the point, immediately before us.

But although Captain Malcolm has admitted the attachment of risk; he speaks a determined resolution to have sent in ships, in defiance of the batteries of Aix, which, he says, "could have "been nearly avoided." (p. 208.) "Had it appeared to me, "that there was no other chance of destroying those ships, but "by such an attack; I certainly think, it ought to have been "made." (p. 211.)

On the subject of that part of Lord Cochrane's statement, relative to "the rubbish" upon the Isle of Aix, which his Lordship mentioned, to shew the weakened state of its fortifications, and which Sir H. Neale (p. 186), Captains Broughton (p. 218), Rodd (p. 90), Mr. Spurling, his Master, &c. have supported, Lord Gambier says, "they were, in fact, materials for improving or "repairing the works;" and his Lordship attempts to maintain his naked assertion, against such overwhelming evidence, by arguments, equally destitute of foundation—thus: "Can it be "natural to suppose, that the enemy, who are so active in forming batteries, and whose Engineers are considered to be equal "to any, would, of all moments, choose that for dismantling or "blowing up works, when they expected those works would be "most required; for it is very certain, that the enemy were as "fully apprised of our intention of attacking their fleet, as my"self." (p. 135.)

Had Lord Cochrane and his Master deposed, that those works had been recently reduced to an heap of rubbish, the reasoning of his Lordship might have appeared plausible; but such was not the case. It is wonderful, that it never occurred to his Lordship, that those works might have been, and in all probability were, dilapidated and become rubbish, long before the Fleet had received its destination: long, indeed, before that destination had ever reached the information of the French Minister of Marine; and in that case, the enemy, apprised of the intended attack by our Fleet upon them, would not have been of the least advantage whatever. The act had taken place, and all that could be done, to remedy the evil, in proportion to the extent of their means, was to throw up temporary works, and run out guns upon platforms: (p. 89) thus giving an appearance of defences, instead of defences themselves; and endeavouring to terrify, where they had not the power to injure. This is a piece of finesse frequently played off by the enemy; and, in the present instance, it seems to have succeeded, to the full extent of their wishes. Captain Bligh says, "he *did not observe* that any of "the fortifications had been blown up and destroyed." (p. 157.) Captain Kerr was equally inattentive to these magazines of *horror;* but he has offered something of excuse: "The situation of "the Revenge was so critical, that I was otherwise taken up." (p. 168.) Yet it is extraordinary, that they should have failed to attract his notice: and the very circumstance, which he draws into an apology for not having remarked on them; is the very circumstance that should have been a most powerful inducement, with him, to examine them minutely. The enemy directed all their fire against his ship; she appeared to Captain Bligh "to "draw the fire of the batteries of the Isle D'Aix from the fri- "gates." (p. 156.) Having got her off, he ran her to some spot, beyond the shot of those batteries, "conceiving it to be his duty "to let her ground, out of range, if possible, rather than "within." (p. 167.) Captain Godfrey was as incapable of giving any information upon the subject of those batteries, as the rest. Asked by the President, "Did you observe any heaps of "earth, *rubbish*, or stones, by the fortifications, on the Isle "D'Aix, which indicated, that any part of those works were in "a *ruinous state?*" He answers, "No." (p. 174.) Such kind of testimony, however, must have been considered as sufficiently satisfactory: as the Court never disturbed it, by any further interrogatory; although many might have been suggested. They may have conceived, as his Lordship, no doubt, did, that it completely defeated the affirmative depositions of Lord Cochrane, and Mr. Spurling; but they should have known, that one affirmative is worth twenty negatives. A thing may be discovered by one man, who remarks on objects, that are interesting in their nature, and likely to be important in their consequences; which shall, notwithstanding, escape the observation of others, nay of hundreds, who have not curiosity to provoke enquiry; or whose taste and judgment are not formed to direct it. This truth proves the principle, that one affirmative is preferred, both in law and in common sense, to twenty negatives; and, if carefully considered, will explain many of the Minutes, to which we are speaking, and which, without explanation of some kind, are not intelligible.

We shall not urge the point any further, persuaded, in our own mind, that, from the testimony of Sir Harry Neale, Captain Broughton, and others, enough has been advanced to refute Lord Gambier's insinuation, which was to have invalidated the Evidence delivered by Lord Cochrane, in reference to the feeble and ruinous state of the batteries of Aix. But as Lord Gambier's friends may yet be a little sceptical, to remove all doubt, we will quote the Evidence, of one of his Lordship's own Witnesses: and the circumstances it connects adds to its weight.

Captain Broughton questioned by the President: "In your "service in Basque Roads, had you any opportunity of making "observations upon the state of the enemy's fortifications, on "the Isle D'Aix?"—*A.* "Yes, I had."

Q. "Narrate what were those observations?"—*A.* "I was on "board the Amelia, when she was ordered to dislodge the enemy "from the Boyart Shoal; and being nearly within gun-shot of "the Isle D'Aix, I observed the fortifications. They appeared "to me to be in a very different state, to what I observed them, "when serving two or three years before, under Sir Richard "Keates; I thought they were repairing the works, from the "*quantity of rubbish* that was thrown up: and I counted, on a "semicircular battery, which commanded the roadsted, where "the enemy lay, between fourteen and twenty guns; I am not "positive as to the exact number."

Q. "Did it appear to you that the enemy were constructing "new works in front of the old ones, and nearer to the sea?"—*A.* "It appeared to me that they were repairing and improving "the old works; I think that the *rubbish* was the remains of "*the old works that had been taken down.*" (p. 219.)

Q

When Lord Gambier's Friends shall have deliberated upon these facts dispassionately, it is to be hoped that they will, in their own minds, at least, and nothing further can be desirable, do justice to Lord Cochrane's accuracy. And should these Notes ever reach the Members of the Court Martial, they may regret that they did not permit their judgment to be informed, by the means that were placed at their disposal; and that they had not time sufficient to take into their consideration, the several parts of the investigation, that bore upon the case, on which they were to decide.

Were we speaking of any other man, than a strictly religious British Admiral, who reduces piety to practice, and does unto all men, as he would that all men should do unto him: we should, occasionally, be much disposed to believe, that Lord Gambier sometimes, allowed the cares of this world, to run away with his Christian doctrines; and in attempting to exculpate himself, in the moment of Trial, suppressed the benevolent dictates of Christian charity.

The extreme solicitude, with which his Lordship endeavours to impress the minds of the Officers, under his command, with a conviction, that Lord Cochrane had endeavoured to traduce their good name, and wrest from them the praise that was due to their zeal and exertion, cannot but appear to every one, as calculated only to promote his own personal interests: which, he might have imagined, would be best aided by inflaming their resentments; and prevail upon them, to make a common cause, with him, against their, supposed, common enemy. But that solicitude is made still more manifest, in a subsequent part of his written Defence, in which his Lordship appears to be aware, that the memory is sometimes unfaithful; and that to keep resentment in its vigour, it is necessary to feed it with an occasional incitement.

He says: "Relative to the service that had been performed, "and what might, possibly, still be further attempted towards "the destruction of the enemy's ships, Lord Cochrane states a "conversation to have passed, between his Lordship and myself, "on his return from Aix Roads, in which he represents me to

" have said: 'that if he threw blame, it would appear like arro-" ' gantly claiming all the merit to himself.'" (p. 135.) "I how-" ever trust the Court will not conceive, that the expression of " '*casting blame*' has any allusion *to my conduct*; for, as I " have before said, Lord Cochrane never expressed one syllable, " from which I could form the most faint idea, that *he felt dis-" appointed, at any thing resting with me*. His Lordship's al-" lusion had reference only, *to the several Officers, who acted with " him in Aix Roads*, upon whom, *generally, he cast blame*; with-" out giving *the smallest intimation*, either by word or manner, " that in the expressions of dissatisfaction, *he included his Com-" mander in Chief*."

The public are not unacquainted with the character of Lord Cochrane, who, although a young man, and with nothing of Lord Gambier's "experience," has not, unfrequently attracted public notice: not by words, for he is reserved, and diffident; but by his actions, in his profession, against the enemies of his country, whom he has often encountered, and invariably beaten. And the public will judge, "under all the circumstances of the case," whether his Lordship is capable of speaking in the absence of any man, that which he would not dare to proclaim in his presence; or say, at one time, what he could not justify at another. How Lord Gambier could assert, that the words he had quoted from Lord Cochrane's deposition "had reference, only, to " the several Officers, who acted with him, in Aix Roads," can be explained only, by his Lordship, or some of his ingenious friends.

Lord Cochrane has clearly and distinctly stated, in *his* Evidence, that the expression WAS used, after he had suggested to Lord Gambier, the propriety of sending in Admiral Stopford, to the inner roads; as his zeal for the service, would accomplish, that which would be more creditable, than any thing that had been accomplished. "I apologized," says Lord Cochrane, "for the " freedom I used with his Lordship, and stated, that I took that " liberty, as a friend; for it would be impossible, *things remain-" ing as they were, to prevent a noise being made about it, in " England*. My Lord, you have desired me to speak freely " and candidly to you; and I have used that freedom. I have

" no wish or desire, but to serve our country. To which his " Lordship replied, that *if I threw blame, it would appear, like " arrogantly claiming all the merit to myself.*" (p. 64).

From this plain and consistent Evidence, it is made perfectly clear, that the expression had no manner of reference, either directly or indirectly, to the Officers, who acted with Lord Cochrane, in Aix Roads; but was, on the contrary, confined to the half measures of Lord Gambier, and conveyed a delicate, though pointed, disapprobation of his conduct; suggesting, at the same time, the adoption of a mode, that might prevent "*a " noise being made about it in England.*" Lord Gambier's attempt, therefore, to pervert the plain and true meaning of it, by a positive declaration, that it was intended to criminate the Officers, who acted with Lord Cochrane, in the Roads of Aix; was not very consonant with the character of an Officer, nor with the dignity of a man.

We know not how the word *blame* may be understood, by Lord Gambier; but if pointing out the misapplication of means, that were within a man's power; and if to represent, that the conduct he adopted, had been such, as was likely to produce a ferment in the public mind, can be considered as implying *blame;* Lord Cochrane gave something more, than the " smallest intimation," of *blaming* Lord Gambier. It is true, he did not deliver himself in the harsh sounds of hostility; unkindness was foreign to his purpose. He spoke in all the mildness of friendship; with the generous purpose of averting the danger, in which he feared "his " Commander in Chief" would be involved, "if things remained " as they were." Still, however, it was in blame of his conduct: and in terms, as strong as the occasion called for; at least they appeared so to his Lordship's mind, who judged of Lord Gambier's feelings by his own. Indeed, his Lordship's grand object, in addressing Lord Gambier, upon the subject, was to serve his Country, by exciting his Lordship to a vigorous exertion, towards destroying the remainder of the enemy's ships, that were, as he imagined, yet assailable. But Lord Gambier had determined, within his own bosom, that, although Lord Cochrane had forced him to risk his Majesty's ships, in one instance; he should not prevail upon him to do so in another. Imagining, however, that

Lord Cochrane, on his arrival in England, learning that his friendly hints, instead of being adopted, were absolutely discarded: and that every thing continued, as he left it, might deliver his sentiments to Government, or promulgate them through such channels, as would convey them to the public ear: policy admonished him, that something was necessary; and he used the menacing expression, which he has aimed at employing in a different sense: "*If you throw any blame, it will appear, like* "*arrogantly claiming all the merit to yourself.*" An expression, which was, of all others, the best calculated to close up the lips of Lord Cochrane; to whom the bare idea of arrogating merit, would carry more alarm and apprehension, than could the batteries of Aix, the two line of battle ships still afloat, and the ships aground, strike into the bosom of Lord Gambier.

Of all this, Lord Gambier was well aware: and with the consideration that the subject suggests, he might have spared himself the trouble of giving his remarks, in relation to his public dispatches to England, which had nothing to do with his Defence, before the Court, unless to confuse it.

Lord Cochrane never could have supposed, that it was Lord Gambier's intention to send dispatches by him: or he must have imagined, that his Lordship meant to punish him, by way of retaliation, for the censure he had bestowed upon his measures, in the friendly advice he had offered, in aid of them, when taking his leave; and no one who reads the conversation, which then occurred, and which we have just gone over, can possibly conceive, that Lord Cochrane could have "expressed evident," or any, "marks of dissatisfaction," when Lord Gambier gave him to understand, that Sir Harry Neale, the Captain of the Fleet, was to bear those dispatches (p. 136), notwithstanding the "positive "declaration" of his Lordship to the contrary.

Lord Gambier is in the habit of making declarations: and, as it may be proper to display the nature of them, we will take this opportunity for the purpose; and an instance or two, drawn from the mouths of his own witnesses, will suffice. His Lordship, asked by the Court, if he had any questions to put to Admiral Stopford, observed, in all the calmness of pious resignation, as to his own fate; and all the acuteness of feeling for the fate of others: "With respect to my *own conduct*, I have no "wish; but I think it due to the Officers of the fire-ships to put "a question as to *their conduct*, which *I* AVER *was highly me-"ritorious.*" (p. 79.) His Lordship then asked Admiral Stopford: whether, "under the circumstances of the time, it was NOT "surprising, that so large a proportion of the fire ships passed "through the enemy's fleet; and that so small a number failed?" *A.* "*Every circumstance was extremely favourable*, for the fire "ships acting; and, therefore, I took it for granted, that when "*properly placed*, they must INEVITABLY go down upon the "enemy's ships. (p. 80). "Some were certainly set fire to be-"fore, it appeared to me, that they had run so near to the "enemy, as others had." (p. 81). Captain Woolf says: "Two "of those vessels got on shore, on the Island of Oleron, *from "bad management*;" and that "his own ship was nearly burnt "by two, that were badly managed, and which were on fire as "they passed;" (p. 126). though the Aigle was, at the time, according to Mr. Fairfax's own Chart, two miles and a half from the enemy.

Thus is Lord Gambier's "*averment*" placed in a distressing predicament. Admiral Stopford and Captain Woolf have both proved it, to be altogether unfounded; and we may add, that his Lordship has contradicted himself, having, in another place, acknowledged that "several of the fire-ships failed in their object;" (p. 124.)

Lord Gambier should, at least, have consulted the strength of his memory, before he trusted himself with the hazardous expedient, of making "averments," and "positive declarations," which, he must have known, would extend themselves beyond the latitude of the Court Martial, and be subject to the consideration of men of intelligence, and common sense: who pronounce their judgment without favour or affection; and render to justice, all that justice has a right to claim. We are, therefore, to conclude, that his Lordship's "*averments*," and "*positive declarations*," were the offspring of error and prejudice. In this conclusion, we are partly justified, by the testimony of the loquacious Mr. Wilkinson, who, notwithstanding the very remarkable attention he received from the Court, and the Judge Advocate: and the encouraging cheers of both; has not said a syllable of the "evi- "dent marks of dissatisfaction expressed by Lord Cochrane," when "given to understand, that Sir Harry Neale, the Captain "of the Fleet, was to bear Lord Gambier's Dispatches to Eng- "land."

Lord Gambier's reflection, upon Lord Cochrane's Evidence, has one claim, that must be tolerably obvious; nor will we withhold from it the merit to which it is fairly entitled—the merit of being in accordance with, almost, every other part of his Lordship's Defence, on which he insinuates much, but proves nothing.

Lord Cochrane, when questioned by the Court, as to a paper which he held in his hand, stated with more candour than he experienced, "that it contained a Copy of the Minutes he made, "during the passing scene, to which they referred;" (p. 33,) "that some of those Minutes were transposed; but that the act "of transposing, had not caused any difference, or alteration, in "the points they embraced: that those stood, as they occurred, "taken down upon different slips of paper, at the moment of oc- "currence; and afterwards formed into the shape of a regular "Log: that there was one, or two particulars he had inserted, "since he came on shore, which, he said, he should remark as "he came to them: that all the circumstances were known; and "that he might appeal to the Logs of the whole Fleet, for their "accuracy." "I could not," said his Lordship, "in the midst "of firing, sit down to write those circumstances." (p. 34.)

Lord Gambier was in the possession of these facts, and, therefore, must have sinned against conviction, when he said, or rather insinuated, that "Lord Cochrane founded his statement on "a narrative Log, compiled since his return to England, and "*on a French Chart.*" Whatever his Lordship might think of a narrative, so composed as we have shewn it to be, and as the same appears on the face of the Minutes, is of trifling moment. Lord Cochrane did not deliver it in with the general and guarded assertion, that the contents were true "to his recollection and "belief:" he looked at it, only, to refresh his memory, in order that he might depose to every fact within his knowledge; convinced, in his own mind, from the complexion of the questions proposed to him, that, unless he proceeded by way of narrative, he would not be enabled to do so. And this was decidedly his Lordship's opinion, as certified by himself. Upon an interruption from the Judge Advocate, and in severe reproof of that Officer's conduct on the occasion, he said, "I am bound to state "the whole truth; and I do not think I can deliver the whole "truth, unless I am assisted by these Notes. If I am to state "the whole truth, I must use these Notes." (p. 40). And towards the conclusion of his Evidence, when again interrupted by the Judge Advocate, he exclaimed, "I have felt, that if I answered "YES or NO, to all the questions, which have been put to me, I "ought to be hung; and that if a Court Martial was held upon "me, and only the answers YES or NO, appeared to those questions, I should be hung for them." (p. 59.)

These facts were also, within the knowledge of Lord Gambier; yet he, notwithstanding, asserted, that Lord Cochrane's Evidence, was no better than a compilation of fancy and imagination, founded on a French Chart. His Lordship was equally well informed, that Admiral Stanhope, one of his judges, held this narrative Log, to be competent to the purposes, to which it was applied; and gave the best reason for admitting it. "Lord Cochrane swears, that all, which he now states, is correct; therefore, "I do not think it material whence it comes." (p. 34). But it must be observed, and we state the fact with sincere regret, that Lord Cochrane was, notwithstanding, refused the benefit of referring to his Notes, in any form. The objection was taken by the Judge Advocate; and he carried the Court with him. (p. 38).

There is, it is true, a vast difference between the "Charts "delivered in by Lord Cochrane, and that by the Master of the "Caledonia;" the latter of which, Lord Gambier promised "should be verified by the Master of the Caledonia;" but it must have escaped his Lordship's memory. We find, indeed, the difference to be so great, "that it is scarcely to be supposed, "they relate to the same transaction." (p. 136). The reason is, that Lord Cochrane's Charts, are verified, by his oath, as correct, as to the objects they were meant to bring within the notice of the Court: namely, the position of the enemy's ships, after their dispersal, on the morning of the 12th of April; (p. 130), and the Master of the Caledonia, has, by his oath, falsified his Chart, established the Charts of Lord Cochrane; and it appears, that, by some unaccountable inadvertency, the Chart, which he delivered, as descriptive of the situation of the enemy, on the 12th, was a Chart of their position of the 13th!!

If Lord Gambier thought it "very fair," to remark a fact, said to have been acknowledged by Lord Cochrane, in his Evidence, "that he had erred no less than five points of the "compass, in the report made to Lord Gambier, before the "attack, of the direction in which the French fleet was moored." (p. 136). Lord Gambier ought to have mentioned the circumstance in which the mistake was made: that it was a mistake of no consequence whatever; and that the bearings of the enemy's ships, from the Fort of Aix, might have been ascertained with nearly as much precision, from the anchorage, at which his Lordship lay, as the spot from which Lord Cochrane reconnoitered them. But, making his Lordship a present of his argument, and all the advantage that can be derived from it: what will it amount to? Why, to the very proposition that his Lordship has, by every studied art, endeavoured to deny; namely, that Lord Cochrane pursued the straight course of honesty, in delivering his sentiments; and candidly acknowledged an error whenever he detected it. In acknowledging this, however, he has used other words than those employed by his Lordship: he has not stated in his Evidence, that "he erred no less than five points of the "compass, regarding the direction in which the French ships "were moored;" but merely, and we quote his own deposition, "that they appeared to be moored, as near as he could judge, "North and South, or nearly so; *although he thought, at first,* "*they inclined considerably more to the North East, and South* "*West.*" (p. 31). This comparative statement, shews Lord Gambier, himself, to have been the most erroneous of the two, and that he has, to answer his own purposes, put words into Lord Cochrane's mouth, which his Lordship never uttered.

Allowing, then, the fact to stand, as Lord Gambier has placed

R

it, it would shew only, that Lord Cochrane had made a mistake, in a matter of no consequence, namely, the relative bearings of the ships from each other: for, in either case, the fleet was equally exposed; and, therefore, did not demand of him any very particular attention. It was not how one ship bore from another; but the bearing of the main body of the fleet: and, especially, whether the whole lay in a situation, that was open to attack: which was, indeed, the grand, if not the sole object of his Lordship's mind; and, to which every faculty of his mind was principally, if not entirely, directed. His Lordship, however, as we have before observed, candidly and very properly acknowledged his mistake. And it were to be wished, that Lord Gambier had better understood this truth: that *to render error culpable, is to persist in it;* and that in the admission of it, we learn that it had no connection with design. This leads us to the following passage in Lord Gambier's written Defence.

" Lord Cochrane has thought fit to represent that the enemy's " three grounded ships, which escaped from off the shoal of the " Pallés, were lying so near together, as to give two of them," which he states to be heeling inwards " the *appearance* of their " Masts and Yards locking. This description of them is certainly well calculated to make a strong impression of their defenceless state; but whatever may have been their appearance to his Lordship, such is not the fact; for, in reality, they " were lying *perfectly separate* and *clear of each other*, as is " shewn by the afore-mentioned Chart, produced by the Master " of the Caledonia, as will also be proved by Evidence." (p. 136). " But, whatever their situation might have been, with respect to " proximity, I must here repeat, that they could not have been " approached by our ships, within the reach of our shot, as " Lord Cochrane has allowed, in regard of the Tonnere, which " was nearer to our attacking force, than either of the three " ships in question." (p. 137).

We will not say, that Lord Gambier persists in error, in this instance; but, to say the least that can be said on the occasion, he has committed an error, that will not admit of extenuation. To deny what another had asserted, without the least ground on which to rest the contradiction, is neither good manners, nor good policy; but, to assert, as a truth, that of which a man has no personal knowledge, is an offence against the principles by which society is governed, and which liberality severely censures. Admiral Gambier did not, in the morning of the 12th, nor in any part of that day, go into the inner Roads of Aix; and, therefore, could not, of his own knowledge, be competent to deny the statement of Lord Cochrane, who was an eye witness of the fact, that those of the enemy's grounded ships, which escaped from off the shoal of the Pallés, " were lying so near together, as " to give, two of them, *the appearance* of their Masts and Yards " locking;" and much less to assert, that " in reality, they were " lying perfectly *separate* and *distinct* from each other." (p. 136). If the Court gave implicit confidence to Lord Gambier's positive declarations: and if they often referred, during their deliberations, to his Lordship's written Defence, as from the issue of " what may be called," his Lordship's trial, it is fairly to be assumed they did: and if his Lordship was impressed with the conviction, that such would be the operation of his Defence, upon the minds of his judges, and such must have been the case; in what light are we to regard his Lordship's sense of justice, and ot right and wrong? We restrain the dictates of our feelings. They would hurry us beyond the bounds of prudence, were we to allow them expression. An enlightened public, will view the fact, in its different bearings, and give to it the designation it deserves. We shall confine ourselves to the task of demonstrating, that Lord Cochrane's ideas were correctly founded; and that Lord Gambier's "*reality*," was the mere phantom of delusion. If, however, his Lordship, or his friends, should insist upon the integrity of the term used by his Lordship; we shall, in that case, give to it both a character and a name. We have no wish to be severe, when we can possibly avoid it; and our only object is, to check misrepresentation, in its progress against truth and candour.

We will now hear the Evidence introduced by Lord Gambier, in the advancement of " what may be called," his Defence, as given by the Masters of his own ship. Mr. Stokes says, " At " day-light, in the morning, I observed the whole of the enemy's " ships, excepting two of the line of battle ships, on shore; four " of them lay *in a groupe*, or *lay together*, on the western part "of the Pallés Shoal." (p. 147). And Mr. Fairfax, asked by Lord Gambier, "Were any of the enemy's ships, that were "aground, lying so close together, as to have the yards of "two of them locked in together?" (p. 143), says, "By perspective "those near the Tonnére, seemed to be *very close*: if you draw "a line they *appear to be in one*; but, by the observation, *by* "*lights*, they were *separate, as I have laid them down*; every "half mile *we went out*, they appeared to be otherwise."

Here the President interfered. "The question is, Whether "these two ships, were lying *so close together*, that their masts "and yards might be locked in?—*A*. They were distinct *at night*, "*I think* their yards were not locked," (p. 144).

Admiral *Young*. "You have said, that by perspective, by "which I suppose you mean by the eye, three of the enemy's "ships appeared to be *near* each other: were you, afterwards, in "any situation, which enabled you to determine, that they were "*not near* each other?—*A. No*. It was *prior*, that I distin- "guished them separate."

Q. "Can you at all determine, how far they were asunder?— "*A*. I *should think not a ship's length* from each other."

Thus do those witnesses prove positively, that the "three "decker, and the other two ships, lay close together;" and Mr. Fairfax, that they seemed so *very close* as not only to give them "the *appearance* of their masts and yards locking," but "to be "*in one*," which, instead of weakening Lord Cochrane's testimony, strengthens and fortifies it. "He *should think* those ves- "sels were not a ship's length from each other:" and such was their situation, with respect to proximity, that he could not take upon himself to depose positively, that their yards were not locked together; he only *thinks* they were not. (p. 146.)

Men, conversant in nautical affairs, will easily determine, whether three ships of the Line on shore: "heeling inwards," (for this fact has not been attempted to be denied), and not a ship's length from each other, would, or would not, have had their yards locked together. Mr. Fairfax, in his Deposition, blends together two distinct periods of time: namely, Night, when he lay at anchor; and Morning, when he was working out. Perhaps we may, by separating them, and giving to each what seems to belong to it, come nearer to the truth. The answer to Lord Gambier's question did not satisfy the Court, that "by perspective "they seemed to be *very close*; so close as to appear to be in "one," which evidently alludes to "the observation" made in the morning. He goes on; but, by the observation of lights, they "were separate, as *I have laid them down*," (p. 144.) which as evidently relates to the Night. The Court, therefore, to reduce the point to greater certainty, proceeded in their interrogation: "Were these two ships, lying so close together, that their yards; "might be locked in?" and the Answer they received was, "They were distinct *at Night*. *I think* their yards were not "locked." (p. 146.) This answer was as indefinite as its predecessor; but it established, by inference, at least, more than seems to have been expected; and in consequence Admiral Young proposed the following question, "You have said, that, by perspective, three of the enemy's ships appeared to be *near* each "other; were you, afterwards, in any situation, that enabled "you to determine, that they were not near each other?"—*A.* "No; it was *prior* that I distinguished them separate," (p. 146), which still refers to the Night; as it was "by the observation by "lights they were separate," (pp. 143, 144.)

Now, how does this Evidence stand, thus detected? The night, to which Mr. Fairfax alludes, was the night of the 11th; the night on which the enemy's ships ran on shore. The flood had then made, only, about an hour; and those vessels, therefore, were, in course, not fixed to the spot, on which they first grounded. So that when Mr. Fairfax, says, "by Lights they were *separate*," and that "they were *distinct* by Night," he must mean before high water, when, owing to the want of a requisite depth of water, they could not move; and then, indeed, they might have been, as he describes them, "separate" and "distinct." But about two o'clock in the morning of the 12th, when it was high water, and when, if they had not themselves attempted to move, the impetus of the rising tide would have forced them to the situation, which gave the appearances on the *Morning of the 12th*, and not the *Night of the 11th*, which Mr. Fairfax was called upon to depose to: and it was then that they "seemed to

" be *very close,* so very close, that they appeared to be in one; " and it was, only, on the preceding Night, that they were *dis- " tinct.*"

Hence arose the confusion between the following Question and Answer: "You have said by perspective, by which, I suppose, " you mean by the eye, three of the enemy's ships appeared to " be *near* each other: Were you, afterwards, in any situation, " which enabled you to determine, that they were *not near* each " other?" *A.* " No; it was *prior that* I distinguished them " separate," (p. 146); *prior* to what? indubitably *prior to the time when they appeared* " *by perspective*" " tō be very close, " not a ship's length from each other;" " *to be in one,*" (p. 146.) And hence the ambiguity and evasion, apparent in the answer to the question: Whether these two ships were lying so close together, that their masts and yards might be locked in; or whether they were distinct? " They were *distinct at Night.*"

We, therefore, are entitled to say that Lord Gambier's assertions are totally refuted; and that the testimony delivered by Lord Cochrane is powerfully sustained, by the evidence of Lord Gambier's own witnesses. The " defenceless state," therefore, of the enemy's ships having been proved; it ought, conformably to Lord Gambier's own notions, to have made a " strong impression" somewhere.

Before we quit this subject, we cannot refrain from saying a few words, upon the mode adapted by the Court Martial, in the course of investigating it, by which the first question, to Mr. Fairfax runs thus: " Were any of the enemy's ships, that were " aground, lying so close together as to have the Yards of two " of them *locked together?*" Lord Cochrane had merely said, that their proximity to each other was such, that their masts and yards were "*apparently* locked," a conclusion, which Lord Gambier's question was, certainly, calculated to destroy: as it goes to the fact *positively;* and not, as it had been stated, " *apparently.*" The question by the President, which immediately followed, was nearly as exceptionable, as it also departed from the fact under Examination: " Whether they were lying so close together, that

" their masts and yards *might be locked in;* or, whether they " were distinct?" (p. 144.) passing over the Answer, in which Mr. Fairfax had said, " they were distinct at Night," (pp. 143, 144.) which gave an important fact, as Lord Cochrane spoke to the point of time, between the signal he made, between five and six o'clock in the morning, of the 12th, until one o'clock in the afternoon, when the Ocean, and the *group*, floated. And, as this circumstance was before the Court; standing upon their Minutes: and impressed, as it may be imagined, upon their recollection: how could they answer to their Country and to their own consciences, in allowing such an answer to be received, and to stand as a part of their proceedings? Why did they not say, that it was not of the *Night of the* 11*th*; but the *Morning of the* 12*th*, between the hours of five and one, that Mr. Fairfax was required to depose to? It was no answer to the questions; but it was such an answer, that, coupled with the one which preceded it, absolutely provoked curiosity to be curious. Why did not the Court remark: you have said, that " they were *distinct* at *Night*;" but how did they appear at five, or six o'clock, in the morning? " You have said that, *by perspective*, three of the enemy's ships " appeared to be *near* each other; Were you, afterwards, in a " situation to determine, that they were *not near* each other?" " No. It was *prior* that I distinguished them *separate*," (p. 146.) Here the question substitutes the words, " *near each other*;" which were not used by Mr. Fairfax, for " *very close*," which were those, he actually did use. Leaving the substituted words, and the motives that induced them, to the discussion and judgment of the intelligent, we submit: whether it was not a matter of course, that Mr. Fairfax should have been asked what he meant by " *prior?*" and to what period he alluded? whether it was to the Night, when he observed by Lights; or to the morning, when he had the advantage of a light, which was less liable to deceive. These omissions will appear the more extraordinary, when it shall be considered, that Mr. Fairfax is the person who marked the position of the ships, in reference, upon a Chart.

It would appear, that the first question to Mr. Stokes, who followed Mr. Fairfax, upon the same subject, drew an answer so unfavourable for his Lordship's object, namely, " Four of them *lay*

" *in a group* or *lay together*" that he did not deem it advisable to press that person any further, (p. 147.) But although Lord Gambier declined asking any further questions, the Court, sitting as Judges, and bound to do justice between " our Sovereign Lord the " King and the Prisoner," might have gone further, and asked, what was meant by " *lying in a group*, or *lying together?* And whether they were *so close*, as to give the " *appearance*" of having their masts and yards locked? especially as Mr. Stokes spoke to the relevant point of time, that is to say, " at day-light on the " morning of the 12th." The Court, however, did not ask a single question of Mr. Stokes; indeed, the President immediately changed the subject, and we will here follow his example.

We have now followed Lord Gambier through the various assertions, propositions, conjectures, and insinuations contained in the body of his written Defence, and trust that we have observed every possible forbearance towards him, consistent with that justice, which is due to the cause we defend—which we beg to be understood is not, in our consideration, the cause of Lord Cochrane; but that of the public, who have been injured through his Lordship; who has, in our humble judgment, experienced unheard-of oppression.

In closing his Defence, Lord Gambier requests the attention of the Court, to four conclusions, drawn, as he says, from the whole of the statements he had submitted to their consideration; and those conclusions, therefore, will receive our particular regard. His Lordship has sufficiently proclaimed their importance, and marked his expectation from their influence. They embrace every matter that preceded them; and are to give the tone to every other, that is to follow. They form the ground on which his Lordship takes his stand, in justification of his conduct; and on which he challenges an honourable acquittal. To the end, therefore, that they may be as conspicuous as they are important, we will arrange them in a manner, different to that in which we have hitherto moved, by stating them separately, and giving to each distinctly, the remarks it shall demand.

First Conclusion.—"*That during the whole of the service, the most* unwearied attention *was applied, by me, to its main object,* the destruction of the Enemy's Fleet." (p. 137.)

The assertion this conclusion breathes, is certainly bold and unqualified; but we must not be satisfied with appearances. Investigation proves very frequently that appearance professes much more than it entertains; and courts our confidence merely to deceive it. Try it by the test of enquiry; and its delusion will become evident. It is a glossy bubble; touch it, and it bursts. The present instance is strongly in point, and we will establish the fact by his Lordship's own testimony. His Lordship having fully admitted, (p. 106) "that from the time of his observing, on the "morning of the 12th, the situation of the enemy, communi- "cated to him also by signal from the Imperieuse, SOME TIME "DID ELAPSE BEFORE THE ENEMY'S SHIPS WERE AT- "TACKED." Which is an admission of the Charge exhibited against him. But to prevent any misunderstanding, we will once more quote that Charge. "And whereas by the Log Books, and "Minutes of Signals of the Caledonia, Imperieuse, and other "ships employed on that service, it appears to us, that the said "Admiral Lord Gambier, on the 12th of the said month of "April, the enemy's ships being then on shore, and the *signal* "*having been made that they could be destroyed*, DID FOR A "CONSIDERABLE TIME NEGLECT, OR DELAY TAKING "EFFECTUAL MEASURES FOR DESTROYING THEM."

Here then, we might safely and truly say, is a complete and ample refutation of his Lordship's first conclusion. We will however, proceed a little further, and illustrate as we go on. At 5. 48' A.M. of the 12th April, Lord Cochrane made a signal "that "seven of the enemy were on shore; and that half the fleet "could destroy them." (p. 125.) Yet such an invitation did not prevail with Lord Gambier; neither were the dictates of his duty, nor a consideration of the pressure of circumstances, at the moment, sufficient to stimulate his Lordship to an immediate attack on the enemy. The fleet did not get under weigh, *even according to his own statement*, until between nine and ten o'clock; and in fact, not until between eleven and twelve; as we have demonstrated in a former page, when describing the point of time, at which the Etna passed the Imperieuse, *with the wind and tide in her favour*. And when he did at last get under weigh, what did he do? Did he run down to the attack of the half-destroyed, and wholly discomfited enemy? No. What object did he attempt? He merely moved towards the Isle of Aix, and anchored three miles to the Northward of it—a position that in prudence and humanity, and for the honour and safety of his Majesty's ships and vessels, and the crews on board of them, he ought to have taken up on the early dawn of the morning.

In this situation he remained nearly four hours, and as far as we have been able to discover, an indifferent spectator of the grand, yet distressful spectacle that lay before him; without any attempt to complete "the destruction of the enemy;" although repeatedly admonished by the signals of the Imperieuse, and by the *preparations the enemy were making to get out of his reach,* which his "experience," and his "judgment," must have informed him, they would most assuredly effect, at the flood tide, if not interrupted.

With all these facts impressed upon his mind, and with a certain knowledge of various others, which in our course we have remarked on, and which stand on the "Minutes:" it is astonishing that Lord Gambier should have asserted in the face of his injured Country, "that during the whole of the service *the most "unwearied attention* was applied by him, *to the destruction of "the enemy.*"

Second Conclusion.—"*That in no part of the service was* more zeal and exertion *shewn, than during the 12th April, when I had necessarily in view two objects: the destruction of the Enemy's Fleet; and, also, the preservation of that under my Command; for the extreme difficulties, on approaching an Enemy closely surrounded by shoals, and strongly defended by batteries, rendered caution in my proceedings peculiarly necessary.*"

If Lord Gambier means "*the zeal and exertion*" displayed by the Officers and Men of the Fleet, who were, unfortunately too late, suffered to attack the enemy, we heartily accord with him; but then, we must observe, that the assertion was altogether superfluous.—Their character for bravery and enterprize, zeal and exertion, has been too long established, to require any panegyric from the testimony of Lord Gambier. Their achievements are best descriptive of their " zeal and exertions: of this their vanquished enemies bear testimony: and the world at large, has long acknowledged it. But if his Lordship has reference to himself, he has misapplied the terms he has used; and our remarks upon his first conclusion establish the fact.

Of the " two objects," which his Lordship says he " had necessarily in view," he seems to have been extremely partial to one; and very neglectful of the other. " To preserve the British fleet," his Lordship adopted the surest means, by keeping them, not only out of the range of the shot and shells; but even out of the possibility of " annoyance." He kept them at anchor with himself; until the most valuable part of the enemy's fleet had escaped beyond his Lordship's power, and bid defiance to every effort that could be made towards *their* " *destruction.*" It was then, and not till then: it was after Lord Cochrane had, without orders, commenced the attack, AND NOT TILL THEN, that Lord Gambier prepared for the accomplishment of his object, " *that had in view the destruction of the enemy's fleet!*" On this head his Lordship's assertion, so circumstanced, must appear in the trappings of ridicule, breathing the language of absurdity.

But his Lordship insinuates, that he could not have approached the enemy at an earlier period; because they were " *closely surrounded by shoals, and strongly defended* by batteries." This reason for delay leads naturally to the following questions: Did those shoals, of which the Minutes do not afford any evidence, retire from their situation: and were the batteries silenced by their own firing, for there was not a shot employed against them, between *forty eight minutes after five* o'clock in the morning, when Lord Cochrane made the signal, " seven of the " enemy's ships on shore, *half the fleet can destroy them,*" and—two o'clock in the afternoon, when a great part of the enemy had escaped, and when some of our *ships did go in to attack those that remained;* if the sands did not shift; and if the batteries retained their wonted powers; to what circumstance are we to attribute, "the extreme *difficulty of approaching the enemy*" which was so terrific in the morning; when an attack upon them held out *prospects* of the most important result: and the absence of that difficulty in the afternoon, at which period our ships actually commenced that attack; and when those *prospects* had become "extremely" diminished? Those grounds, then, on which his Lordship has advanced to defend a conduct charged with "neglect or delay," are indeed most extraordinary, and shew Lord Gambier's "*zeal and exertion*," so pompously emblazoned in his second conclusion, to be in a similiar predicament with the "*most unwearied attention*," so proudly boasted by its elder brother.

To the third and fourth Conclusion, we must premise, that Lord Gambier has made a distinction between them, with only a shade of difference; and therefore, that we may not further unnecessarily trespass upon the time of the public, we propose the consideration of them as one.

1. Third and Fourth Conclusion.—"*That* THREE *out of* SEVEN *of the Enemy's ships* aground on the Pallés *were from* their first being *on* shore, TOTALLY OUT OF THE REACH OF THE GUNS OF ANY SHIPS OF THE FLEET, *that might have been sent in, and that at* no other time WHATSOEVER, EITHER SOONER OR LATER could they have been attacked."

2. "*That the* OTHER FOUR *of the* ELEVEN SHIPS *of which the Enemy's fleet consisted, were* never in a situation to be assailed, AFTER THE FIRE SHIPS HAD FAILED IN THEIR MAIN OBJECT."

When we refer to the premises, whence these conclusions are drawn, we confess ourselves, utterly incapable of reconciling the one with the other: as they are in hostile opposition, and maintain totally different facts; although we have little difficulty in penetrating his Lordship's motives, aided, as we essentially are, by his Lordship's own statements and declarations. His premises are intended to evidence, that, owing to existing circumstances, he could not have gone into Aix roads, at an earlier hour than two o'clock: as appears from the following passage, extracted from his Lordship's written Defence. " Lord Cochrane " has expressed an opinion, that two or three sail of the line, " sent in on the morning of the 12th, might, by running up on " the verge of the Boyart Shoal, have passed to leeward of the " two French ships, remaining at anchor. This, I declare to " have been absolutely impracticable: as well from the raking " fire of the two ships afloat: of the upright ones on shore, in our " approach: and the fire of the batteries: as from the shoal " water close under their lee;" (p. 134,) and, consequently, the delay, which took place, was not only justifiable, but deserving praise also. And his conclusions are advanced with the view to convince the Court, that had he sent in a force, at the time suggested by Lord Cochrane, that is to say " on the morning of the " 12th," it would not have been attended with any other advantage, than, that which was afterwards obtained, in the destruction of the Ville de Varsovie, Aquilon, and Calcutta; as all the other ships, that is to say, " *three out of the seven*" " and the other " *four of the eleven ships,* of which the enemy's fleet consisted, " were never in a situation to be assailed."

His Lordship does not seem to have been aware, that by such his endeavours to avoid *Scylla* he would be engulphed by *Charybdis*. If, as his Lordship asserts, all the enemy's ships, *except the three destroyed,* were " NEVER IN A SITUATION TO " BE ASSAILED," because " totally out of reach of the guns of " any ships of the fleet, that might have been sent in," how could they have *raked us in our approach,* had their destruction been " attempted *in the morning?*" His Lordship could not allude, to the three ships, that were afterwards destroyed, as capable of raking any of ours, " that might have been sent in;" as we are entitled to say, from the silence of evidence before us, on that subject, they were not in a situation or state to have, even " an-

"annoyed" any of our ships, at that or any other time, between the time in which the signal was made by the Imperieuse, and that chosen by his Lordship for the attack.

His Lordship however is supported, by the testimony of Mr. Fairfax, in answer to a question from himself: that *before the enemy's ships had moved up the Charante* "they certainly lay "in a favourable place" to "*annoy any of the King's ships* "that might have been sent in to attack them," (p. 144.) Captain Bligh also deposes, that "early in the morning" the ships, that were aground, "lay with their *broadsides towards* the en-"trance, and were capable of *annoying* the British ships," (p. 154.)

But while these witnesses maintain Lord Gambier's premises, they totally destroy his conclusions. His Lordship ought to have considered the consequences that inevitably follow contradictions in a statement of facts; and that a sword with two edges is a dangerous weapon to meddle with.

To elucidate the subject before us, as far as possible, we will refer to the evidence of Mr. Stokes, who, deposing to the situation of the enemy's ships, that were on shore, says, "at day-light" four of them lay *in a group*, or lay together, on the western part of the Pallés shoal: "*the three decker* was on the *North-*"*west* edge of the Pallés shoal, *with her broadside flanking* "*the passage, nearest the deep water*;" (p. 147.) and that the FIRE "*of the three decker,*" "would have been directed" on any of our ships, had they been sent into Aix Roads. (p. 152). This is the "group," that Mr. Fairfax describes, as in appearance "*so very close,*" that they appeared "*to be in one,*" (p. 143). and "as he thought, not a *ship's length from each other,* "*those three.*"

All this is in aid of his Lordship's premises; but strike another mortal blow at his conclusions: the more so with respect to *the three decker*, (the Ocean), as she did not haul off until about two o'clock (p. 202); of course, could not have moved up the Charante previous to that period; and consequently, was until then, WITHIN THE REACH OF THE GUNS, *of any ships of "the fleet*, that might have been sent in," to attack them. We speak particularly of the THREE DECKER, as in relation to her departure for the Charante, we have specific testimony, advanced in consequence of his Lordship's own interrogatories; but we might say, that *the whole group,* to which Mr. Stokes, and Mr. Fairfax, have deposed, (and in complete corroboration of Lord Cochrane's Chart, and oral testimony) were also, "WITHIN "REACH OF THE GUNS *of any of the ships of the fleet, that "might have been sent in.*" Thus has his Lordship defeated his own purposes; and, by attempting too much, lost every thing.

We might continue this subject, with similar disadvantage to his Lordship; but we refrain, in the thorough persuasion, that enough has been already shewn to evince, that his Lordship's THIRD and FOURTH conclusions, are not better constructed than the *first* and *second;* that the whole are totally destitute of foundation; and that, instead of assisting, are most injurious to his Lordship's purposes. Yet SUCH "ARE THE POINTS," on which his Lordship says, HE RESTS HIS JUSTIFICATION: trusting that it would appear to the Court "upon their review "of the whole case, that he had taken the *most effectual mea- "sures,* for *destroying the enemy's fleet.* (p. 157). This however, he, immediately afterwards, virtually refutes by suggesting, "that *it was owing to the time,* CHOSEN BY HIM, for sending "a force in, to make the attack, that the service was accom- "plished with so very inconsiderable loss." (p. 138). "The time "chosen" to use his Lordship's words, without adopting their purport, was *some minutes after two o'clock*, all the means devised by Lord Cochrane, having failed to prevail on him to "make the attack" earlier, and at that *time*, the time chosen by Lord Gambier, only three of the enemy's fleet remained, within our reach, the others * had all sailed for the Charante. We, therefore, cannot comprehend the motive, that could have actuated Lord Gambier to hazard the proposition, that *he "had taken the "most effectual measures to destroy* THE ENEMY'S FLEET."

* Of this number were the Ocean and group, Cassard and Foudroyant; the only ships spoken of by the witnesses as being capable of annoying the British ships.

Upon the whole, we submit, that if his Lordship stated, at *one period*, that the enemy's ships *aground*, could *have raked our ships*; and at *another*, that they *could not*, as they *never were within* " *reach of the guns of any of our ships*, "that might have " been sent in:" for the purpose of persuading the Court (contrary to the fact, as established by his own witnesses, and by himself); first, that he did not use unnecessary delay, in so much as it was " *absolutely impracticable for our ships to have gone* " *in earlier than they did*:" and, secondly, *that no more of the enemy's ships could have been destroyed, than were destroyed*, for that thé whole of them, except the three that were destroyed, " were *never assailable, after the failure of the fire ships*," an event that took place on the night of the 11th: and by such means, induce a firm belief, that, " it was owing to the time chosen " by him, for sending a force to make the attack, that the service " was accomplished with so little loss." If such were his purposes: and if his various, though unsuccessful attempts, on a variety of grounds, to depreciate the character, and injure the reputation of Lord Cochrane, were calculated to aid and assist them; " it is " just," we here employ his Lordship's sentiments, as our own, " they should vanish before the superior considerations, attendant " on a service, involving the naval character, and most important " interests of the nation." (p. 138). This is due to " the naval " character;" and the most important interests of the country demand it.

We should have been unfeignedly and sincerely happy, had means been afforded to us, to have bestowed the palm of praise on his Lordship's merits, during the affair of Basque Roads; and, with heart-felt satisfaction, congratulated the country, on the valour and skill displayed by their gallant and zealous Commander: for, whatever may be his Lordship's opinion of our sentiments, we can assure him, that we experience all the distress, that can possibly arise, out of the task we have imposed upon ourselves; but having engaged in it, it is our duty to pursue it to its proper termination: or rather, so far towards it, as time and circumstances will permit; and we have to lament, that we cannot proceed to the extent we originally intended.

We shall now hasten to another view of our subject, that has been glanced at, in the preceding pages of these Notes. Lord Gambier, as we have noticed, more frequently than we wished, but we trust, not more frequently than his Lordship's statements rendered necessary, has been extremely anxious, throughout every part of the extraordinary, we had almost said alarming, MINUTES before us, *to justify the delay, which he* has confessed (p. 106) took place, between the time the first signal, that was made by the Imperieuse, on the morning of the 12th of April, and the afternoon of that day, to take EFFECTUAL MEASURES FOR DESTROYING THE ENEMY. And his Lordship has resorted to various expedients, to ensure success to his object. He has also endeavoured to injure the reputation of Lord Cochrane, and, as far as in his power, deprive him of every merit, connected with the destruction of the enemy's ships, in the Roads of Aix, both by assertions and insinuations. And in order, as it would seem, to induce the Officers to make a common cause with him, against his Lordship, has introduced matter into the Proceedings, that was altogether impertinent, and totally irrelevant to the matter in issue; and such as could tend, only, to rouse resentment into the utmost rancour and violence against him. He has produced Charts to shew *distance* and mark *shoals*, and demonstrate, that the *enemy's fleet were out of the reach of ours*—But all in vain: as these Charts have been proved groundless, even by the fabricators of them.

He has talked of the most alarming dangers: such as would have been destructive to his Majesty's ships, had he sent them in, in consequence of the signal, made by Lord Cochrane, or in any part of the morning in which those signals were repeated:—of *the two line of battle ships afloat:* those of the *grounded vessels*, that were sufficiently upright to have flanked the passage: of the dreadful force of the batteries of the Isle of Aix; and of the impediments, that a combination of the wind and tide opposed to his wishes. To give plausibility to all those points, he has examined unnecessarily, several witnesses. He has spoken of his zeal and caution; and of the preparations he had made, for attacking the enemy. In aid of all this, Admiral Stopford has deposed, that the general signal was made to prepare for battle; and that he witnessed the Commander in Chief's impatience and disappointment, at circumstances, not allowing him, immediately, to go in with the fleet. His Lordship also submitted to the Court, "Whether it was not his duty, as Commander "in Chief, to be governed by a general view of circumstances, "rather than yield to the suggestions of one, and that a very "Junior Officer; and whether an earlier attack, could "have been attended with greater advantages." And he has, also, exultingly exclaimed: "I will venture MOST POSITIVELY "*to assert*, that the destruction of the three ships, would "not have been effected; if I had not delayed the attack until "the time I did," (p. 128); and that, "owing to the time "chosen by me, for sending a force in to make the attack, the "service was accomplished with so very little loss." (p. 138).

That Lord Gambier has obtained, all that he could possibly have wished, from the conduct he has pursued, is evidenced by the sentence, of the Court Martial, which, after premising, that his conduct "was marked with ZEAL, JUDGMENT, and ABI-"LITY;" declares him MOST HONOURABLY ACQUITTED.

It now remains to shew, from his Lordship's own witnesses, that ALL his *statements, declarations*, and *averments* which we have briefly touched on, in our remarks on his *four conclusions*, and those, previously and more at large discussed, are totally unfounded. That so far from CHOOSING the hour, of ten minutes after two, or any other period, for the attack, that was made upon the enemy's ships: such an attack would not have been made, even at the time in which it took place, had not Lord Cochrane, without orders, dropped down upon the enemy, some short time after one o'clock; and, subsequently, made the signal for assistance.

To establish this proposition, we take that part of the evidence of Lord Cochrane, in which his Lordship says, "The Etna "bomb passed: I enquired, by hailing, if any attack was intended to be made on the enemy; and was answered, by the Commander, that he was *directed* TO BOMBARD THE ENEMY." Hence it appears, that no other mode of attack was meditated.

It was a few minutes before two o'clock, that Lord Cochrane made the signal for assistance, which, as we have before remarked, is coupled with that of distress; and Captain Newcomb's testimony, in reference to that fact, is of very considerable importance. He says, "Being under weigh, on the 12th of April, " and it being reported to me, that a signal was made, by the " Commander in Chief—THE FRIGATES, to go to the ship, " making signals of distress, in such a quarter.—I felt it my " duty to proceed, after the Imperieuse, to Aix Roads." (p. 196.)

If this testimony should not be sufficient, we have the further evidence of Lord Gambier, himself, as given in his Letter of the 10th of May, addressed to the Secretary of the Admiralty.— " *Observing the Imperieuse* TO ADVANCE ; the Indefatigable, " Unicorn, Aigle, Emerald, Pallas, Beagle, Etna, and gun-brigs, " were ordered, by signal, in *to the attack.*"

Without noticing the MISTAKE made by his Lordship, and which is rendered palpable, by the deposition of Captain Godfrey, as to his pretended cause or reasons for ordering in the vessels, he has named; we submit, that we have substantiated the proposition we had lain down: namely, that the attack *would not have taken place, even at the time* it actually commenced; if Lord Cochrane had not run down upon the enemy, and afterwards made the signal for assistance.

But we have the means of shewing, in combination with the foregoing arguments, that his Lordship would, not only, not have sent the ships to the attack, at the time they did go in, had he not been compelled so to do, by the acts of Lord Cochrane, on the spot; and that it was not within his intention or purpose, to have made any other attack, than by a bombardment.

This proposition we shall endeavour to support, by the evidence of another of his Lordship's Witnesses: Captain Broughton, examined by the President.

Q. " Are we to understand, then, that you would have recom- " mended the measure, of sending ships in, against the batteries

" in the Isle d'Aix, upon a presumption that the batteries must " be silenced; without adverting to what would befall the ships, " in case they should not be silenced?"—*A.* " I did not give it " that consideration, at the time: I only speak to my opinion, " that I conceived it was practicable, to acquire that anchorage; " although disabled. And *I heard my Lord Gambier, the same* " *morning, state,* it HAD BEEN *his intention, to have gone* " *against the batteries,* I now speak of, with the Caledonia, and " some other ship; BUT AS THE ENEMY WERE ON SHORE, *he* " *did not think it necessary to run any unnecessary risk of the* " *fleet,* WHEN THE OBJECT OF THEIR DESTRUCTION " SEEMED TO BE ALREADY OBTAINED." ! ! ! (p. 222.)

Here we pause—nor dare we urge a word farther.—The public will judge: the public will decide;—and from that judgment and decision—Justice will receive those dues, that have been withheld from her claims.

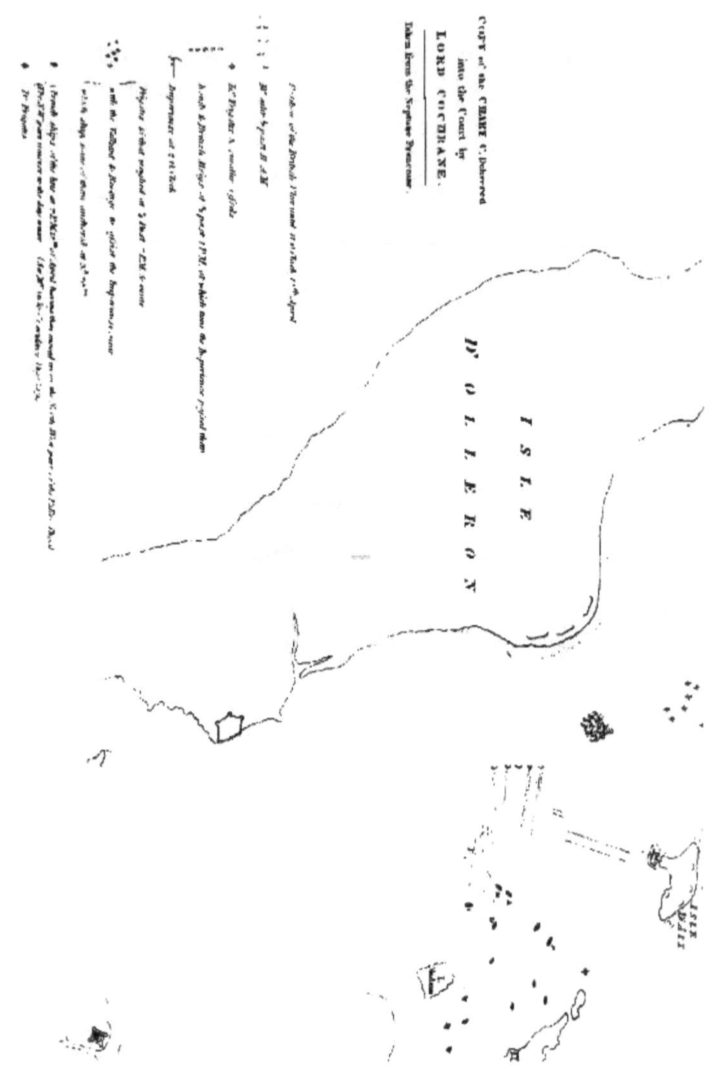
COPY of the CHART C. Delivered
into the Court by
LORD COCHRANE.
Taken from the Neptune François.
ISLE D'OLLERON
ISLE D'AIX

EXAMINATION

OF THE

EVIDENCE.

EXAMINATION

OF THE

EVIDENCE.

"*It is not material whether the thing sworn be* TRUE OR "FALSE, *when the person who swears it in truth* KNOWS "NOTHING *of it.*"——Hawkins' Pleas of the Crown, p. 175.

MR. FAIRFAX, THE MASTER OF THE FLEET, AND ONE OF THE MASTERS OF THE FLEET.

This is a person who, from situation, and the mention Lord Gambier makes of him, as one who is to give authenticity to Charts, by verifying them, (p. 136,) might be expected to convey, the most accurate and perfect information, upon every point, relative to the soundings, in the inner road of Aix; of the situation of the enemy's ships, " on the 11th and 12th of April," and subsequently.

He commences his Evidence by stating: that he was, previous to the 11th of April, sounding and surveying Basque Roads: mostly on the long sand, of which the Boyart is the southern part: that the " Neptune François, was the only Chart they had, as " a guide:" that it was incorrect; and that " the variation was " pourtrayed, in the Chart produced by Mr. Stokes:" that " he " gave Mr. Stokes the marks; and that he had all the different " angles in his pocket, with the different soundings." (p. 140.) And in answer to the following, one of the most leading and, therefore, highly improper, questions, ever allowed to be exhibited to a witness: " Is the space for the anchorage of large " ships very much confined, and the water round it shoal?" he says, in a kind of echo, " *The space* is much confined;" but immediately afterwards, observes, " I have not sounded, myself, " there." (p. 140.) Here is assertion and contradiction in a breath; at least Mr. Fairfax deposes *positively* to a fact, of which he *had not a personal knowledge*. He, however, qualifies the circumstance; although in a way, that must be very unsatisfactory, to minds informed upon such subjects. " I must state," says he, " how I ascertained, that the space was small; and, likewise, the " position. In the first place, I went to the NNE of the Isle " d'Aix, till I brought the enemy's line, touching the citadel. I " then took the direction, that they bore from that point; and, " afterwards, the direction of their line, which was nearly South " by West, by compass. After ascertaining that, I went to the " Boyart, in such a situation as to bring the Northern part of the

U

" Isle d'Aix, to bear East; and the Citadel ESE, by compass. " *Having the distance from the citadel.* It then became a question in trigonometry, to ascertain the distance from the ships, " and the space which they occupied." (p. 140.)

From this statement, we may venture to assert, that Mr. Fairfax could not have ascertained any accurate, or essential point, in reference to the space of the anchorage. Circumstanced as he was, he had it not in his power to obtain any more, than a suppositious conjecture of his distance from the citadel of Aix. He knew not, even, the strength of the tide, (p. 146,) that affected his boat, whilst he was in the act of measuring his base line, on which all his calculations were, of necessity, to be founded:—he could not work an angle without it; nay, even, if he had correctly ascertained his base line, the distance measured, between the extreme ships of the enemy, would not have afforded any proof that "the *anchorage* was *confined*, and the water, round it, " *shoal*." We must also remark, that Mr. Fairfax, though speaking of the Roads of Aix, surveyed, only, *Basque Roads*, SEVERAL MILES REMOTE from them; and that his soundings, as appears by his Chart, were taken near to the ground, on which our fleet originally lay, that is to say, " the long sand," of which " the Boyart is the Southern part."

Mr. Fairfax then, produced a Chart, to shew the Position of the enemy's ships, " at day light," in the morning of the 12th, which, he deposes to have been correctly stated; " except, that " the head of the Calcutta was placed, by the Engraver, too far " to the southward." This observation was, no doubt, intended to evince, that Mr. Fairfax was accurate in his details, even to minutiæ: it is, therefore, to be lamented, that this critically delineated Chart, should have been for some, and we may conclude, very cogent, reason, omitted in the publication of the " Minutes" before us; otherwise the public would have been enabled to judge, as well as the Court, of the merits it possessed.

Mr. Fairfax would not, however, condescend to enter into particulars, respecting the Chart; for when he is desired to " state the " situation of the enemy's fleet, on the morning of the 12th, of

"April?" he says, somewhat indignantly, "I have described "them in the Chart*, produced by me (p. 143);" and the Court, good natured people, suffered the Answer to pass, without notice. In the absence of this extraordinary Chart, and of the information it contained, we must adopt the slender means we possess, to ascertain its worth; and to that end again, have recourse to Mr. Fairfax's parole testimony.

Mr. Fairfax was, on the Morning of the 12th, when Lord Cochrane made the Signal, that "the enemy were on shore, and might be destroyed," "working out" of Aix in the Lyra brig; and says, that "that Signal was made, about 5 o'clock in the morning;" it is, therefore, fair to infer, that he had got under weigh *before it was light*. How then, was it possible, that he could have so nicely examined the situation of the ships on shore, as to lay them down with minute exactitude, without even the help of a glass, as he says, he had not one? (p. 143). He however proceeded with his Deposition swimmingly for some time: when, unfortunately for him, he was asked, in reference to the signal: "whether it was day light, at five o'clock?" Here his discriminating powers failed him; and he could not say, whether DARKNESS, or LIGHT prevailed. His answer is an obvious evasion; and delivered in evident confusion. "I cannot say *to the time:* "I was *working* out of Aix; *and picked up some men under* "*the batteries.*" (p. 145). Now what the *working* out of Aix, and *picking* up those men, had to do with the question, cannot easily be imagined; but it must prove, that, if the combination should have so completely embarrassed his mind, and so totally deprived him of sight, that he could not distinguish whether it was day-light, or darkness: what are we to suppose of his Chart, the materials for which, must have been collected, in those distressing moments, when it was so dark, that he could only judge of the apparent distance of the enemy's ships, from each other, by their own lights; which enabled him to say "they were distinct *at night*;" (p. 144) or when he was working out, and so bewildered, that he could not comprehend the difference between black and white.

* This Chart, we are told, by very high authority, is the copy of a Chart, published, 31st July 1809, by Joyce and Gold, 103, Shoe Lane.

Whatever the friends of Lord Gambier, may say of Mr. Fairfax's veracity, we doubt, whether they will be disposed to panegyrize his coolness, and presence of mind.

Asked, if the Navigation of Aix Roads is very difficult for large ships? he answered *positively* "VERY MUCH SO:" (p. 141) although he had, just before, spontaneously acknowledged, that "he had not sounded it himself." (p. 140.) In this particular, therefore, his *bearings* and *distances* cannot avail him. It is also in proof, by himself, that he did not take such sounding, even at any time after the 12th of April: interrogated whether he knew, previous to the 12th of April, of any anchorage, above the Boyart Shoal, and near the Pallés Shoal, for line of battle ships, out of range of the enemy's shells? he answered, "I know of no "anchorage." (p. 142). *Q.* "Have you acquired a knowledge of "such, since,"—*A.* "I have not," (p. 142.) which demonstrates clearly, that Mr. Fairfax possessed little zeal, and less exertion towards acquiring that knowledge, which it was his duty to possess. If, therefore, Mr. Fairfax should again be Master of the Fleet; he will be equally as ignorant of the soundings, as if he had never been near the Road of Aix. Even common curiosity, might have induced him to become acquainted with those important points, that so many officers have spoken to, upon Lord Gambier's Court Martial. But there was a consideration, paramount to curiosity; it was his duty, to have informed himself upon these subjects.

Such is the intelligence of the highly extolled Mr. Fairfax: and such his exertions in the discharge of his duty, to procure information, for the Commander in Chief, in prosecuting the views of the public service. But to continue: required to state "how the "wind was," on the 12th, he gives its direction: and questioned by Admiral Young, "Whether he meant to say, that it blew "strong, at the time?" he answered, "yes, for two or three "days." (p. 143.) Here it is to be observed, that much depended upon the winds; and that the state, in which they appeared to Mr. Fairfax, should be favourable to Lord Gambier's Defence; but it appears, that Mr. Fairfax's judgment, was equally as deficient in this instance, as it was in that respecting the day light, or no light; or of the distance or contiguity of the enemy's ships, that were on shore. Captain Newcomb says, the wind on the 12th was *rather light*: he brought up with his stream-anchor; "the wind being, *then, moderate enough to ride by it.*" (p. 196). Captain Godfrey sailed in the Etna bomb, between 10 and 11 o'clock, in the morning, and passed the Imperieuse, about one: so that with both wind and tide, in his favour, he was nearly three hours and an half, in sailing as many miles; which infers, that the wind must have been *very light* indeed. In corroboration of this fact, Captain Rodd says, "the *wind was light*;" and that he, and the other ships, with him, "went in *with all* "*sails, royal and top-gallant-studding-sails,*" (p. 89). and Captain Malcolm, on being asked: "How soon, after the bomb "and brigs were sent in, were the other ships ready?" he answered, "the Imperieuse and Beagle very soon followed; and that "the reason why the whole did not join the Imperieuse," so soon, as might have been expected, was; that the *wind failed*, and the tide was no longer in their favour." (p. 212).

Thus stands the veracity of Mr. Fairfax, and, so circumstanced, to what credit is his testimony entitled? Will it be endured, that his Chart, so constructed, as we have shewn it, and kept back, as it has been, from observation, should be considered as evidence? But we have not yet finished with Mr. Fairfax.

Q. By Lord Gambier. "Could any line of battle ships have "run to leeward, of the two ships of the enemy, that lay at their "anchorage?" (p. 144). *A.* "MOST CERTAINLY NOT. I have "laid them down *accurately*, on the Chart; and it will, THERE, "be seen, *they could not*," (p. 145). This mode of reference, to the Chart, was commonly made by Mr. Fairfax, as if aware, that it would not have been safe to speak without it, and is another reflection upon the Court, who, having once found him evading a question, should have compelled a definite answer.

Q. By Admiral Young. "If any part of the fleet had got "under weigh, immediately after the making of that signal; at "what time of the tide, would they have arrived in Aix Roads, in "a situation to attack the enemy?"—*A.* "Upon the last quarter "ebb; they could not have attacked the enemy, without en-

" deavouring to go into the anchorage the enemy had left. " They could not have gone within reach of them; without pur- " suing that deep water line, which was protected by the bat- " teries of the enemy, and by the enemy's ships on shore." (p. 145).

Yet, notwithstanding this positive assertion, we have learnt from Mr. Fairfax himself, that he was *totally ignorant* of the subject it embraces: that he never sounded the anchorage, it describes: that he entered the Roads of Aix, at night; and that he left them, before day light, the next morning.

We know not what opinion Admiral Young could have formed, of Mr. Fairfax's capacity, after the specimens he had witnessed; but, if we are to judge by the Questions, that the Admiral proposed to him, he must have considered it as " passing strange;" which is precisely our opinion of the Admiral's questions. Although Mr. Fairfax had declared positively, that he had never tried the strength of the current of the tide, in the Roads of Aix: still Admiral Young, required information from him on that head.

Q. " Was it such, as far as you did observe it, as would admit " of a fast sailing ship working over it, and beating out against " the flood, as the wind was, on the 12th of April." (p. 146). *A.* " By *report* I should *imagine*, that no ship could."

Q. *What report?—A.* By what I have HEARD FROM PILOTS *of the narrowness* of the channel." (p. 146).

Q. " If, then, a part of the fleet had gone into the Roads of " Aix, when the Imperieuse made the first signal, on the morning; " must it have remained, within three quarters of a mile of these " batteries, till the ebb made in the afternoon?"—*A.* " They " might have shifted by the flood; *but then they would have* " *been in a worse situation!*"

That Admiral Young could have proposed such questions, " so circumstanced," is inexplicable. Did he, or could he, suppose, that these answers were admissible by the world? Or did he calculate for the meridian of the Court only; and flatter himself, that they would never encounter the penetrating eye of the public. What became of the determined resolution of the President; the animated zeal of the Judge Advocate; and the vigilance of the Court, to guard against the admission of hearsay Evidence, of this, worse than hearsay Evidence; the workings of the imagination, of a witness, upon the report of persons, whom, even he, does not name! The President had, here, no excuse arising from an idea, that the witness had gone too far: and, therefore, must be allowed to go further, as in the case of Mr. Wilkinson; (p. 181); nor could the Judge Advocate apprehend any thing from the "*Reporters for the Newspapers.*" (p. 181). Why did not the President say, as he did upon the Evidence, delivered by Lord Cochrane, who actually spoke of his *own knowledge*, for it was repeating, what he had himself said, on a former occasion, and which was pertinent and relevant; why did he not exclaim, as he then did, "It really is not evidence; it is on "facts, the Court must found their opinion?" (p. 50). Why did not the Judge Advocate act, as he did when Admiral Stopford was giving Testimony, that militated against the Defence, or rather, against the assertion of Lord Gambier? (p. 81). Why did he not state, of Mr. Fairfax's testimony, as he then did of Admiral Stopford's; "what the Admiral heard, is not strictly "Evidence." In the one instance, he caused the Answer to be erased; (p. 80,) and why did he not do so in the other? How could the Court, consistently with their own dignity: the impartial administration of justice: and the rules and principles they had, themselves, laid down for their guidance, give their tacit acquiescence, in such a contradictory mode of proceeding.

If Admiral Young, for reasons best known to himself, could, in the very teeth of decisions, that had been made by the Court, prosecute such an examination: how could the Court and Judge Advocate permit him, without stating, that he was violating those decisions: and that he pushed important questions, which, as he well knew, could be answered only, by what the witness *imagined*, from what *another* had *said?* Do not these facts, drawn, fairly drawn, from the Minutes of the Court, in which others, of a similar nature, abound, evince in the strongest terms, that the trial, of Lord Gambier, was a mere mockery of justice? Well might the President say, "*what is called the Prosecution,*" and " *what may be termed the Prosecution*," when speaking of that trial. And well might he, in coincidence with such feelings, at the close of what " might be termed the Prosecution," (p. 91,) and preparatory to " what may be called" the Defence, thus address himself to Lord Gambier: " Your Lordship will *do us the* " FAVOUR, *to meet us* to-morrow morning." (p. 91).

Although we are no advocates for addressing an Officer, on his trial, by the appellation of *prisoner;* yet, to sink a public duty, into individual " favour," is an act which we certainly cannot applaud. Certain forms are to be preserved in all Courts: not merely as necessary to keep up that respect, which should ever encompass the Judges; but for the purpose of preserving rigid and impartial justice. So that the witnesses, to be produced on one side of the case, should not be led to believe, from appearances, that the Court favoured the proceedings, which they were called to support; and that those on the other, should not be borne down, by impressions, originating in the same source, that the Court turned their backs upon those facts which their testimony was to establish. In the case in question, the proceedings of the Court were published daily, in all the Newspapers: of course the Proceedings were known, and their tendency understood by those, who were to give their testimony; and they would come forward boldly, or dismayed, as they might perceive the disposition of the Court, towards the party, on whose behalf, they were subpœned. Mr. Fairfax told the Court, that he had seen the Report of Lord Cochrane's Evidence in the Newspapers, (p. 142), and he manifested, that he knew how to take an advantage of it. When Lord Gambier had finished an Address to the Court, in explanation of a question he had asked, and which, he stated, went to oppose a proposition, made by Lord Cochrane, for attacking the enemy's two ships, that remained at their anchorage, Mr. Fairfax, without any question or cause whatever, to induce him, burst forth into the following strain. " I beg leave to ob- " serve, that no ship or ships, could have hove-to, upon the lar- " board tack, with the wind, as it was, but what they must have " fallen off, so much, as to bring themselves into a position to be " raked, by those two ships of the enemy. *There was not room* " *to go under their sterns.*" (p. 145). This spontaneous explosion, of Mr. Fairfax's zeal, however, hurried him into a situation, not the most enviable. Without taking upon ourselves to contradict Mr. Fairfax's professional statement, we submit to those, who are versed in Naval Tactics, the following proposition. The wind, at the time, as stated by Lord Gambier and others, blew directly into the Roads of Aix. With such a wind, a ship brought to, upon the larboard tack, would come up with her head to the NNE: and having her driver set, with her main and mizen-top-sails full: her fore-top-sail square, and her head sails down, would not vibrate two points. Of course she would not bring the wind abaft the beam; nor, consequently, pay off, so as to fill the fore-top sail. The French ships, therefore, which lay to the SE., could never rake her; whilst, on the other hand, her guns would bear directly upon them. If this reasoning be correct, we imagine that Mr. Fairfax's assertion must fall to the ground; or be a monument of his rashness and ignorance, spurred on by rancour, in attempting to injure Lord Cochrane, at all events, and at all risks.

But, whatever might have been the impression made upon the Court, by Mr. Fairfax's volunteer observation, it is of minor consideration, compared with his positive and altogether unqualified assertion, that there was not room to go *under the sterns of those ships*, " without taking the ground." "I have laid them down," says he, " *accurately* on the Charts; and it will be *there* seen, " they could not." (p. 145); a fact, of which Mr. Fairfax could not have had any *personal knowledge*. It was dark, during the whole time, that he was in the Roads of Aix: and had it been otherwise, the case would not have been altered; as he never made any soundings. So that, whether the bank he has thought proper to lay down, as contiguous to the two vessels, which, at dead ebb, had on it from nine to thirteen feet water, was or was not, as he had traced it, he was wholly incompetent to depose to it of *his own knowledge*. The bank being from nine, to thirteen feet under water, he could not see it; and he never sounded it. And as that part of his deposition, is material to the matter at issue, he has placed himself in a situation, that subjects him to very unpleasant consequences; and at once destroys his Evidence.

X

Similarly circumstanced is his assertion, respecting the distance of the British fleet, in Basque Roads, from the citadel of Aix, which he says, *positively*, "was 11,900 yards, nearly six nauti-" cal miles;" (p. 142), as it was deposing to a fact, of which, as we have shewn, he could not have had *a personal knowledge*. Again, speaking of the explosion vessel, with a view of shewing the distance, at which she was, from the enemy's ships, when she exploded, he says, "she was about two cables length from the "Lyra." (p. 177). Now he could only have judged of her distance, by the blaze she made, when she blew up, as, agreeably to the account given by Lord Gambier, the night was extremely dark; and it blew a strong gale, with a high sea. (p. 124). Admiral Stopford shews, it was so extremely dark, that one of the fire-ships, could not discern the explosion vessel, though close to her, until she exploded and killed two of the people on board of her, (p. 80); and Mr. Fairfax has, himself, acknowledged, that he had not the assistance of a glass. (p. 143.)

Q. "Where were you when the explosion took place?"—*A.* "*In the Lyra.*" (p. 177.)

If we could make use of our own Memoranda, taken during the Trial, we might suggest, that Mr. Fairfax was, by his own admission, below at the time the explosion occurred. But the fact does not appear on the Minutes, and "we must not travel "out of the record."

Upon a second examination, Mr. Fairfax was asked, by the President, and a very extraordinary question it was, coming from the Judge of a Court, "Who set fire to the explosion vessel?" and he answered, "THE BOAT'S CREW OF THE IMPERIEUSE." (p. 178.) A fact of which he could not, possibly, have had any, the least *personal knowledge*. This answer, however, was not satisfactory; and the President continued: "What I am desirous of knowing is, "by *whose directions*, she was set on fire, in *that situation?*" Here Mr. Fairfax became more cautious: he says, "I can an-"swer that, only, by mentioning a *conversation* with Lieutenant "Bissell, when he was on board, the next day. Lieutenant "Bissell and Lord Cochrane were together; and I asked, what

" was the reason, that you set fire to the explosion vessel *so* " *close?* he said, the fuze only burnt six minutes and *an half* " instead of twenty. *Lord Cochrane, himself, lighted the* " *fuzes!!*" (p. 178). This is another positive assertion, of a fact, of which he was totally ignorant, as to *his own knowledge* of it; and shews a palpable contradiction of facts, almost, in the same breath: one moment, he swears *positively*, that the *Boat's Crew*, of the Imperieuse, set fire to the explosion vessel; and the next, that *Lord Cochrane, himself*, set fire to her.

We will now look at the conduct of the Court, in this curious examination; it appears fully as glaring, as on any other occasion, that we have hitherto noticed. They knew, that as the explosion vessel, even by Mr. Fairfax's own confession, was " a " quarter of a mile from him:" (p. 173,) he was totally incapable of answering a question, relative to the person who set fire to the fuze, by means of which, she exploded; and they also knew, that he must have been equally incapable of stating, " by whose " direction, she was set fire to, in *that situation*." (p. 178). It is possible, however, that the President asked the question, without thought, and we are ready to admit he did so; yet, when Mr. Fairfax said, " I can answer that, only, by mentioning " a conversation with Lieutenant Bissell," it is more than surprising, that the President did not immediately protest against further proceedings; as such testimony was contrary to the rules, that the Court had laid down, for their guidance; and which they had scrupulously acted upon: that " conversations with " Officers," was not evidence: that hearsay evidence was not admissible; and that " it was from facts, the Court must form " their opinion." (p. 50).

No doubt the Court, and the acquiescent Judge Advocate, expected some such decisive language from the President; and that he would have further said, " I have already solemnly pro- " nounced, in the course of Lord Cochrane's examination, that " ' the conversation with Officers was not evidence,' and, in con- " sequence, directed a part of his Lordship's answer, in reference " to such conversation, to be ' struck out.' How, then, can I per- " mit the very description of evidence, that I have over-ruled, in

" one instance, to be given in another? It would be most shame-" fully inconsistent; it would be disgracefully unjust." BUT, instead of advancing such liberal and correct, such equitable and just doctrine: he allowed the witness to go on, until he had rashly stated, that " Lord Cochrane, himself, lighted the fuzes of the " explosion vessel:" (p. 178,) and not only allowed him to go on; but even asked a question, that arose out of such illegal testimony.

Q. *by the President.* " By being so *close*, you meant *so close* " *to the Lyra*, NOT TO THE ENEMY?" Which was, also, actually putting words into the mouth of the witness, and that he saw, and profited by their bearing, is apparent by his answer, and the elucidation he connected with it. *A.* " Yes. I said, you had like to " *have blown me up; and not the enemy.*" As to the motives which directed the question, we shall not presume to give an opinion, nor can it be necessary.

If the proceedings we have thus sketched, be looked at, in whatever light they may be placed: they must be thus considered: as the President was well aware, that Mr. Fairfax could not, in the nature of things, have known, *of his own knowledge*, who set fire to the explosion vessel: his positive assertions on that head could not be of any validity; yet anxious, at the same time, to fix the act with Lord Cochrane, he proposed a question, which would naturally lead Mr. Fairfax's recollection, to *what passed* in conversation between him and the boat's crew of the Imperieuse; and thus give a colouring, at least, to the insinuation—that Lord Cochrane, by setting fire to the explosion vessel prematurely; produced the failure of the fire ships. Lord Gambier asser s, that" *the explosion* WAS TO POINT OUT THE " TIME to the Officers commanding the fire ships *to set fire to* " *their vessels.*" (p. 123.)

The public will judge of the tendency of the whole; and that they may have the necessary information before them, we quote, somewhat in repetition, the following parts of Lord Gambier's Defence. After mentioning, that owing to the weather, and other untoward circumstances, several of the fire ships had failed; and that he could not discover any blame imputable to the Officers commanding them, he says: "The explosion vessels, conducted "by Lord Cochrane, in person, also failed in their object; as "will be seen, by reference to the small Chart I now deliver "into court, which points out where two of them blew up. The "third broke adrift, and did not explode. The situation in "which, and the time when those vessels blew up, proved pre-"judicial to the enterprize, in several respects. Their prema-"ture explosion, *contrary to the expressed intention* of Lord "Cochrane, that they should blow up in the *midst of the enemy's "boats*, to deter them from towing off our fire ships, in their ap-"proach; served as a warning to the enemy, whose ships were "observed instantly to shew lights: and several of the Officers, "who commanded the fire ships, not doubting, that the explosion "had taken place, near to the enemy's fleet, *steered their ships, "and set them on fire accordingly*, by which means several were in "flames, at a greater distance from the enemy, than was intended; "and so as to endanger our advanced frigates. In fact, had not "Captain Wooldridge, and some of the other Officers, *wholly "disregarding the explosion*, taken their fire ships in a proper di-"rection for the enemy; it is more than probable, that none of "them would have produced any effect whatever, on the enemy's "fleet," (p. 124.)

Such being the facts, with which the examination, above noted, was intended to unite; we forbear any further comment, and observe, only: that the assertions contained, in the passages quoted, from Lord Gambier's Defence, are completely refuted, partly by his Lordship's own Orders, as they appear upon the Minutes of the Court Martial, and partly by an original document, of which we have obtained a copy, and which will be found in the Appendix; the authenticity of which, we shall leave to the candour and prudence of Lord Gambier to deny or admit as he shall think fit. This is the document Lord Gambier had in his mind, when he said in his letter, of the 10th of May, to the Secretary of the Admiralty:—"I furnish-"ed them," the Officers commanding the fire ships, "with "full instructions for their proceedings in the attack, *according "to Lord Cochrane's plan.*" (p. 8.)

In calling the attention of the public to the evidence of Mr. Fairfax, we had in view, only, to expose its nakedness; in order, that Justice might not be defrauded by specious appearances, and plausible assertions. We have shewn that his imposing situation as Master of the Fleet, and the high mention made of him, by Lord Gambier, serve, only to raise the expectation merely to disappoint it: that the whole of his evidence has shrunk from even a cursory investigation: that its inconsistency and fallacy have been rendered apparent; and that his boldness of intention, alone, remains untouched.

With this witness, we have perceived the conduct of the Court, to deviate from its own principle; and trample upon its own rules: the Judge Advocate, tacitly approving of practices, which, in other instances, he had, with pertinacity, objected to, as incorrect: and Mr. Bicknel, as usual, every inch a nominal prosecutor, and altogether so regardless of the manner in which the prosecution, "as it "may be called," proceeded—that there is some reason to imagine, he was fast asleep the whole time; until, like the lethargic clerk, who awakened only, when it was necessary to say Amen, roused by a question from the Court, "whether he proposed any question to Mr Fairfax?" he answered, "None," then went to sleep again. And as that question was never offered to him, or any mention made of him, after the examination of Mr. Stokes, who followed Mr. Fairfax, it is presumable, that he then took his departure: leaving the Court and the Defendant to manage the business, as they might think proper; and Justice to take care of her own cause, single handed.

Mr. STOKES, Master of the Caledonia.

This is another of the persons, who, as Lord Gambier has told us, in his written Defence, were to verify the Chart, on which the positions of the enemy's ships are said to have been marked, as they appeared on, and previous to, the 12th of April, (p. 23,) "from angles measured, and observations made "on the spot." (p. 133.)

After Mr. Stokes had authenticated the Log of the Caledonia, the following Examination took place, and which is of a nature and description to require particular observation.

Q. by Mr. Bicknel. "Produce a sketch or drawing of the "anchorage, at Isle d'Aix."—It was produced accordingly, and connected, as it appears in the Minutes, with a marginal note in these words, (in italics) "*See the two Plates corresponding with* "*that produced by Mr. Stokes, which accompany this Pub-* "*lication.*"

Q. "Did you prepare this drawing, and from what docu- "ments, authorities, and observations; and are the matters and "things, therein delineated, *accurately described,* according to "the *best of your judgment and belief?*"—*A.* "I prepared "that drawing, partly from the knowledge I gained, in sounding "to the Southward of the Palles Shoal; and the Anchorage of "the Isle d'Aix: the outlines of the Chart are taken from the "Neptune Françoise; and *the position of the enemy's fleet, from* "*Mr. Edward Fairfax,* and *from the French Captain of the* "*Ville de Varsovie;* and the British Fleet from *my own ob-* "*servations.*" (p. 23.)

His own observations, therefore, were confined to the situation of *our own fleet,* a thing altogether immaterial; and "the *po-* "*sition of the enemy's fleet,*" the grand and only important object, was left naked and destitute; resting on mere matter of hearsay, which Mr. Stokes gathered from divers persons.

We should have imagined that any person, acquainted with the proceedings of a Court, however slight that acquaintance might be, would, on the first blush of such a paper, so constructed, decide, that it was such as could not be received in evidence. The Court, however, seem to have been of a different opinion; and, therefore, asked Mr. Stokes: "Whether the "matters and things therein delineated, were accurately de-"scribed according to the best of his knowledge and belief?"—*A.* "They are." But, as if Mr. Stokes had, himself, some compunction of conscience, or was admonished by his apprehension of consequences, he adds: "There is one thing it may be "necessary to explain, respecting the Chart. It cannot be ex-"pected, that, from the opportunities I had of sounding, in "this place, I could accurately point out *the distance between* "*the sands:* therefore, for any thing respecting *that*, I must "refer the Court to the Chart, which I copied from a French "manuscript, which will be produced here; and that, I take to "be correct." (p. 24.)

It might have led to a very important discovery, had the Court asked Mr. Stokes: Why he did not, in his sketch or Chart, conform to the scale of the French Chart, which he "took to be "correct;" particularly as he expressed his ignorance of the soundings in the Roads of Aix, and referred the Court to *that* Chart to supply the deficiency? We do not pretend to assign any reason for the silence of the Court on this head; and the motive that actuated Mr. Stokes will be too obvious to require one, when the public shall have compared this sketch or Chart, with the Neptune Françoise, published for the use of the French Navy. It will therein be found, that the space in Aix Roads, is nearly three times more extensive, than as it is "delineated" by Mr. Stokes: and we may be allowed to say, that this Chart or sketch, thus manufactured, is no more the genuine Chart of Mr. Stokes, than it is of Lord Gambier, who was not near the scene described during the whole of the time it was passing; and with the single exception of a voyage, which, Mr. Stokes informed the Court, he had made into the mizen-top of the Caledonia, his Lordship was equally competent, with that gentleman, to give it authenticity.

But, although Mr. Stokes confessed, that he was ignorant of "the distance, between the sands;" he some time afterwards deposed positively to those sands; and as particularly, as if he had been perfectly well acquainted with them.

Q. by Lord Gambier. "*Is there not* a Bank between the "Boyart, and the Pallés Shoal?"—*A.* "YES."

Q. "What depth of water is there, generally, upon that bank, "at low water?"—*A.* "From twelve to sixteen feet, in the "DEEPEST part; but that part IS VERY NARROW."

Q. "If there are only sixteen feet, line of battle ships could "not pass over it, at all times?"—*A.* "*No; not until near two* "*thirds flood.* You must reckon on going over that part, *at* "*twelve feet.*"

Q. "To get to the anchorage, it is necessary to pass over the "bank just mentioned?"—*A.* "IT IS."

Q. by Admiral Young. "Is there a channel of sixteen feet, "all across?"—*A.* "*There is a channel of sixteen feet, all across;* "but that is NARROW: there are about the middle of it patches "of twelve feet.

Q. by the President. "*There is* no going into the channel of "sixteen feet, without, in some instances, passing over that of "twelve feet?" (p. 148)—*A.* "You may go over the channel of "sixteen feet; but *it is so narrow,* that I should calculate going "over that part, which is only twelve feet."

Q. "*It is* so intricate, you must count on passing over some "part, with only twelve feet?"—*A.* "I should calculate on "going over part of the twelve feet; because *it is so narrow,* "it is *difficult to hit* the passage of sixteen feet."

Mr. Stokes has also asserted, that "the deep water was very "much limited;" and, by his answer to a question from Lord Gambier, "that the space for anchorage, of large ships, was "very much confined, and the water round it shoal." (p. 149.)

Such testimony, even thus contrasted, will make a strong impression on the thinking mind. Mr. Stokes, in the first instance, declared his incompetency to point out "the distance between "the sands;" and in the second, speaks of that fact, with all the positive certainty of an intimate and accurate knowledge of them.

But what will the world say, when it is made manifest, that Mr. Stokes could not have believed, although he so deposed, that "the matters and things" delineated on the Chart, or sketch, delivered by him to the Court, were "*accurately described.*"

Q. by Lord Gambier. "State the situation of the fleet on the "morning of the 12th of April."—*A.* "Four of them lay in a "groupe, or lay together, on the WESTERN part of the Pallés "Shoal; the others on the *Eastern* side of that shoal. The "three *decker* on the *North West edge* of the Pallés Shoal, with "her broadside flanking the passage; the *North West part* "NEAREST THE DEEP WATER." (p. 147.)

On a reference to the Chart, or sketch, it will be seen, that some of those vessels are thereon traced, to the South East of that shoal; and *the rest* nearly due East. This, however, is not all. To prove a part of the danger, that opposed themselves to Lord Gambier, and which, together, prevented his attack of the enemy, at an earlier hour than two o'clock, he is interrogated by his Lordship,

Q. "Could any of the enemy's ships, on the 12th of April, "before they ran up the Charante, have annoyed and raked any "of the King's ships, that might have been sent in to attack "them?" (p. 149.) He answers: "The Foudroyant and Cassard "both lay afloat: the Cassard, about one third of a mile distant "from the Isle of Aix. The Foudroyant lay, I suppose, about "*three cables distant from the Cassard,* &c."

If any one will take the trouble to place one end of a pair of dividers on Mr. Stokes's sketch, or Chart, and the other, occasionally, on the Foudroyant and Cassard: he will find that *the farthest* is *upwards of a mile;* and that the *nearest* is considerably more than *three quarters of a mile* from the Isle d'Aix.

Hence it is demonstrable, that Mr. Stokes's sketch, or Chart, and his deposition, are at total and fatal variance with each other; and as the former was supported merely upon the inconclusive words, to "the best of his knowledge and belief," we must place our reliance on the latter, which is without any reservation; direct and positive. It was upon these grounds we assumed the fact, that when deposing to his Chart, or sketch, Mr. Stokes *did not*, nor could *believe* the matters and things therein delineated, to have been "accurately described," notwithstanding his assertion to the contrary: and we trust that we have made out our case.

From the evidence we have quoted, we trace another result, of still higher consequence; and, in order to make this evident to those, who may not have leisure to pursue minute investigation, and go forwards and backwards, which, from the complicated and confused state of the Minutes, is essentially necessary to a perfect understanding of them; we must restate that part of Mr. Stokes's testimony, which describes the position of the fleet, on the morning of the 12th of April, "Four of them lay in *a group*, or "lay *together* on the WESTERN part of the Pallés Shoal," the three decker "was on the NORTH WEST EDGE of the Pallés "Shoal, with her broadside *flanking the passage*, the NORTH "WEST part *nearest the* DEEP WATER." We must, also, once more beg that the Chart, or sketch, may be referred to: and it will thereon appear, that the vessels just mentioned, are laid down in the sketch or Chart, not on the *North West* edge, but on the *South East side* of the Pallés Shoal: and instead of being *nearest* are *farthest* from the *deep water*; and *not one of them* FLANKING THE PASSAGE. Here, then, is the result we suggested—a complete falsification of Mr. Stokes's Chart, or sketch, by Mr. Stokes's own evidence.

In going a step further, we have another part of Mr. Stokes's depositions, strengthening and illustrating our conclusion: The Foudroyant and Cassard, both lay afloat: The Cassard about one third of a mile from the Isle d'Aix; *and close to the edge of the bank* which extends from the Isle d'Aix to the NW part of the Pallés Shoal; "the Foudroyant" *lay, also, near the edge of that bank,* and about three cables length from the Cassard.

These two ships are very ingeniously placed in a corner, on the *edge* of the shoals, for reasons, that will not require any other explanation, than such as is furnished by that part of Lord Cochrane's deposition, in which, after stating that the enemy's ships *were incapable of resisting an attack;* and that two or *three sail of the line* were quite sufficient to have destroyed them: his Lordship says: "Ships of the line, by passing *near the Boyart,* " and putting their helms a lee, their fore or main-top-sails being " to the mast, would have brought their heads towards the North " East; which would have enabled them, at a distance at which " *the shot of Aix would have been of no effect,* to have brought " all their guns to bear on the enemy's two ships," " until they " approached them: or until *so far to leeward,* that they would " have been enabled, by putting their helms up, *to run under* " *their sterns,* BETWEEN THEM AND THE SHIPS ON SHORE, " and thereby capture them, or force them to cut and run aground " likewise." (p. 45.) And it was with a view of combatting this part of his Lordship's evidence, that Mr. Fairfax stept out of the course of his examination, a volunteer, as we have already noticed: " I beg leave to observe, says he, that no ship or ships could " have hove to, on the larboard tack, with the wind as it was, " but what they must have fallen off so much as to bring them- " selves into a position to be raked by those two ships of the " enemy: *there was no room to go under their sterns,*" (p. 145.)

Having thus disposed of the famous Chart or sketch, we shall take a transient review of some other parts of Mr. Stokes's evidence; to enter into a minute examination of the whole, after the traits we have already noticed, would be both tedious and superfluous.

Q. by Lord Gambier. " Could any of the enemy's ships, " on the 12th of April, before they ran up the Charante, have " annoyed and raked, any of the King's ships, that might have " been sent in, to attack them?"—*A.* " The Foudroyant and " Cassard both lay afloat: the Cassard about one third of a mile " from the Isle d'Aix; and close to the edge of the bank that " extends from the Isle d'Aix, to the North West part of the " Pallćs Shoal. The Foudroyant, also, lay near the edge of

" that bank, and, I suppose, about three cables length from the " Cassard: the three decker lay, with her broadside flanking the " passage; they all three would have fired, with complete effect, " on any ships, that might approach," (p. 149.)

Further questioned, he said: " Had four sail of the line run " into Aix Roads, when Lord Cochrane made the signal, they " would have met a force equal to themselves: the fire of the " Foudroyant, Cassard, *and the three decker*, would have been " directed to them*."

Lord Gambier here quits this subject, and goes to another, as if satisfied with Mr. Stokes's information.

Q. " Could the three French ships, that were aground, upon " the Pallés, and afterwards warped off, and run up the Cha- " rente," (of which the three decker was one), " ever have been " attacked by line of battle ships?" *A.* " THEY COULD NOT: " *They never could have come near enough to have fired upon* " *them with effect,* FOR THE SHOT TO REACH." (p. 150.) and this is in confirmation of Lord Gambier, who says, " THREE, " OUT OF SEVEN, of the enemy's ships, aground on the Pallés, " were, *from their first being on shore, totally out of reach of* " *the guns of any of the fleet,* that might have been sent in;" " and that the OTHER FOUR, of the eleven, never were in a

* The following facts as they dance before us, can only be explained by those who produced them—they make a figure that would puzzle a ballet master. Mr. Stokes says: " The only time the enemy's ships could have " been attacked, with any prospect of success, was the time the attack was " made, *the tide had then ebbed,*" (see his other reasons, which are curious, p. 151); and Mr. Fairfax informs us, that the time of high water on the 12th of April, by calculation, was about *five minutes past* 2 o'clock, (p. 143,) but Lord Gambier, in his Defence, asserts, that " the ships took a position to be in " readiness to proceed to the attack, *as soon as the tide had sufficiently* " FLOWED, and that in consequence of *strong Northerly winds,* the tide con- " tinued to run, until PAST THREE," a circumstance which his Lordship very justly observes, " Lord Cochrane has not noticed in his evidence," (p. 127.) This unusual flowing of the tide, is supported by the complaisant Mr. Fairfax, who deposes that " it blew strong," (p. 143), notwithstanding that Captain Rodd " went in with royals and top-gallant studding-sails set," (p. 89,) and Captain Newcomb " brought up with his stream anchor," (p. 196.)

" situation to be assailed, after the fire ships had failed!" (p. 137).

Here then we perceive, as the result of our enquiries, a substantive fact, asserted in the *most positive manner*, and the same fact denied in the same positive manner, by the same witness.

We shall close our remarks on Mr. Stokes's testimony, with his examination, by Admiral Young.

Q. " Were you consulted by any person, on the practicability " of going into, and coming out of the Road of Aix, on the 12th " April."—*A.* " I was not *particularly* consulted; but Sir H. " Neale, on the morning of the 12th, seeing the enemy's fleet on " shore, asked me, what I thought, (or words to that effect) " could be done, as to taking the line of battle ships in, to attack " the enemy? I told him, perhaps, he might destroy some of " their ships; but that we should sacrifice our own; there " being no idea whatever, of the ships being able to return."

Q. " Are you quite clear, that you gave that opinion to Sir " Harry Neale, on the morning of the 12th April!" (p. 151).

We have quoted this testimony to remark, that the Court on this, as on other occasions, not only allowed evidence of the " *conversations with officers;*" but courted and solicited it: and not only received "*opinion*" as evidence, instead of "*facts;*" but endeavoured to fix that opinion, by forming a question on it.

Had the same practice been pursued generally, we might have been silent; but that has not been the case, and it is an abuse, that demands attention, when a Court, of Justice and honor, draw distinctions between parties before them; peremptorily refusing to the one, that which they readily granted to the other.

From the premises we have collected, we can draw this conclusion, only: that the ground-work of Mr. Stokes's Chart, which was received by the Court, is, confessedly, not drawn from his own survey: neither is it copied from the French Chart, *to which he refers, " for the distance between the sands ;"* (p. 24.) and consequently false, to his own knowledge. Yet a printed Chart, delivered by Lord Cochrane, and *fac simile* copies, were rejected, on the plea, that his Lordship could not authenticate the original: another proof of the *consistency* and *impartiality* of the Court. That Mr. Stokes's Chart has been clearly proved, by his own evidence, to be *totally invalid ;* that he himself had no knowledge of the most essential objects, which it professes to delineate, namely, the position of the enemy's ships ; and that some parts of his evidence contradict other parts ; amongst others we will notice the following instance, which is very glaring : "THE " THREE DECKER, *the Cassard and Foudroyant,* would ALL " have fired with complete effect, upon any of our ships, that " might have approached them." (p. 149). Yet in another part of his evidence, he says; " *our ships never could have come near " enough, to have fired upon them with effect,* FOR THE SHOT " TO REACH." (p. 150).

Mr. Stokes was eager and anxious throughout, to give information. His zeal, heated and ardent, outrun his discretion: ignorant, unfortunately, of the most important facts; and labouring under the defects of a bad memory; he found himself struggling with difficulties, into which he incautiously plunged; and where he meant to render a service, involuntarily committed an injury. If further proofs were necessary to fix the falsity of this *fabricated* Chart; he has furnished it, and here it is.—" The " ONLY SHIPS *marked on it, on the 12th April,* ARE THOSE " DESTROYED;" (p. 147).

Mr. RAVEN, Master of the Cæsar.

It is a matter of some surprise, that Lord Gambier should have examined this person, except he imagined that the multitude of his Witnesses would compensate for the deficiency of their information; as he really knew nothing of the points to which he was interrogated. Like Mr. Fairfax and Admiral Stopford, he went into the Roads of Aix, when it was dark; and left them, on the next morning, before it was light. His diligence in acquiring local knowledge, and the success he met with, can be expressed in a single sentence: the Cæsar ran on shore in Aix Roads; he was then in her, and " sounded round her, NEARLY " A CABLE EACH WAY!!" (p. 170.)

Thus ignorant of every material fact and circumstance: how could he have known, what would have been *the fate* of ships of the line, *had they been sent into the Roads of Aix*, in the morning of the 12th of April? Or whether the two Ships afloat, *could, or could not, have been approached by British line of battle ships;* yet to such points was he interrogated, by Lord Gambier. The Chaplain of the Caledonia, who never left the side of his Lordship, might have been called upon, with equal propriety.

It was a cruelty to bring forward this poor gentleman, who, whilst demonstrating, that the disposition was powerful, proved, also, that the ability was weak; and his mind, partaking of these contrarieties, was in a state of continual perturbation and confusion: as the following facts will sufficiently evince. Having shewn to the utmost extent of his means, and very far beyond his knowledge: that if our Ships had been sent in, on the morning of the 12th, to attack the enemy, they could not have returned during the day, he was asked: " Would they have been " within the range of shot, from the enemy's batteries, whilst they " remained there?" he answered; " The greatest part must " have been:" And the Cæsar having been on shore, and her danger still haunting him, he added, " PARTICULARLY THE

"Cæsar." Again: "When the enemy's ships, that had been "aground, and the two that were afloat, ran to the entrance of "the Charante, could they have been approached by British line "of battle ships, or large frigates?"—*A.* "*From the knowledge I* "*have of the place*, I do not THINK, they could have been ap- "proached, by large ships; I am not *positive*, as to the large "frigates." (p. 169.) Why not? Why could he not speak as positively in the one case, as in the other? Here is his reason: "*I did not know the depth of the water!!*" (p. 170.) He had surveyed the great and little Basque Roads; but had "little or no "knowledge of the Roads of the Isle d'Aix; having been, only, "in there, in the Cæsar; that night after the ship was aground." (p. 170.) Unfortunately for Mr. Raven, the reason he assigns, for not being able to speak *positively*, respecting the large frigates, evidences equal incapacity, to speak of the line of battle ships; and argues as much for his embarrassment as the incident, we have just noticed, when he combined the danger of the "enemy's batteries" with the fate of the Cæsar.

These specimens of Mr. Raven's knowledge, on which we might considerably enlarge, would have been enough for any reasonable person; but not so with Lord Gambier, who most unmercifully carried him from Dan to Bethshebah, and required him to state: "Whether he had not been in the Cæsar, under "the flag of Sir Richard Strachan?" (p. 170.) He answered in the affirmative, and his Lordship proceeded to question him, relative to any *observations* he might have made, on the anchorage of the enemy's squadron; which was referring to a period, nearly two years prior to the time of his examination.

Such a question, to such a man, who had shewn himself so very incurious, regarding objects and circumstances, in which he ought to have been deeply interested, and anxiously inquisitive; that when the Cæsar, the ship to which he belonged, "was "aground," and in, what has been termed, "a perilous situation," he did not sound round her *quite* a cable's length: (p. 170,) although so much depended on finding a depth of water, in which she might float; and although he was stimulated to prosecute his search, for that purpose, by having found four fathoms

Z

and an half, in a North West direction (p. 170), close to the spot on which the Cæsar lay. As to the observations, which Lord Gambier's question extracted from him, they were, as might have been expected, insignificant—"the enemy's ships," said he, "came out to manœuvre; and were chased in again by ours!!" and like Mr. Wilkinson, he conceived another man's intentions, without having heard them expressed: "I conceive it was the "intention of Sir Richard Strachan to have attacked the enemy; "but from the strength of the batteries, and the manner in "which the ships were laid, we worked out again!!" (p. 170.)

Lord Gambier, following up his interrogation, asked: "Did "they ever appear to take the ground, at low water, at the an- "chorage?"—*A.* "It appeared frequently, from the Cæsar, that "they did, at low water, at spring tides." It is to be recollected, that this observation was made in Basque Roads, at a distance of at least five miles; and possibly, in the same manner, as Mr. Stokes made his observation, *from the mizen-top.* But what will nautical men say, of ships of the line, striking the ground frequently, in a heavy sea, occasioned by strong winds, blowing from the North West? (p. 170.)

Mr. Raven was also examined to Mr. Stokes's Chart: but to what end we cannot collect, either from the question on the occasion, or the answer it received, as no precise time is mentioned, either by the one, or the other; consequently, both the Chart and the deposition, might have referred to the evening of the 12th, or the morning of the 13th; or, indeed, any other period.

Such is the testimony of this persecuted Officer, who, in pity, ought to have been spared the unequal trial, to which he was cruelly exposed; and whose confessed total want of information, should have pleaded successfully, in his behalf.

But this examination of Mr. Raven, whilst it betrays his ignorance and confusion, reflects no credit, either on Lord Gambier, the President, or Admiral Young, who conducted it.

JAMES WILKINSON, ESQ. LORD GAMBIER'S SECRETARY.

Lord Gambier tells us, in his Defence, " that it was found, " altogether impracticable to proceed to the attack, on the night " of the 10th, though much pressed by Lord Cochrane; and it " might be considered a most fortunate circumstance, that the " attempt was deferred, for it appeared, *by a general order,* " *found on board one of the enemy's ships,* and now delivered " into Court, that the French, to protect their fleet from attack, " had equipped 73 launches, and other boats, in five divisions, " to guard it from surprize, during the night, and to tow off " our ships on their approach: and the tranquillity of the night " of the 10th, would have afforded the enemy full opportunity " of availing themselves of this protection; but of this, they were " deprived, by the very blowing weather, on the subsequent " night, when the fire ships were sent in." (p. 122). Mr. Wilkinson, was called upon to authenticate this singular document, which was to support the assertion his Lordship had raised on it. But his answer to the first question, on the subject, shews him to have been totally ignorant of every circumstance connected with it. He saw it, for the first time, *on board the Caledonia,* on the 13th or 14th of April: and yet, he says, " It was found *on board* " *one of the French captured ships,*" (p. 139), which ships, are proved to have been destroyed on the 12th, one day, at least, before the paper was known to him. Admirable, Mr. Wilkinson! Thus has his zeal, in the service of Lord Gambier, placed him in a disagreeable dilemma, and contaminated the whole of his testimony. He has deposed, *positively,* to a fact of *the truth of which,* he had, of himself, *no manner of knowledge.*

Mr. Wilkinson is a second time brought forward, on the subject of a conversation between Lord Cochrane and Lord Gambier.

Q. by Lord Gambier. " Did you hear Lord Cochrane, on his " coming on board the Caledonia, on the 14th of April last, say " any thing to me, respecting the loss, he calculated on, of any of

" the King's ships, if I had sent them in, to the attack of the " enemy, agreeable to his signal?—*A.* Yes, I did. Lord Coch- " rane, in conversation, told the Admiral, that if he had sent in " the ships, *agreeably to his signal*, he calculated, or reckoned, " upon three or four of them being lost; or words to that effect. " THIS ALLUDES TO THE SIGNAL OF THE 12th—Seven of " the enemy's ships on shore—HALF the fleet can destroy them."

Q. " Did he say any thing respecting my own conduct, or " misconduct; or, that of any of the Officers of the ships?—*A.* " He said nothing of your Lordship's conduct, in my presence: " he spoke, generally, of misconduct of the *sloops*, and *small* " *vessels*; and of a *great many of the fire ships*; and he par- " ticularly noticed *the gun brigs,—small vessels was the expres-* " *sion*. I am confident the *men of war sloops*, were INTENDED " *to be referred to*, from the circumstance of *the Beagle being* " *mentioned*." (p. 179).

So that Mr. Wilkinson, after having, upon his former examination deposed, as a truth to that, of which he was wholly ignorant, now asserts, first, that Lord Cochrane " spoke, generally, of " the misconduct of the *sloops*:" secondly, that his Lordship did not speak of those vessels, but confined himself to *small* vessels; " *small vessels* was the expression." To crown the whole, he, with faculties peculiar to himself, penetrates Lord Cochrane's mind, and speaks, not only of what he said; but also of what he INTENDED to have said: " I am confident the *men of war* " *sloops were* INTENDED to be referred to; from the circum- " stance of the Beagle being mentioned."

This illustration, which Mr. Wilkinson, no doubt, *intended* should give the colouring of plausibility to his testimony, effectually destroys it: and thus his positive assertion, is rendered dependent on what another never said, but what, in Mr. Wilkinson's calculation, he INTENDED to say; and that, when Lord Cochrane spoke of *one*, he meant *half a dozen*.

But how was the subject of the Beagle introduced, in the conversation, to which Mr. Wilkinson alludes? Not by Lord Cochrane. Mr. Wilkinson says, that " Lord Gambier expressed his

" regret, that Lord Cochrane entertained so bad an opinion of " *the small vessels*, and particularly asked, his Lordship, as to " *the conduct of the Beagle*," and that, Lord Cochrane observed, rather abruptly, according to Mr. Wilkinson's statement: " but " my Lord, I cannot make an exception, respecting the conduct " of the Officers, commanding THE GUN BRIGS!! (p. 181).

Here, then, the *Beagle*, which seems to have been brought forward, as giving foundation to the statement, that Lord Cochrane had spoken, generally, of misconduct of the sloops, &c. is treated by both noble Lords, as a distinct and separate topic; and THE GUN BRIGS, *which are not sloops*, are the *only vessels*, of which Lord Cochrane had spoken, even according to Mr. Wilkinson's own statement, in terms of dissatisfaction.

Thus does the deposition of Mr. Wilkinson, carry, upon the face of it, assertions, that, in the eye of the law, constitute an offence, of no slight consideration: it abounds, also, with contradictions, in terms and in fact; and those are involved in such confusion, as to throw suspicion over every part of it.

Yet, whatever may be the opinion, formed upon the view we have offered, every generous mind will feel a glow of indignation, when contemplating the purposes, that such testimony was intended to promote. Certainly not the exculpation of Lord Gambier. Had such been its object, however overcharged it might have appeared, it would have been susceptible of some extenuation: as allowances are made, where friendship or interest, influence the actions: at least, in those instances, in which truth is not violated, nor justice totally suppressed; but it had in view, only, to kindle in the breasts of those Officers, who served with Lord Cochrane in Aix, the most violent passions: and excite and enfuriate the most powerful resentments against him, by impressing upon their mind: that he had endeavoured to cast blame upon their conduct: to rob them of the reward, due to their merits; and by such means, secure " all the credit," of the affair, in Basque Roads, " to himself." In short, Mr. Wilkinson's testimony, combining with the insinuations of Lord Gambier, could have no other object, than to provoke quarrels, and produce bloodshed. And is it possible, that any endeavour can be directed to a more malignant end? Whilst involving his Lordship in incalculable distress: it promised, in its consequences, an essential injury to the interests of the state; by creating inveterate animosity in the service, in which the utmost harmony is indispensibly requisite.

Of all this, the Court must have been very sensible; yet they allowed such testimony to be given. It is true, the President did stop it, in its course, for a moment, with this just and legal remark: "Mr. Judge Advocate—There appears to be some "doubts entertained, as to the strict propriety of this. It is "commenting upon the conduct of Officers, *whose conduct is* "*not called in question;* and, I think, it might be attended "with *very unpleasant consequences.* I am not SINGULAR in "my opinion; *some members* around me, have also *doubts, of* "*the strict propriety of it.*" (p. 179). But, with this conviction of an highly important truth, pressing upon his judgment, the President allowed himself, to be led away, by the following most perverted and iniquitous reasoning of the Judge Advocate: "I understand the bearing of it to be, to shew *some* CONTRA-"DICTION *to Lord Cochrane*; certainly, this, as to the con-"duct of other Officers, does not appear to be relevant: *unless* "*it is in* THAT POINT OF VIEW." (p. 180).

We will tell this learned gentleman, *en passant*, and it may be of service to him, on some future occasion, that such Evidence is *not* "admissible," in any "point of view." Indeed, the President, after the Judge Advocate had pronounced the strange doctrine, seemed to continue in his original sentiments. Nay, Lord Gambier, himself, appeared to be confounded, by the irregularity; and ashamed to proceed in it. "If the Court," said his Lordship, "have any doubts, as to the propriety of the Evi-"dence: if Mr. Wilkinson will state, whether he heard Lord "Cochrane express any *dissatisfaction with my conduct,* that "will be quite sufficient," (p. 180), which, by the by, was rather an ambiguity, on the part of his Lordship, as Mr. Wilkinson had *already* deposed, to that fact, *in the negative.*

But, notwithstanding, such the objections of the President, and of "other Members round him," and notwithstanding the concession of Lord Gambier, Admiral Stanhope suggested the propriety, of continuing the examination. "The difficulty now "is," says he, "as Admiral Campbell observes, that we have "gone a great way into the conduct of another Officer; and it "may not be pleasant to leave it as it stands, at present." (p. 180). Never was such an argument urged, by a Judge of any Court; nor one more fallacious. What, because the Court had confessedly fallen into an error, that "might be attended with "very unpleasant consequences," they were still to persist in it; in order to render those consequences inevitable!

This is indeed, "to know the right, and still the wrong pursue." There was no "difficulty," the Court might have expunged the whole of the obnoxious evidence; and it was their bounden duty to have done so. What right had they with the conduct of any "Officer," not embraced by the Charge "before" them? Let us look at the principle, and consider its ruinous, and destructive operation. Suppose a Court Martial, suffering such testimony, as Mr. Wilkinson's, to criminate an officer, not before them: What would be the consequence? That officer would of course, demand a Court Martial. And then, what would be his situation? Instead of fairness and candour, in his Judges, he would have to encounter all the evils, of deeply rooted prejudice; and all the obstacles, that decided partiality could throw in his way. He would be judged before he could utter a word; and condemned before he should have entered upon his defence. Such are the baneful effects, that Admiral Stanhope's principle is calculated to produce.

Whether Admiral Stanhope's argument had any weight with the President, or whether he had not been previously determined, by the sentiments of the Judge Advocate, are questions, that we are not prepared to enter upon, nor is it necessary; the fact is, he altered his opinions, which were correct, and worked down his own judgment to the following remark, which is as puerile as it is absurd. "The question appears to be, whether Mr. "Wilkinson, having gone so far, he shall proceed with his nar-

" ration." (p. 181.) This was enough for the subtle Judge Advocate, he immediately seized upon it, and in his province of advising the Court, said, " I think it would be better he should " proceed now, to the close of whatever passed, as to Captain " Newcomb; *for it will be published*, and it is very unpleasant, " that it should stand, as it does *at present;* there are several Re" porters for the *papers* present; and it will be published, as " imperfect, if it stands as it does." (p. 181). The Judge Advocate's reason, for going on then, turned entirely upon the *probable publication* of the evidence, (as it stood) in the newspapers. And thus, were the best established rules, that govern Courts, and the principles of justice, by which the dearest rights of man are protected, to be sacrificed to the *probability* of a *publication in a* newspaper. But was there no means of getting over this stumbling block? or was it a mere pretext, to give a colouring to the prosecution of illegality and injustice! Yes, the means were ready, and might have been easily and successfully employed: the Court had only to desire the "several Reporters" to expunge from their notes, the whole of the matter in discussion: and those men, who are men of liberality, for they are men of education, and acquainted with the laws of their country, would have yielded a ready and cheerful compliance. But the Court could have demanded the act, and this all parties must have very well known. Was not the learned Judge Advocate aware of this fact? If not, he ought to have been. There is no excuse for his ignorance; nor can he plead it, in mitigation of his offence: an offence, that is rendered infinitely outrageous, by a recollection of the conduct he observed towards Lord Cochrane, in that part of the proceedings, which, " may be called the Prosecution," objecting, upon every occasion, to every thing his Lordship brought forward in support of the Charge, that could, by any possibility, be considered, as not strictly within the rule of evidence. The Chart, which his Lordship delivered into the Court, to shew the relative situations of the British and French fleets, (p. 32). and the rise and fall of the tide, was objected to by the Judge Advocate, who exclaimed: " This Chart is not evidence " before the Court; because his Lordship cannot prove it is " accurate:" (p. 35). although it was proved, as accurately, as any French or English *printed* Chart could possibly be, unless the surveyor, who made it, had been called upon to verify it; and far more accurate than the *Paper*, called a General Order, produced by Lord Gambier, to Mr. Wilkinson; who when called upon to substantiate it, clearly proved, that he had never seen it, until he saw it in the Caledonia; and that he did not know how, or by what means, it had made its appearance there. Yet that *paper* was not objected to by the Judge Advocate; but received as unimpeachable evidence, and now stands upon the Minutes, as an authenticated document!!

Lord Cochrane had thrown some Notes together, which he had taken on the 11th, and subsequent days, of April, (p. 33). and copied them into the shape of a narrative, some time in the month of June following, for the purpose of refreshing his memory: but to these the Judge Advocate raised an opposition. (p. 40). Although Lord Cochrane declared, that he was bound to tell the whole truth: and that he did not think he could do so, unless assisted by those Notes: and although the point had been previously settled by the Court, upon a suggestion of Admiral Stanhope, who said, "Lord Cochrane swears, that which he now states is "correct; therefore, I do not think it material, whence it "comes." (p. 34).

Many other objections came from the Judge Advocate, to the evidence offered by Lord Cochrane, and which we shall keep in our memory, for a future occasion. For the present, we shall select only one other instance, in addition to those already noticed. We have seen the Judge Advocate struggling to introduce the hearsay testimony of Mr. Wilkinson, as to language that Lord Cochrane is said to have advanced, regarding the conduct of an officer, with whom, as not being a party named in the charge, the Court had not, nor could possibly have, any the least right of interference. We will now view him, pressing in a diametrically opposite line.

The President, alluding to something, that had fallen from Lord Cochrane, restated the following question: "If the frigates "could do the thing at two o'clock, why could they not do it at "ten?" (p. 49). Lord Cochrane, in his answer, proceeded to

A A

state the preparations he had made, to go down upon the enemy; and that he had no longer expectations of any other attack, by the directions of the Commander in Chief, than merely throwing shells. "That the Calcutta and Varsovie, and most of the "other ships, were pressing sail, to force them on towards the "Charante, and out of our reach; and that the confusion of the "enemy, was then so great, that it was upwards of an hour and "an half, before the Aquilon could get a single gun out of her "stern ports:" and after pointing out, that he had already answered the question proposed, and given his opinion, that "the most judicious plan would have been, to attack the two "sail of the line, that continued at anchor," and "*this opinion*, "founded upon the situation in which they were, and the con-"fusion in which they appeared to be, *I expressed, a little* "*after day light in the morning*, in conversation, to the offi-"cers; and, I think, to *Captain Woolf, who then came on board:* "*who likewise expressed to me his opinion*—"

His Lordship was here interrupted, by the Judge Advocate, but certainly in the mildest manner. "I am afraid, that is not evi-"dence:" to which the President added, "Nor is the con-"versation with the officers any evidence," (p. 50). and although Lord Cochrane remarked, that "it would give the Court an op-"portunity of proving the fallacy of what he had stated, by "calling these persons;" the latter part of the evidence was struck out, from the words "equal to the task."

How will the Judge Advocate defend himself upon such grounds; to exculpate himself is, in our opinion, utterly impossible. Mr. Wilkinson's evidence was totally irrelevant to the matter at issue; and tended only to injure individuals, and the public service. Lord Cochrane's deposition, on the other hand, was perfectly relevant; and in support of his own consistency. He mentioned a conversation with officers, in corroboration of an opinion he had just given to the Court, of the situation, in which the enemy were; and the confusion in which they appeared to be at the moment; it was also intimately connected with the charge, that the Court were then investigating: and it will be found, that, in referring to those officers for the purpose he mentioned, his Lordship was completely within the rule of evidence, laid down by Chief Baron Gilbert, "Though hearsay be not "allowed as direct evidence, yet it may be, in corroboration of a "witness's testimony, to show, that he affirmed the same thing "before, on other occasions; and that the witness is still con-"sistent with himself." (Law of Ev. p. 135.) This seems to be more particularly applicable to the circumstances of the case, in which Lord Cochrane stood. He was subject to have every part of his testimony rigidly scrutinized, and certain, from what he had experienced, that every endeavour, would be most strenuously exerted, to refute it, by witnesses, whom his Lordship would not be allowed to cross-examine: nor was there any one who would cross-examine for him, or for the country.

The nominal prosecutor, Mr. Bicknell, who was indeed nominal: if our information be correct, took his final leave, as we have already suggested, of the witnesses, on the part of "what may be called" the defence; very shortly after Lord Gambier had entered upon it. But this was certainly of no importance, as he never thought fit, to cross-examine the witnesses produced, either on "what may "be called" the defence, or on what may be "termed the "prosecution," although he had an ample field, and provoking opportunities for the purpose. And in the course of what may be called, "the prosecution," instead of exerting his efforts, to establish the charge, he allowed Admiral Stopford, avowedly the witness on the part of Lord Gambier, to give evidence in favour of his Lordship, of a fact, of which the Admiral had not any personal knowledge, (p. 80). and, with equal disregard and inattention, allowed the Judge Advocate to check that Admiral, when stating another fact, similarly circumstanced, that carried with it a shew of destroying an assertion made by Lord Gambier, because, as the Judge Advocate observed, "what the Admiral *heard* "is not evidence." (p. 81).

Indifferent, however, to these facts, and seemingly despising the considerations arising out of them, the Judge Advocate, the adviser of the Court and the expounder of the law, in which double capacity we have frequently listened to him, with more astonishment than edification, rejected the testimony of Lord

Cochrane, both as to his charts and reference to Officers, and not only admitted, but warmly and assiduously contended, with the President and the Court, for the admission of Mr. Wilkinson's narrative, on the subject of the pretended *General Orders,* pretended to have been found on board one of the enemy's ships: and on the subject of over-heard conversation, said to have taken place between Lord Gambier and Lord Cochrane, on board the Caledonia. And all this he did contrary to his own rules, laid down by himself; of course contrary to his own judgment: contrary to the decisions of the Court, solemnly pronounced; and certainly, contrary to every principle of equity and the law.

The public will decide on these and other traits, that we may hereafter lay before them, relative to the impartiality of the Judge Advocate; and how and in what manner he discharged the duties imposed on him by his office. They will, at the same time, take into their consideration the conduct of the President, in coinciding with the Judge Advocate, regarding the expunged evidence of Lord Cochrane. We allude to the first part, for which we solicited attention. We will now touch on the second.

The President stated, as above quoted, that "conversations "with Officers were not evidence." Yet on the behalf of Lord Gambier, and to favour his views, he allowed it, and in a matter not in the least connected with the Charges: nor capable of affording any aid to the Defence set up by Lord Gambier; but evidently to injure the character of Lord Cochrane, by arraigning his conduct; as will be seen by the following examination of Captain Beresford.

Q. by Lord Gambier. "Did you ever understand by whose "orders the Calcutta was set on fire," (p. 162.)—*A.* "The only "thing I know, with respect to the Calcutta being fired, was by "a conversation between Lord Cochrane and myself, *in the pre-"sence of Captain Bligh, Captain Maitland, and others,"* (p. 163.)

The conduct of the President, in this instance, whilst it destroys his claim to consistency and impartiality, displays the motives of the Judge Advocate in the strongest and most glaring colours. The moment, as we have above remarked, that Lord Cochrane referred to two or three Officers, in corroboration of an opinion his Lordship entertained, of the weakness of the enemy, and the mode and means, by which they were to be attacked; the Judge Advocate objected, that that was not evidence; and the President gave to the objection his concurrence; but here he admits it, as "legal evidence:" and why? because the Judge Advocate had said, "I conceive it is to affect the evidence of "Lord Cochrane. In that point of view, I think it is legal "evidence!!" (p. 163.)

Adverting again to the Judge Advocate, we will ask, What could more decidedly and distinctly demonstrate his determined partiality towards Lord Gambier, and his equally determined oppression and injustice towards Lord Cochrane? than that, A conversation with Officers, and hearsay evidence, was decided to be good evidence, because he conceived it *would impeach the evidence of Lord Cochrane*; but bad, when it supported his Lordship's accuracy and consistency. Again, it was perfectly well known by both the Judge Advocate, and the Court, that the question respecting the fate of the Calcutta was not calculated to affect; and consequently the answer it was to receive, could not by any construction be tortured into a meaning to affect, the testimony delivered by Lord Cochrane. It was, as it plainly shews upon the face of it, directed against his Lordship's conduct, and *not to contradict or impeach any part of his testimony;* nor to establish the *innocence*, nor in any way to exculpate Lord Gambier. It was with the sole view of injuring Lord Cochrane, in the estimation of his country, by inducing the belief, that he had carelessly allowed one of the enemy's ships to be destroyed, which might have been brought off: and we challenge the conscientious Judge Advocate, to contradict our assertion.

We have now finished with the testimony of Mr. Wilkinson, and trust, that we have demonstrated its worthlessness, and the malevolence of its tendency. In the course of dissecting it, we have supposed, that the Judge Advocate, unmindful of the trust reposed in him, by the office he held, had lent himself to the unavailing, and equally illiberal recriminating purposes of Lord Gambier, which, with the fullest assurance, that his Lordship could derive no possible benefit himself, by the pursuit of them, had in view to destroy the reputation of Lord Cochrane: and that the President, and the Court, departed from the line pointed out to them by their duty: sacrificed their own consistency; and violated the best principles, both of the law and of justice, in carrying into practice the precepts of their Judge Advocate.

THE END.

ADMIRAL STOPFORD, OF HIS MAJESTY'S SHIP CÆSAR.

It must be recollected, as it has been more than once noted, that Mr. Bicknel, the nominal Prosecutor, was desirous of closing what "might be called" the prosecution, before it was in any shape prepared for that measure; and closed it certainly would have been, on the evidence of Lord Cochrane, had not the President's delicacy towards Lord Gambier, and his Lordship's misconception of the important benefits it was calculated to afford him, prevented it. Mr. Bicknel threw out an intimation, that he purposed asking a *general question* of Lord Gambier's Captain and some others, whom he understood his Lordship meant to call on, as his witnesses. Lord Gambier, however, wished to know what that question was; because it might be necessary, he observed, to explain in his Defence, the point referred to by that question. And as his Lordship persisted in this wish, although Mr. Bicknel very kindly and most obligingly said, "it is not as "to any particular circumstance, which will CRIMINATE YOUR "LORDSHIP; it is *only* a general question."

Mr. Bicknel, in compliance with his Lordship's wish, called upon Admiral Stopford: and for reasons, which will be better understood hereafter, we shall give this *general question* at length, and entreat it may be always kept in the recollection, when the questions put to Witnesses by the Court, shall be under consideration. This question, which was not "to any particular circumstance, that "would criminate his Lordship," Mr. Bicknel gives in the following legal shape: "Having heard the orders, from the Lords "Commissioners of the Admiralty, to the Commander in Chief, "to attack the enemy's fleet in Basque Roads: and the letter "stating the result of such an attack: and the Charges preferred "against his Lordship, read:—you will be pleased to state to the "Court, whether you know of any neglect, or unnecessary de"lay, on the part of the Commander in Chief, in taking effec"tual measures for the destruction of the enemy's ships; or any "deficiency in any part of his Lordship's conduct, between the "17th day of March, and the 29th day of April, 1809. Or

B B

" whether, it appears to you, that he used every means in his " power to carry into effect the above mentioned orders?" (p. 70.)

Admiral Stopford is extremely guarded, and somewhat ambiguous in his answer, " by giving to the Commander in Chief " the free use and exercise of that discretion, which every Com- " mander in Chief must possess, in the execution of those mea- " sures for which he, alone, is responsible." Admiral Stopford ventured to "THINK," and he would go no further, that there " was not any delay or deficiency on the part of the Com- " mander in Chief." After delivering such an inconclusive and unsatisfactory opinion, Admiral Stopford was allowed to make obscure allusions to conversations, between himself and the Commander in Chief, respecting the " making a shew of the " fleet getting under weigh, in order to deceive the enemy, pre- " vious to the fire-ships going in." (p. 70.) This idea of frightening the enemy might have been amusing to the Court, but it was the very reverse of that which was entertained by Captain Kerr, who thought, if we had sent in ships, when only two of the enemy's remained afloat, with the melancholy reflections, that their consorts were aground, they would have blown us out of the water, or something like it, " and prevented the " two ships that were afterwards destroyed from being so." (p. 168.)

Admiral Stopford, after acknowledging, that the signals of the Cæsar were not put down correctly, nevertheless states the signals as *reported* to him by the Captain of the Cæsar; and amongst others, that first made by the Imperieuse: thus " Seven of the enemy's ships on shore: THE FLEET can de- " stroy them." (p. 70.) But Mr. Sparshot, Signal Lieutenant on board the Caledonia, says, the first signal was, that HALF the fleet could destroy them: Lord Gambier supports him; (p. 125,) and further, that it was made at 48 minutes after four o'clock, (p. 125) and not at HALF PAST SIX, as Admiral Stopford deposes. (p. 71.) So much for the accuracy of hearsay, and of recollection!

When Admiral Stopford spoke of a signal made by the Imperieuse, that she "was in distress, and wanted immediate "assistance," he might have explained that the signals in the Navy are so very imperfect; that those two points are unnecessarily and preposterously coupled together in the Signal Books. This signal, he says, "was made between half past twelve "and one o'clock," when the Imperieuse "was standing in "towards the enemy." And what notice did Lord Gambier take of that signal? Did he manifest all "the zeal, judgment, "and ability," and all that "anxious attention to the interests of "his Majesty's service," for which the Court, in their sentence, have given him credit; and on which they pronounced his MOST HONOURABLE ACQUITTAL? (p. 231) He who has talked so much of the care he bestowed upon his Majesty's ships, and kept them at anchor, from the apprehension that sending them in, to the attack of the enemy, they might forsooth be "*annoyed.*" Did he, at the instant the signal was made by the Imperieuse for immediate assistance, take the necessary steps to give her all the succour that was necessary, in such a situation, to prevent her from falling a prey to the "superior" force of the enemy?

Captain Rodd has shewn, that the signal to the Indefatigable for rendering that assistance was not made, until a few minutes after two; (p. 89) and Captain Bligh says, not until half past two. (p. 154.) In the mean time the Imperieuse, full five miles distant from the fleet, was left to her fate, and to the mercy of the enemy. So much for "zeal and anxiety."

Lord Gambier, in his written Defence, referred to "the high "professional character of Admiral Stopford, and Captains Beres- "ford, Bligh, and Kerr," who, his Lordship says, "cannot for an "instant be supposed likely to omit any circumstance that could "effect the object, for which they were sent into Aix Roads;" and, continues his Lordship, "I am morally certain they did not with- "draw their ships, until it was wholly impracticable to annoy the "enemy further." (p. 129.) Admiral Stopford, however, to whose high professional character, we, as readily subscribe, as Lord Gambier, went into the roads, when IT WAS DARK (p. 72), and left them the next morning before IT WAS LIGHT; carrying out with him all the other ships, that were in the roads, except the Pallas and Imperieuse, which two ships *voluntarily*, and according to newly broached opinions, improperly remained; when asked his reason for such a measure, without directions from the Commander in Chief, he answered: "the imminent danger to "which the ships were exposed by a longer continuance in that "anchorage; also the certainty they could not be employed with "effect in the further destruction of the enemy's ships, and "from the badness of the anchorage." (p. 72.)

It remains, however, to be explained, how he was capable of ascertaining those important facts. Surely not by ocular demonstration,—and we know of no other means. That he was mistaken on one point is evident, as it is proved, that the Pallas and Imperieuse continued in the roads until the 14th, (p. 190) without any injury; either from the anchorage or the batteries; and Captain Woolf, of the Aigle, who was ordered in on that day, to take the command from Lord Cochrane, remained on the station several days afterwards, without "*imminent" or any danger*. As to the fire *from the batteries*, that must have been of no account, if we may judge by the little damage sustained by our ships, that were exposed to it, during their attack upon the enemy on the 12th. Indeed the Admiral himself says, "they "did not fire their guns fast." (p. 82.)

Whether our vessels could, or could not, have been employed with effect, against the enemy, is another question; and such as might, or might not, have authorized Admiral Stopford to take upon himself, to order them away to the outer anchorage. All, however, that we contend for is, that Admiral Stopford has spoken of "*imminent*" danger, that could not have come within his view; and it is proved by Captains Malcolm and Broughton, and many others, that there was in the vicinity of the Roads of Aix, a good anchorage, not only for frigates; but even for ships of the line; with five fathoms at low water. This, Admiral Stopford admits: but says, "the fact was not within his knowledge, "when the frigates went in;" he however, might have known it. He had charts, no doubt, as well as Lord Cochrane and Captains Malcolm and Broughton; and had he consulted those

Charts, they would have instructed him, as they did those officers. (pp. 57, 214, 221, 223, &c.) But Admiral Stopford says: "that HAD HE KNOWN OF SUCH ANCHORAGE *be-" fore he went in, he should have expected* little good to arise "*from any of the ships going there;* as it was completely out " of the reach of annoyance to any of the enemy's ships, that " were on shore." (p. 73.) And why not have expected any good from such anchorage? Our ships might, at least, have rid there, and been perfectly secure from the batteries, the dangers of which were the grounds, upon which he founded *one* of his *two reasons* for withdrawing the ships, that were under his authority. The other rested entirely upon the enemy's ships being, at the time, out of our reach. So that our ships " could not be em-" ployed with effect in the further destruction" of them. And how has he explained this point?

Q. "Were you, before it was dark, in a situation so to see " the enemy's ships, as to feel quite satisfied, that ships of the " line could do them no mischief?"—*A.* " Before I went in, and " on going in, I observed the enemy's ships, that had not struck, " had gone in SO NEAR TO THE BATTERIES OF THE ISLE OF " AIX; and being also in a part of the anchorage with which we " were imperfectly acquainted, except from having seen a " French ship wrecked upon the Pallés Shoal, some weeks before, " I was of opinion, both with respect to the navigation, and " the exposure from the batteries, the ships could not have been " employed with effect without imminent risk of their safety." (p. 73.)

Whoever regards this part of the Rear Admiral's evidence, will naturally conclude, that he actually saw the ship he speaks of wrecked; but he saw only the wreck of a vessel, that had met such a misfortune, some time before our fleet had arrived in Basque Roads. And if the other part of his statement carries a plain meaning, it will be pretty evident, that notwithstanding his surmises to the contrary, our ships could have been " employed with " effect in the farther destruction of the enemy's ships." Whether this would have been done " without imminent risk of our own," is a point which we might pass by; as our object is merely to shew that the Rear Admiral had not, conformably to his own propositions, any reason for going out himself, or of ordering out, as he did, the ships that were in Aix, on the night of the 12th.

But taking as a guide, the wreck of the French ship, as she was situated on the Pallés, and which assisted the "very im-" perfect acquaintance" the Admiral had " with the anchorage :" and referring to Mr. Fairfax's Chart, we shall find a bason " with " five fathoms at low water," not much further removed from the batteries than the Boyart, and it will be easily and satisfactorily comprehended, by any mind not determined to refuse its belief to the existence of truth, that the vessels, which Admiral Stopford says, had gone in so near to the batteries of the Isle d'Aix, must of necessity have been within reach of our guns: or the Rear Admiral must have seen only, the apparitions of those vessels about three o'clock in the afternoon: or have confounded time and circumstances together, and alluded to the two vessels, that remained the last afloat; although they sailed between one and two o'clock, and the Rear Admiral speaks to about, four or five o'clock.

The Admiral is then examined on another point.

Q. " When the Imperieuse made the signal in the morning: " 'The enemy's ships on shore, and *the fleet* might destroy " 'them:' would he, with the experience he had, as a Flag officer, " have thought it prudent or proper to lead in *the fleet*, to de- " stroy them? *A.* In my opinion, the dislodgement from their " anchorage, of the enemy's ships by fire ships, removed but a " *very small part* of the obstacle which ever existed in my mind, " and in those of other officers, who have commanded before " me, towards the British fleet, going in to attack them; the " difficulties of the navigation*, and our imperfect acquaintance " with it, with the wind right in, would, I think, have made me " unworthy of command, if I had risked a fleet or a squadron,

* The Admiral acknowledges, that the passage was more than a mile and a half over. (p. 74.)

" entrusted to my charge, in a situation, where our's would " have been only the loss, and the enemy's all the advantage." (p. 73.)

The question is certainly worthy of such an answer; and such questions and such answers make up a great part of the materials, of which the Defence of Lord Gambier, if a Defence it can be called, is composed. The Court must have been aware in this, as in many other cases of a similar nature, in which such a question has been asked, that Admiral Stopford had never been in the inner road of Aix, during the period of day light; and that, consequently, he must have had the most imperfect knowledge of the position of the enemy's ships, that were on shore: how then could he be competent to give an opinion upon the subject, a subject, that could not have been traced in the hour of darkness; nor understood without infinitely more attention, than Admiral Stopford was allowed to bestow on it? The greatest impediment, however, that seems to have occurred to his mind, as to the undertaking pointed out by Lord Cochrane, was, as he tells us, the difficulties of the navigation; " in a passage *more than a mile* " *and a half in breadth.*" (p. 74.)

But if such difficulties, arising out of ignorance, could so operate to the prevention of an heroic, a glorious achievement: Why were not those Charts consulted, of the excellency of which Lord Cochrane and Captains Newcomb, Broughton, Malcolm, &c. have spoken? Those difficulties would then have vanished. Or, why did the Admiral, and Lord Gambier, remain in Basque Roads, from the 19th of March until the 11th of April, seven miles at least, from the enemy's ships, without taking any one step towards ascertaining the means, by which those ships might be attacked? But above all, when those ships had been dispersed, and driven upon the shore, like so many victims, bound hand and foot: and when the Imperieuse made the signal, that they could be destroyed, whether with " a part," or " half," or " the whole" of our fleet; why did not Admiral Stopford and Lord Gambier, or one of them, immediately repair to the spot, and learn from their own personal observations, the accuracy or fallacy of Lord Cochrane's report? Dispatching at the same time small vessels and boats in all necessary directions, to sound, and shew by signals, the depth of water they might find, which must have occurred to every one "ignorant of the "anchorage" as indispensably requisite: yet, this important proceeding was neglected; and the golden opportunity that offered itself, tamely suffered to pass by unnoticed, from forty minutes after five o'clock in the morning, until two o'clock in the afternoon. If then any difficulties existed, they were imaginary; and the fact has been proved so by experience.

Our frigates went in, nay, some of our line of battle ships went in; and though they did touch the ground, they returned to the anchorage without injury. How then could Admiral Stopford, without a perfect knowledge of the subject, state that *the navigation was difficult;* and that that circumstance, together with the wind, as it was, (that is, not a beating wind, but as fair as it could blow for going in), operated such powerful difficulties and obstacles, that "he would "have thought himself unworthy of command, if he had risked "a fleet or a squadron entrusted to his charge," in a situation, as he says, "where ours would have been all the loss, and the "enemy's all the advantage." To risk a fleet, in *such a situation*, would, certainly, render a man unworthy of command. But how has Admiral Stopford shewn, that such a situation existed? It is one thing to assume a fact; and another to support it. The Admiral has furnished a well turned and exceedingly lofty period: Lord Gambier admired it, he has called it "emphatical," and quoted it in his Defence. But it is sound without force; or rather it is an insensible sound, that probability disclaims, and practice has destroyed. Again, when stating a possible risk, how could Admiral Stopford state the consequences of it, as positive and certain. Had our fleet encountered a risk of all the dangers that Lord Gambier has conjured up, will not Admiral Stopford admit, that there was a possibility of escaping them: and if he does, how could he have so positively stated, that ours would have been all the loss? Will he not also admit, from what he has witnessed, in the destruction, four of the enemy's ships, attacked between one and two o'clock, that had a part of our force been employed at an earlier hour, namely, between eleven and twelve o'clock, it was possible a *sufficient* number of holes might have been made in their bottoms, exposed by the ebbing of the water, so as to prevent their floating with the rising tide? If he admits this possibility, and we do not see how he can deny it: How would "the enemy's have been all the "advantage?" It is only from causes direct and certain, that we are enabled to pronounce positively, as to effects.

Admiral Stopford, however, seems to have been as fluctuating in his opinions, as people in general are, who found themselves on the delusions of the imagination, without the aid of experience to inform, or knowledge to direct them: He says, to a question relative to a second signal, made by Lord Cochrane, "In this, "as in the former answer, I must be considered as speaking to "the state of the wind chiefly; and that my conduct as com-"manding officer of the squadron would have been governed "chiefly by the state of the wind." (p. 73.) So that, "the "broadsides of the ships, that were afloat," and of "those "aground, that were sufficiently upright, to rake the passage "going in," and "the batteries of Aix," and various other dangers, on which Lord Gambier has so feelingly, and frequently expatiated, were, in the mind of Admiral Stopford, of very inferior consequence. The wind was, with him, the primary consideration; he "would have been governed chiefly by the state "of the wind," of which he can have no right to complain: it was fair for him when he went into the Roads of Aix, at night, and changed, during the few hours he lay there, so as to become fair for carrying him out again. Thus do great men differ.

It seems, however, that Admiral Stopford had mistaken the question; or that his answer did not meet the expectations of Admiral Young, who proposed it, as he says, "my question "was under the circumstances, at the time." In noticing this observation, Admiral Stopford added, "the broadsides of three "ships still commanding the passage."

But notwithstanding he had thus become doubly fortified: instead of *thinking* that he would have been unworthy of command, if he had led a fleet or squadron into such accumulated

C c

danger, he only *thinks*, that he should not have *risked* the attack; (p. 74,) nor does he say a word, that "ours would have "been only the loss, and the enemy's all the advantage." Such are the happy consequences of second thoughts. We have only to add, that in whatever way the different statements and opinions of Admiral Stopford were received by the Court, on the subject of our ships going in to attack those of the enemy, it does not amount to any justification of the conduct observed by Admiral Stopford, in taking upon himself to order out those, that had gone in. We do not pretend to investigate the instructions, which he received from Lord Gambier; whatever they might have been, we are led to imagine, that they did not embrace the measure in discussion, if we are to judge from the language held by his Lordship, upon the subject, in his written Defence. "At the close of the afternoon, says "his Lordship, I judged it adviseable to attempt to follow up "our success, by an attack upon the five ships, that had escaped "to the mouth of the Charante, which I thought it might be "possible to effect, during the night; I therefore sent Admiral "Stopford in the Cæsar with the Theseus," line of battle ships, "and fire ships: and boats of the fleet, with Mr. Congreve's "rockets," which it must be confessed were excellent engines to be employed against single ships in a dark night!! "and gave the "Rear Admiral discretionary orders, to proceed as far as he should "judge proper." What will the world say of this, to us unintelligible, proceeding, after what his Lordship had said, in his plea for disregarding Lord Cochrane's signal, made at six o'clock in the morning?—Line of battle ships sent into the Roads of Aix, to hunt in the darkness of the night, after the enemy who had escaped beyond our reach! that were withheld during the day, when they lay at our feet, incapable of moving, and when fortune with a smile, pointed to the captures she had placed within our power!! Or did the wind, which continued to blow "right in," serve better in the night, and "the difficulties of "the navigation" exist only, in the day time?

If his Lordship had been "desirous of following up our success," there were already frigates in the Roads, and those declaredly better calculated than ships of the line which Lord Gambier would not risk at a time they had an object every way worthy of their attack, and adequate to the consequent risk: but which he is here seen precipitating into dangers without any object at all; nay, when "all circumstances considered," they could only be a drawback upon the exertions of others. The result evidenced the folly of the measure. The whole of the expedition was thrown into confusion, and Admiral Stopford, "very "judiciously, before day-light on the 13th, availed himself of a "providential shift of wind," and come out precisely as he went in. If this be not a farce of blunders, it is very like one; and if this be the method adopted to follow up success; it can be pursued only, if we are to regard an old proverb, when "deeds are evil." It has however one merit, it is original, with the fairest chance of being preserved to its author; as we may venture to believe, that no one will ever pirate it.

Unfortunately there is a complete and very material variance between this effusion of Lord Gambier, and that offered by Admiral Stopford. His Lordship says, the five ships of the enemy "had escaped to the mouth of the Charante." Admiral Stopford has deposed that they had gone in so near to the batteries of the Isle d'Aix, that our ships could not give "annoyance" to any of them; and this, is one of his reasons for ordering out the ships, that left the roads with him. It is not within our means to reconcile these inconsistencies: we must therefore, leave them to themselves.

Admiral Stopford was called in a second time, and examined to matters of mere hearsay. Some questions he answered, to the best of his *recollection*, of what others *recollected;* and it is to be remarked, that official reports, declared not evidence, when coming from one witness, were allowed, when delivered by Admiral Stopford. "Did you receive it, *as the official report* of "the commanding Officer of the boat?" "I did, *as nearly* "*as I can* RECOLLECT." (p. 80.) And on one occasion, Lord Gambier was permitted by the Court to preface a question in the most extraordinary manner: Asked if he had any question to put to Admiral Stopford, he observed, "With regard to my own "conduct, I have no wish; but I think it due to the Officers of

" the fire ships, to put a question, as to their conduct, which *I* " *aver* was highly meritorious." (p. 79,) And this too! in the presence and hearing of Admiral Stopford, his second in command! And if Admiral Stopford had, at that time, any thing to hope or fear from Lord Gambier's situation, interest, or influence; to what a painful situation, would it have reduced him! his Lordship had AVERRED in his presence and hearing, that the conduct of the Officers, to which he was required to bear witness, WAS HIGHLY MERITORIOUS; so that having no alternative, he was either obliged to sacrifice truth to Lord Gambier's solemn declaration: or by maintaining it, contradict his Lordship's averment, positively made, and solemnly delivered; he followed the dictates of his own honourable feelings, and in consequence the " averment" of the Commander in Chief was refuted, (p. 80, 81.) although some pains were taken by the Court to give him an opportunity to recollect, and correct himself.

Hence we learn the fatal effects of giving way to inconsiderate warmth, and rashly pledging veracity to a fact, that must, with his Lordship, have rested on hearsay; and as his Lordship is fond of inferences, we will follow him, and, in nearly his own words, suggest " that if he could thus pledge himself to a fal- " lacy in one instance, have we not some reason to doubt his ac- " curacy in every other, that is not supported by proofs?"

Four days after the second examination, and after the Defence had been read, and several witnesses on the behalf of Lord Gambier examined, Admiral Stopford again appears before the Court, at his own desire, and as we are informed, by the President, " to " correct a *little inaccuracy* in his evidence," (p. 182.) Lightly, however, as the President has treated the subject, we are induced to think it of very considerable import; that is if the subject out of which it arose be of any import. It connects with an answer to a question from Lord Gambier, respecting the hazardous undertaking of the fire ships, on the night of the 11th. In giving his former testimony, Admiral Stopford, speaking of the fire ship fitted out by the Cæsar, says, " the explosion vessel blew up " close to her, and damaged, and indeed ruined one of the boats, " in which the men were to come away from her." In his corrective evidence he shews, that the boat was not "destroyed;" it was only "damaged." Again, his first deposition states, that "the men were crowded in the remaining boat;" in the *correction* it stands thus, "the men were therefore, much crouded "in the other *boat*, few only were able to come away in *the damaged boat*." Once more, "the acting Lieutenant, and one man "died in the bottom of the boat, from fatigue; and the others "were picked up by the Lyra." The correction has it, "the "acting Lieutenant and one man died from fatigue, in the bottom of *that boat*, i. e. the damaged boat;" and the boats were "*both picked up by the Lyra*," (p. 182.)

These are errors in substantive facts, and in circumstances connected with them; but both in the one, and the other, the Admiral speaks positively to occurrences, as if he had been present at the time, and examined them, as they passed; the truth is, that *of his own knowledge*, he knew nothing of them, and this he himself admits, in answer to the following question, by Admiral Young, "As that, which occurred, *did not pass under your own* "*observation*, inform the Court how you came by a knowledge "of it?"—*A.* "From the *individual* and frequent examination of "the Officers and men *who returned, and comparing their ac*"*counts together*," (p. 80.) What will the public think of such testimony, and of the conduct of the Court in permitting it? It is another proof of the glaring impropriety, and dangerous consequence of hearsay evidence. And it may become a question with thinking men, by what means Admiral Stopford acquired those new lights on his second examination, that enabled him to discover and correct the errors of his first, as the facts did not originate with his observation. And why he did not correct this "*little inaccuracy*" in his evidence, on the day on which it was committed? There was sufficient time for the purpose: or on the next day, when the Court did no more than ask Lord Gambier, on what day he would be ready to enter on his Defence; (p. 104.) Or, the next day after that Defence had been read, as there was on that day, many witnesses examined; or on the day following? We have no doubt, that the Admiral could have assigned a reason: although he did not give any to the Court; possibly *because he was not asked.*

We will use the freedom to say, that such corrections so circumstanced, were never before heard of in any Court, and it is to be hoped they never will occur in future. In the course of this, his third examination, Admiral Stopford was interrogated by Admiral Young, " Whether Lord Gambier had been guilty of " any neglect, misconduct, or inattention to the public service?" —*A.* " So far from it, that it always appeared to me, the Com- " mander in Chief was actuated by a warm zeal, for the desire " to discharge the duties entrusted to him, with punctuality and " effect." On this point we have never expressed a doubt; on the contrary our belief accords with the fact, and we say with Lord Cochrane, that " the feelings of Lord Gambier for the honour " and interest of his country were, and are, as strong as those " manifested by his Lordship," and with Admiral Stopford, " that he was anxious in the extreme:" yet his zeal wanted energy; and his extreme anxieties were confined to expressions.

Like Captain Kerr, Admiral Stopford was before the Court at four different periods. On his last examination he deposed to some papers of intelligence said to contain particulars relative to the state of the enemy's ships, that had escaped up the Charante; and the President very properly observed " it was material to " insert, how such information was obtained," adding, " *I know,* " *no names ought to be mentioned.*" (p. 204.) "The information," says Admiral Stopford, " was received *from a Seaman,* belonging " to the French ship Foudroyant, who called himself *an American,* " and who DESERTED to the squadron in the Basque Roads on " the 22d of May!" Where had this equivocal American lain concealed from the 12th of April, until the 22d of May; or by what means, did he escape from his lurking place, to our ships in Basque Roads? But this as it may, if he had been an American, and a deserter, there could not have been any cause for alarm in mentioning his name; nor any reason to forbid his examination. He ought to have been produced as a witness to verify his own information, and without such verification the paper was not evidence. He might have written the paper himself, as no one could say how it came into his possession, nor does Admiral Stopford state how it found its way into his own; as he says only, it was received from a seaman. This wretched document, however, was received as evidence, at the Court Martial of Lord Gambier, that would have been rejected by any other Court in his Majesty's dominions, merely to support an assertion contained in Lord Gambier's written Defence, regarding the differences between his prudence and Lord Cochrane's impetuosity; although it does not appear to have had any relationship with either the one, or the other.

In making a few cursory remarks upon this Testimony, we shall only say, that it is chiefly composed of hearsay; and is sometimes inconsistent, and contradictory: that Admiral Stopford has spoken very fully to several points, as if they had come within his own immediate knowledge; whereas they were in fact, collected from the reports of others. The Court, in allowing the correction we have remarked on, in a part of Admiral Stopford's evidence at the time, and under the circumstances in which it was made, would appear to have been unacquainted with the rule that obtains in giving evidence; and the Judge Advocate did not think fit to instruct them. As to the question itself, it was altogether irrelevant and impertinent, and appears to have been calculated solely, for the purpose of stamping an odium on the character of an Officer, whose conduct the Court were not empowered to investigate. (p. 179, 180.)

SIR HARRY NEALE.

Much of information as we expected from Mr. Fairfax, the Master of the Fleet, ushered in as it was by Lord Gambier; still much more was to have been expected from Sir Harry Neale, the Captain of the Fleet. But the Court, far from seeking that information, took the most effectual means to suppress it; and we have been disappointed. Sir Harry Neale seems, himself, to have been aware, that such expectations were entertained; and, anxious to act with propriety, solicited of the Court those instructions, which he deemed necessary, for the regulation and guidance of his conduct.

"I would," said he, "beg to address a few words to the Court, "before I am sworn. Upon taking this oath, which I have read, "and of which I understand the extensive nature: am I to state "to the Court *every thing*, which may occur to me, as to "*proposals* and *private communications* with the Commander "in Chief; or solely to answer the question put to me? I take the "liberty of asking *that*; because I stand in a peculiar situation "with the Commander in Chief."

To this appeal the President stated, that he "was not "called upon to relate PRIVATE *conversation* he had with the "*Commander in Chief, in his intimate and particular situa-* "*tion.*" (p. 185). This however did not appear satisfactory, and Sir Harry Neale proceeded. "There were continual *conver-* "*sations*, between the Commander in Chief and me. I had "given him *my opinion* ON DIFFERENT SERVICES: *some of* "*those* he may have *approved*; and some HE MAY NOT HAVE "APPROVED."

These, something more than hints, of Sir Harry Neale's knowledge of matters, then under investigation, manifested that his knowledge was not confined to *private conversations*, on points of *a secret and confidential nature*; but extended also, to PUBLIC TRANSACTIONS "on *different* SERVICES," and ought to have roused an honest and honorable curiosity in the Court, to question him on points, most essential to the furtherance of truth, and the due administration of justice. Independent of every other consideration, it was the duty of the Court, to have sought information from a gentleman, whose situation gave him those peculiar and fair advantages, that others had no means of acquiring: and whose respectability added weight to his testimony; but when he invited them, as it were, to receive it, tha duty became infinitely more imperious: and the neglect of it, as it deprived the public of the benefits of the best information, that could possibly have been attained, rises so very high, that we dare not speak of it, as our feelings dictate. The public will give it all the attention it claims, and decide upon it, with their accustomed impartiality.

But let us hear the Court upon the subject. In reference to those " opinions *on different* SERVICES," which Sir Harry Neale said he had given to the Commander in Chief, " some of which " he might *not have approved.*" The President exclaimed " CER- " TAINLY ! I apprehend *these are* NOT TO BE STATED." And why not? Did not Sir Harry's own words shew, that he had drawn the line between PRIVATE and PUBLIC matters; and did he not call the attention of the Court to the discrimination he had made! In the first instance, he was desirous to have the aid of the Court, to direct him in a point of conscience, on a consideration of " *the extensive nature,*" of the Oath he was about to take, regarding proposals and " *private communications* " with the Commander in Chief;" and having heard from the President, that " he was not called upon to relate *private con-* " *versations.*" He then suggested, that there were conversations of a PUBLIC NATURE, for no other construction can be attached to the words, " I have given him my opinion upon *dif-* " *ferent* SERVICES." And what were those *services*? Doubtless PUBLIC *services*; the services, in which the public were interested, and which justice required to be revealed.

We cannot for an instant suppose, that the Court were ignorant of those points: or we should impeach their understanding, which has impressed us, with a very different sentiment. We

D d

have witnessed its vigour on some occasions, and the depth of its sources in others. But to whatever the neglect, we have spoken of, be assignable, it has intertwined itself with doctrines, the promulgation of which, we could not have imagined, was possible, had we not seen it, in the authenticated Minutes of the Court.

Admiral Young, following the President, and addressing Sir Harry Neale, thus expresses himself. "If you are DIRECTED "to detail any circumstances, you THEN are to say *all you know*, "OF THE CIRCUMSTANCES, or events you are DIRECTED to "detail: but if you are asked SPECIFIC questions, your oath, "I should imagine, will only OBLIGE you to answer SPECIFI-"CALLY and DIRECTLY, and as fully as you can, the QUES-"TION which is proposed to you." (p. 185.)

Of the SPECIFIC questions, that were asked of Sir Harry Neale, we have to remark, they were so framed, and pointed to such objects; that however much he might have deviated into detail, his answers could scarcely have affected Lord Gambier. They related only to the signal of the 14th of April, and the incidents connected with it; which signal, Lord Cochrane has asserted to have been made on the 13th. And in this assertion he is borne out by documents, under the hand of Lord Gambier; and by other circumstances, the occurrence of which is not denied.

But did Admiral Young, when he expressed himself, in the words we have quoted, seriously consider their tendency? Was he aware of the mischief he was doing, by the precedent he was establishing; and that the rule he was then laying down might be quoted by future Courts Martial: to the suppression of truth, and consequently, to the violation of justice? "If you are "asked a SPECIFIC question, your oath, I should imagine, will "*only* OBLIGE you to answer SPECIFICALLY, and DIRECTLY." (p. 185.)

Is such the language of a Member of a Court Martial, to a witness brought before it? Is such the construction of an oath, which the legislature has framed, with the nicest care, to prevent the operations of partiality, the influence of habits, and the consideration of self-interest, when a man should be standing before a Court Martial, as a witness, between our Sovereign Lord the King, and the party to be tried? Is it not telling the witness, that, although he might know much that would criminate one party, and support the integrity of another, he was not to bring forward all the facts, within his knowledge necessary to those salutary ends; nor even to suggest an idea, upon the subject, that might compel the Court to enter upon it; unless he should be SPECIFICALLY interrogated?

To what intent, is the charge, against the Defendant, read to every witness, previously to any question being asked of him? Is it not with the view, that he should be made acquainted with the offence, under investigation; and, by such means, be enabled to render to the Court, for the guidance of their opinions in the dispensation of justice, every information touching, or in any wise materially connecting with it, that might be within his knowledge! And are not those points in conformity with the plain, simple, and equally perspicuous and comprehensive mandates of the Oath, administered to every witness*?

With the Oath before us, and such an Oath too! we conceive it utterly impossible for a witness to tell the whole truth, and so discharge the most solemn duties to his country, and to his God; if he be bound down by SPECIFIC QUESTIONS, and restrained from passing their limits. What does he swear? "I will, whether *demanded of me* BY QUESTION OR NOT, and whether favourable or *unfavourable to the Prisoner*, declare the truth, THE WHOLE TRUTH. Are not the restrictions then, that we

* That the public may have a perfect conception of the consistency, with which the Court, and Admiral Young in particular, gave these instructions to Sir Harry Neale, on the duty required of him by the Oath he took, we have thought it necessary to transcribe that Oath:

I, A. B. do most solemnly swear, that in the Evidence I shall give, before the Court, respecting the present trial, I will, *whether* DEMANDED *of me by* QUESTION *or not*, and whether FAVOURABLE *or* UNFAVOURABLE *to the Prisoner*, declare the truth; *the whole truth*, and nothing but the truth. So help me God!

have quoted, in direct and gross violation of this particular, and most essential part of the Oath? And how is it possible, that the Members of a Court Martial should perform the duties imposed upon them, by the situation in which they are placed, and by the Oath administered to them, if they do not hear, from the witnesses produced, the TRUTH: and not only the TRUTH; but the WHOLE TRUTH, that may be within his knowledge, and pertinent, relevant or material to the issue trying; Nay if they do not exert every power of their faculties to obtain from him the WHOLE TRUTH, by employing such questions as may be requisite to that important end.

Yet we here see a witness instructed by the Court to *restrict* his evidence; unless "*directed* to detail any circumstances," to points contained in a SPECIFIC question. Is such a fair or correct interpretation of the Oath? Could such have been the intention of the legislature when framing it? A trial so shackled, and so circumstanced and embarrassed, must operate to place truth in the most humiliating situation, deprive justice of her well entitled rights; and be, at once, the reproach and contempt of mankind.

This rule or opinion laid down by the Court, and more particularly by Admiral Young, in application to the testimony of Sir Harry Neale, may be traced, also, in the instance of Lord Cochrane, a witness on the part of "what may be called, the Prose-" secution." His Lordship was frequently checked by the Court, and by the Judge Advocate, when in the act of detailing, in strict conformity to the dictates of the Oath he had taken, the occurrences, that were connected with the charge, to which he was deposing. His Lordship was sensible, that the interruption was highly improper; and, therefore, fully impressed with the conviction, that, as he says himself, "he was bound to tell the " WHOLE TRUTH," (p. 40). persevered in his course, which however, was very soon impeded. In answering a question from the President, which regarded the explanation of a fact, his Lordship was entering into a narration of circumstances, necessary to the purpose in view, when he was interrupted by Admiral Young. "*This is really very improper: this has no* "*sort of connexion whatever, with the* QUESTION, *which was* "*asked; and is only a series of observations to the* DISADVAN-"TAGE *of the Prisoner**." I wish, replied his Lordship, to speak the truth, the WHOLE TRUTH, and nothing but the truth. Admiral Young continued, "this has really nothing at all to do "with the QUESTION, which is asked you, which arises merely "out of the statement, which you had made." (p. 47). Lord Cochrane replied, if a QUESTION be put by a person ignorant of the whole proceedings, and which does not lead to get the *truth and the* WHOLE TRUTH; I hold, that I am to give the truth: and that I must depart from an express answer to the question, in order to give it. (p. 48.)

We will not stop to examine the serious manner in which the Court discussed the part of his Lordship's deposition, in allusion: we shall observe only, that they wholly misconceived his Lordship's evident and true meaning; and go on to shew, that the Court acted in more than one instance, on the illegal and unjustifiable doctrine laid down by Admiral Young, for the guidance of Sir Harry Neale. Lord Cochrane having insisted on another occasion, that he was bound to speak the WHOLE TRUTH, the language he used, though to us decorous, and inoffensive, gave umbrage to the Court, which was, in consequence, cleared for deliberation. On re-opening, Lord Cochrane was severely, and we may add, unjustly censured. His Lordship, in justification of himself, said, "Had I used the expression, in the sense supposed by the Court, I should be reprehensible; but, I believe, I said it would leave the Court in ignorance, if I answered merely to the question put to me; in ignorance of those things which ought to be put to the Court; that is, as to my reason for not weighing at half past eleven o'clock; and that it would tend

* If the Admiral had said the point, on which Lord Cochrane had dilated, was *impertinent* or *irrelevant* to the matter investigating, he might have been correct; but as he did not found his strictures on that ground, we have a right to assume that he was actuated solely, by his apprehensions, that the testimony his Lordship was giving, would tend to the DISADVANTAGE OF THE PRISONER. We will not press this subject further: what might be said in addition to that which we have advanced, is obvious. Does such conduct evidence that strict and inflexible impartiality which should be the characteristic of a judge trying a cause.

" to criminate myself. That it would be said, why, if the fri-
" gates were equally capable of weighing at half past eleven, as
" at one, did I not do it? and I, therefore, found it necessary to
" give that explanation."

President. " That was not the impression made upon my
" mind, or that of any one of the Court; for it did not infer,
" that the reply you should make, would be involved in igno-
" rance; unless you elucidated it. But, the observation was
" that, if persons ignorant of the circumstances, proposed ques-
" tions, they would not be informed."

Lord Cochrane. " Then that was really not my intention."

Admiral Young interposed; which brings us to our object.
" With respect to the answer you are giving, in a supposition that
" another question would be *asked,* the *answer you are giving*
" *would be* VERY PROPER, *when* THAT QUESTION WAS
" ASKED; but it is in no measure an answer to the question now
" asked; but *if that question* WAS NOT PUT, there is NO REA-
" SON WHATEVER *for giving* THAT ANSWER." (p. 49.)

If this should be considered not sufficiently strong to support our proposition, we will supply the deficiency from the examination of Captain Seymour, who, although commanding one of the attacking ships, in the afternoon of the 12th, and, consequently, well acquainted with very important points and transactions, that took place, on that occasion, was only asked half a dozen short questions: as to what time the enemy's ships last afloat, cut and run, and what time the three ships, aground upon the Pallés Shoal, removed; although others, without his means, or indeed scarcely any means at all, of acquiring the knowledge he possessed, were examined and re-examined to a very considerable length. When, however, Lord Gambier, on whose behalf he had been called, told the Court, that he had no further questions to ask Captain Seymour—Captain Seymour, from an impulse of honourable feelings, and conscientious rectitude, addressed the Court in the following words: " Am I bound, by the oath, to relate every
" circumstance which comes within my knowledge, relating to

"the proceedings of the fleet?" This unexpected address required some notice: it could not be passed over in silence; nor negatived by a naked monosyllable. The President answered it; but in a manner, that would have appalled many men, even of a far more advanced period of life.—"*If the* QUESTIONS, *that* ARE "ASKED YOU, should not seem to embrace all the circumstances "which you know, respecting *the matter to which* THEY *refer*, "you are bound still, to relate them?" (p. 190.) Leaving him, of course, to conclude, that whatever circumstance might be within his knowledge, he was not to communicate it to the Court, unless some QUESTION should require it; and that Captain Seymour so understood the President's meaning, is evident, from his immediately saying, "I know no other circumstance on "THIS subject."

With such an impressive remark, it became once more impossible that the Court should be silent: they therefore, examined him further; but instead of desiring him to relate EVERY *fact*, that had come *within his knowledge*, regarding the CHARGES exhibited against Lord Gambier, he was asked: "Whether all "the vessels of every description, employed against the enemy, "were conducted with every becoming zeal and judgment, for "the benefit of the public service?" (p. 190) which, departing entirely from the Charge against Lord Gambier, aimed at supporting one, that his Lordship had raised against Lord Cochrane: and on which the Court had wantonly, illegally, and cruelly examined several witnesses. Captain Seymour, however, desired to be informed by the Court, "from what period he was to give "his answer?" and was told by the President, "*from the time* "*of his being sent in to attack the enemy, and his remaining* "*there.*" "What!" asked Captain Seymour, apparently astonished at the restraint thus imposed on him, "*without going* "*back* TO THE ELEVENTH." The President answered, "No. "I take it from your going in, ON THE 12TH; because then "you became *an immediate spectator;*" (p. 193) which indicated, that the testimony of any other person, than an immediate spectator, would not be received, in relation to the conduct of vessels in the affair of the 11th. Yet Admiral Stopford was examined to these and other points, of which he had not been *an immediate spectator;* and of which he could not give any information *of his own knowledge.* Such distinctions in the proceedings, on the part of the Court, must appear very extraordinary: as altogether irreconcileable with every known principle of justice; and perhaps those who employed them, may find it a very difficult task, should they be bold enough to attempt it. The liberal and impartial will now determine, how far we have established the proposition with which we set out, regarding the rules laid down by the Court, and particularly Admiral Young, in restriction of evidence.

Returning to Sir Harry Neale, we will take a rapid review of his examination, which is, in itself, of very little, if any, consequence; either in support of the Charges, or of the Defence set up by Lord Gambier; but of the highest importance, in demonstrating the conduct observed by the Court.

On the subject of the signal, said to have been made by Lord Cochrane, on the 14th, which his Lordship has denied, he was asked by Admiral Young:

Q. "Was any thing done in consequence of that signal?"—*A.* "Yes."

Q. "What was done?"—*A.* "Captain Woolf, of L'Aigle, was "directed to proceed, and take the command of the in-shore "squadron."

Q. "Did L'Aigle go into the roads in consequence of that sig-"nal?"—*A.* "Yes."

Here Sir Harry Neale has fallen into an error*, as it appears by Lord Gambier's letter to Lord Cochrane, that Captain Woolf had received *that direction,* on the preceding day; and that L'Aigle went in, IN CONSEQUENCE OF THAT DIRECTION, and not otherwise, as Lord Gambier's letter is dated the 13th, and has these remarkable words:—"It is necessary that I should

* In justice to Sir Harry Neale, and to our own feelings, we have to remark, that the error noticed, must have been owing entirely to inadvertency. His Deposition carries on the face of it the genuine traits of honour and integrity; and of such qualities is his character composed.

"have some communication with you, before I close my dis-"patches to the Admiralty: I have THEREFORE, *ordered Cap-"tain Woolf* TO RELIEVE YOU on the service you are engaged "in." (p. 51.) And the fact is farther confirmed by Lieutenant Hockings, Signal Lieutenant of the Caledonia, who, adverting to the signal in question, shews, that Captain Woolf was not sent in to take the command of the in-shore squadron, *in consequence* of THAT *signal*. "The Aigle," says he, "had been ordered "to go in, SOME TIME *before*; but in consequence of her hav-"ing made a signal, that her prisoners, on board, were suspi-"cious, she was detained to send the prisoners, on board the "Theseus." (p. 183.) The evidence of Mr. Hockings and others, on the subject of the signal, said to have been made by Lord Cochrane, on the 14th, was intended to prove, that, that signal was improper; and that Lord Gambier was so highly displeased, that, without answering it, he immediately ordered Captain Woolf to relieve his Lordship.

To those, who may have been led to entertain such an opinion, we would recommend the perusal of Lord Gambier's letter to the Admiralty: (p. 4,) "I cannot," says his Lordship, "speak "in sufficient terms of admiration, and applause, of the vi-"gorous and gallant attack, made by Lord Cochrane, upon the "French line of battle ships, which were on shore; as well as "his judicious manner of approaching them, and placing his "ship in a position, most advantageous to annoy the enemy, and "preserve his own ship; which could not be exceeded by any "feat of valour hitherto achieved by the British Navy." This letter was written, when his Lordship was free to speak the genuine sentiments of his bosom *, unbiassed by prejudice, and free from resentment; a tranquil moment, in which his Lordship ingenuously described, what he saw and felt; it was written, when his Lordship had no thought of a Court Martial; nor had he then heard any thing of opposition, to a Vote of Thanks.

* It was written on the 14th of April, after the pretended signal is said to have been made: and all we ask is, that the extract we have given of it, may be contrasted with that part of his Lordship's written Defence, which treats of that signal, and the testimony deduced to support it.

E E

In the progress of our humble duty, we have seen his Lordship, at one period write in the highest strains of panegyric; and, at another, in the most unqualified reprobation, on the self same subject. In what state of his Lordship's mind, then, are we to expect sound reasoning, and correct opinion? Is it when inflamed by passion, and seeking gratification for resentment; or when no boisterous storm prevails, to agitate and distract him: when reason directs the understanding, and informs the judgment? To those who best know the workings of the human heart, we leave the decision.

We have noticed, that Sir Harry Neale was interrogated by the Court, to the signal only, said to have been made on the 14th, and to the measure by which it was followed up: points totally insignificant in their nature, and such as it was highly irregular and improper to have introduced; because irrelevant to the matter in issue, and unjust and injurious in their tendency. But Lord Gambier called Sir Harry Neale's attention to another part of his Lordship's case, and examined him to a conversation, he had held with Lord Cochrane, respecting French Charts.

Q. "What did he state, as to their accuracy or inaccuracy?" —*A.* "I was conversing with Lord Cochrane, about the 6th of "April, respecting the distance, that the British Fleet was anchored from the French Fleet: his Lordship stated, that the "fleets were nine miles from each other; I replied that they "were only six. It had been ascertained by angles, as well as "by cross bearings upon the Chart; his Lordship replied, the "Chart was not to be depended upon. I was speaking of a "French Chart. I had marked the situation of the fleet, upon a "French Chart."

Q. "Did it happen to be, what is called the Neptune François?"—*A.* "That was what I was speaking of. I had that in "my cabin; and concluded from what followed, that, that was "what he alluded to. His Lordship said, that the French were "in the habit of giving *a smaller space upon their Charts,* than "was true; and that he had an instance of it, upon some former "occasion when standing in to the Pertuis Breton, he expected

" to have found, by the Chart, that the space was small; and he " found it near five or six miles broad." (p. 186.)

The intention, then, of these questions was to prove, that the French Charts, to which Lord Cochrane had referred, in the course of his deposition, as capable guides, were generally incorrect; and that Lord Gambier was justified in treating them with contempt, when urged to the attack of the enemy on the morning of the 12th. But as their inaccuracy consisted in shewing a *smaller space*, and, we may presume, *less water* " than was " true," his Lordship's intention is defeated; and Lord Cochrane's apparent inconsistency, perfectly reconciled.

The part of Sir Harry Neale's examination immediately before us, was commenced by Lord Gambier; but for some reason, that does not appear, taken out of his hands by Admirals Young and Stanhope, who proceeded to interrogate Sir Harry Neale on other subjects. They were, however, very soon interrupted by his Lordship, in the course they were pursuing, in the following very extraordinary manner:—" Under the peculiar circumstances in " which Sir Harry Neale stands, as my confidential friend, and " first Captain of the Caledonia, I do not think it proper to ask " him any further questions." (p. 186.)

Had Lord Gambier been the person examining Sir Harry Neale, something might have been said in apology for his Lordship's precipitancy; but as Sir Harry was, in fact, under the examination of the Court, such conduct assumes a very different aspect, and admits of no excuse. It was telling the Court, that they had examined the witness quite long enough: that if it pressed further, it might give rise to something unpleasant; and therefore, and as his confidential friend, and first Captain of the Caledonia, he did not think it proper, that he should be further questioned. It must, in justice to Lord Gambier, however, be remarked, that he had some kind of encouragement to the step he took, by the conduct of the Court, in the advice and opinions, they had delivered to Sir Harry Neale, regarding the information he might withhold: and as the Court did not take any notice of the interruption they experienced, we do not think it would be proper to offer any opinion on a subject, from which we turn, in order, that we may render to the President, the same measure of justice, that we this instant dealt out to Lord Gambier.

The President notwithstanding, and, as it seems, unmindful of the check the Court had received from his Lordship, thought fit to interrogate Sir Harry Neale a little further.

Q. "You have stated the observations Lord Cochrane re-
" ported to you, as to the number of men, and furnaces; did
" he state to you, how many guns he saw mounted on the bat-
" teries of the Isle of Aix?"—*A.* "No, he did not; he re-
" ported the West end of the battery to be in a state of *rubbish.*
" *It was visible from the fleet, that it was* NEWLY FORMING.
" The West end pointed towards the Boyart." (p. 186.)

This answer does not seem to have been expected, as the President ceased his enquiry; and Sir Harry Neale was not troubled with any other question. To Lord Gambier's Defence this answer was as hostile, as it could have been conceived: it was equally favourable towards "what may be called the Prosecu- " tion;" and, considered with the testimony which Lord Cochrane had given, of the ruinous state of those batteries, which it seems was visible from the fleet, together with that delivered by Captain Broughton, completely establishes the fact as his Lordship had stated it.

It might have been imagined that the President, furnished with such new light, would have endeavoured to acquire further information upon a subject, of the first importance: as Lord Gambier had, to a very great extent, founded his justification of his acknowledged delay, in attacking the enemy, upon the *strength* of those very batteries. But instead of asking Sir Harry Neale, whether he had ever reported the circumstance to Lord Gambier? he turned away from him, rather abruptly, to tell Lord Gambier, that "the Court were ready to hear any other witness " he had to produce." (p. 187.)

Almost every witness had been questioned, upon the important subject of going into Aix Roads, on the morning of the 12th; as well those who did proceed thither, as those who continued in Basque Roads; amongst the latter, of whom, we may venture to reckon Admiral Stopford: for although he did go into the Roads of Aix, it was at night, when it was dark, and he returned the next morning, before it was light; so that, any observations he could have made, could not have been of much estimation. And why was not Sir Harry Neale further interrogated, on the subject, and particularly as he had shewn, that he possessed some knowledge of it? Those witnesses were also interrogated, whether they knew of any unnecessary delay, on the part of the Commander in Chief, in taking effectual measures for the destruction of the enemy's ships; or any deficiency, on the part of his Lordship's conduct? or whether it appeared, that he used every means in his power, to carry into effect the orders of the Lords Commissioners of the Admiralty; whether there was any blame imputable to his Lordship, for any part of his proceedings; or whether, under all circumstances of the wind and tide, did it appear, that on the morning of the 12th April, " when the enemy's ships on shore, and the signal had been " made, that 'half the fleet could destroy them,' there was, on " the part of his Lordship, any neglect or unnecessary delay in " taking effectual measures to destroy them?" (p. 188.) And the better to enable some of those witnesses to give their answers, they were, for the moment, made Commanders in Chief! Why were not such questions, or some, or one of them, proposed to Sir Harry Neale: who, as was well known to the Court, and to the public, was continually at the elbow, of course an eye witness of every part of his Lordship's conduct, and consequently was, of all other men, the best calculated to give the most full, distinct, and satisfactory evidence upon every point, they could possibly wish to obtain. There must have been some very cogent reason, some very powerful motive for the omission, which appears to us altogether inexplicable.

Were the Court apprehensive that Sir Harry Neale's answers " would have affected" the Defence of Lord Gambier, or "pro- " duced a contradiction to it?" If such was the feeling of the Court, that feeling was not displayed towards Lord Cochrane.

In his Lordship's case many witnesses were examined, on points, not in anywise connected with the Charge; nor capable of aiding the Defence in any shape whatever. Such examination could have been intended for no other purpose, than to create an undeserved, and unjust prejudice; with a view to injure his Lordship's professional character, and detract from his merits. Some of these points were so glaring, that the Court felt themselves compelled to notice their impropriety; yet allowed them to stand as part of their proceedings. And the Judge Advocate, in delivering his opinion on one of them, said: "I conceive it is to "*affect* the *evidence* of Lord Cochrane. In THAT POINT OF "VIEW, I think it *legal* evidence." (p. 163.) Although it must have been known, both to the Judge Advocate and to the Court, that Lord Cochrane had not given any evidence on the subject, then in discussion, namely, *by what means the Calcutta was fired;* yet Admiral Young did not say on that, as on another occasion, "it is only a series of observations to the disadvantage "of Lord Cochrane *."

We will here quit a subject, which we fear, we have already dwelt on too long. Circumscribed as we are with regard to time, we are unable to condense it. The public will judge of the merits submitted; and be, we trust, kindly indulgent to the dress in which we have presented them.

* Vide Admiral Young's comments on Lord Cochrane's deposition. (p. 47.)

CAPTAIN BLIGH.

The maxim, "*humanum est errare*," was never more pointedly illustrated, than in the Minutes of Lord Gambier's Court Martial; and it is, upon the face of them, equally apparent, that prejudice can blind the understanding, and hold the judgment in suspence.

Captain Bligh, on looking at Mr. Stokes's Chart, thinks the enemy's ships were, on the morning of the 12th, as *there represented*. (p. 153.) This paper was offered to Captain Bligh, by the authority of the Court, and it is therefore presumable, that he considered it to have been perfectly correct. We have already shewn that this scribbled paper, which cannot, without a glaring impropriety, be denominated a Chart, is totally erroneous in every material part of it: even according to the testimony of its inventor (p. 147); and that testimony is corroborated by other witnesses. So that Captain Bligh's conception on this point, was completely illusive; nor are his ideas, on some others, better founded. Asked, if "there were any of the enemy's ships, "that were aground, capable of acting against ours?" (p. 154,) He says, "Early in the morning, they lay with their *broadsides* "*towards the entrance;* and, I think, *were capable of* ANNOY-"ING *the British ships*."

In another part of his examination, however, we find him of a different opinion.

Q. "Were all the enemy's ships, which were on shore on the "Pallés Shoal, *near enough* to the British ships to be destroyed "by them?" (p. 159.)—*A.* "No. The three ships, that moved "up the Charante, were lying to the Southward and Eastward of "the Ocean, and she *was* NEVER *within gun shot* of the Va-"liant, or Revenge *."

* This is evidently an evasion of the question, in two different instances: in the first, instead of embracing the *whole* of the enemy's ships, Captain

Q. "Do you mean, that they were not within reach of the guns "of the British squadron, BEFORE THEY MOVED UP THE "CHARANTE?"—*A.* "In my opinion they were NOT WITHIN "REACH."

Thus it appears the enemy's ships "WERE, and WERE NOT, "capable of annoying;" and WERE, and WERE NOT, "within "reach of the guns of the British ships."

Lord Gambier has precisely asserted the same facts, and as precisely in opposition to each other. When his Lordship aimed at giving a reason for *not attacking* the enemy's ships, on account of their superior strength: his Lordship brings their *broadsides* to RAKE *the passage;* and when endeavouring to shew an excuse for not sending vessels in, at an earlier time than *two o'clock* (pp. 134, 135,), he insists, that the enemy's *grounded vessels* were BEYOND THE REACH of our guns. (p. 137.)

Captain Bligh, examined on a following day, on the supposition, that the two ships, which remained longest afloat, "had "moved towards the Charante, at *half past* 12 *o'clock*," is asked: "Whether the frigates *alone*, assisted by the smaller "vessels, could have succeeded in their attempt, to destroy the "whole of the seven ships of the enemy, that were on shore, on "the Pallés?" Answers (p. 157), "No, I am *confident*, they "would not have made *any impression* on the ships; but on the "contrary, *I think* it would have been attended with the LOSS "OF SOME OF OUR OWN SHIPS!!"

But how our ships could have been destroyed, by the enemy's, without making any impression on them, is a matter that has not been satisfactorily explained; and such as we cannot comprehend. Captain Bligh has given something, in the shape of a reason, raised on the supposition, that the two of the enemy's ships of the line, that had moved towards the Charante, were in a situation to protect those, that were on shore. This reason, did not

Bligh *particularises the* OCEAN; and in the second, he says, she was not within reach of *the Valiant and Revenge*, taking no notice of the OTHER *British ships*.

appear satisfactory, even to Lord Gambier, the two ships in allusion, having sailed about one o'clock; and his Lordship, imagining that Captain Bligh had mistaken the question, gently hinted, that "it was *after* those two ships had run up."

This remark seems to have roused the Judge Advocate, to the following elucidation: "Your *supposition is*, that they had "moved *towards* the Charante *?"—"Yes: my answer is on "the ground, that the two ships had moved *towards* the Charante; but were *still in a situation to have assisted the* "*enemy*." (p. 158.)

Q. "Were these two ships *in your mind*, after they *had moved* "*up, so far removed*, that they could not give any assistance, or "have opposed our frigates?"—*A.* "The impression on my "mind"——

Here Captain Bligh was interrupted by the following observation:—

Admiral Young. "I think, as far as possible, Captain Bligh "should speak to what he felt, and thought at the time." (p. 158.)

This observation was doubtlessly intended to relieve Captain Bligh from the confusion in which he appeared to be, but it lead to the substitution of conjecture for a statement of facts; which is a singular mode to obtain certainty, and in opposition to the rule laid down by the President, that the Court were to decide on facts only.

Why Admiral Young should have interrupted the witness, is not for us to explain. He had an indisputable right, in common with other Members of the Court, to interrogate Captain Bligh, or any other witness; but we submit, he rather exceeded his powers, when he took upon himself to stop a witness, in the midst of his answer to a question, not in any way objectionable.

* We may here say, without the hazard of contradiction, that the Judge Advocate's interference was highly irregular; and that he absolutely put words into the mouth of the witness.

It is remarkable, that Lord Gambier frequently proposed questions to witnesses, who were ignorant of the matter, to which they were pointed, yet plausible, and, sometimes, positive answers were given; such as met his Lordship's wishes. Amongst others, his Lordship interrogated Captain Bligh, "Whether the "frigates and small vessels, could have destroyed those ships of "the enemy, that were on shore, after the Cassard and Foudroy-"ant had gone up the Charante?" and Captain Bligh answered positively, "No;" adding: that "he was confident, they would "not have made any impression; but, on the contrary, he "thought it would have been attended with the loss of some of "our own ships;" (p. 158) which was carrying the thing further than Mr. Stokes; who, when giving his advice upon the subject to Sir Harry Neale, the Captain of the Fleet, signified that "WE "MIGHT destroy the enemy's fleet; *by the sacrifice of our* "*own*." And this advice was given, at a time, when the enemy's two ships were still at their anchors, with their "broadsides "flanking the passage." But Sir Harry Neale was not asked a single question in any way connected with the subject in discussion; and yet, as Captain of the Fleet, he was, of all distant spectators, the best qualified to give information.

In the very brief statement we have given, connected with the dissection of Captain Bligh's evidence, we trust enough has been shewn to convince the public, that such evidence is invalid and nugatory; that there is a variance in both immaterial and material points: and we submit, that even in matters of opinion, when fluctuation is perceived, consistency is lost, and credibility destroyed. We shall mark one very extraordinary part of Captain Bligh's evidence: It respects the works of Aix, which Lord Cochrane had reported, and afterwards deposed, were in a state of rubbish. Captain Bligh says, the fortification appeared to him to be perfect; and he had the help of a good glass. "If "there had been any heaps of stones or rubbish, he must have "seen them." (p. 159.) In addition to Lord Cochrane's testimony on this point, we have Captain Broughton's; not equivocally, but positively. (pp. 148, 149.) And Sir Harry Neale says, it was visible from the fleet!! that it was newly forming. (p. 186.)

How then could the works of the Isle d'Aix have appeared to Captain Bligh to be perfect?

Some questions were put to Captain Bligh by Lord Gambier, relative to the *zeal* and good *conduct* of Captain Kerr, of the Revenge, for the purpose of assisting an assertion, made by his Lordship, in his written Defence, that Lord Cochrane " cast " a blame generally upon the officers who acted with him in Aix " Roads." (p. 135.) We notice this, however, merely to express our regret, that an examination, so foreign to the matter, before the Court, and having in view an object, neither liberal nor correct, should have been permitted.—Captain Bligh was not the only person questioned to this highly exceptionable point; Mr. Wilkinson, who has deposed in favour of his Lordship, was also interrogated to the same point; but all he could shew was, that Lord Cochrane must have meant more than he expressed; that when speaking of brigs, he must have included sloops of war; and because he spoke in the singular number, he certainly intended the plural. Grounding ourselves upon the Minutes before us, we boldly assert, that Lord Cochrane never " cast" that blame which is imputed to him. It is Lord Gambier alone, to answer ends, too obvious to require any explanation from us, who has brought the zeal and exertion of those officers into question. Lord Cochrane well knows, and the Country at large with gratitude acknowledges, the worth of our naval heroes; and that they require no other testimony of their zeal or exertions, than such as is furnished by their own acts.

The Court, however, not only permitted Lord Gambier to examine to such points; but followed his Lordship's example in the evidence, now under review.

Q. by the President. " You have stated, that the Revenge was " very judiciously placed, and you have described the conduct " of that ship, as having been highly meritorious, on the occa- " sion; were not the other ships and vessels engaged with the " enemy placed as judiciously; and did it appear to you, that the " Captains and Commanders of them, conducted themselves with " equal zeal, in the public service." (p. 156.)

If the Court had ever been authorized to enquire into the conduct of those officers, it should first have been shewn, that such conduct had been impeached; to set up a defence of its integrity, before accusation had breathed suspicion, or reproach on it, is new in description, and will very probably never be quoted as a precedent. It is purifying the pure, and cleansing the spotless. Who were the Court trying? Was it the Commander in Chief or his officers? Against whom was the charge preferred? Was it against the officers of the fleet, whose zeal and exertions were highly meritorious? or against the Commander in Chief? We say, the Charge had reference only to the conduct of Lord Gambier *; nor is there a single syllable, in any part of Lord Cochrane's evidence, relative to the conduct of any other officer, that could have justified the examination, to which we have objected. It was not, therefore, in refutation of the Charge; nor in the least to assist Lord Gambier in his Defence, on those fair and honest principles, allowed, or allowable to any party, before any Court in his Majesty's dominions, that such an examination took place. But the Court, in the plenitude of their power, or for certain considerations, allowed and encouraged such examinations, which could tend only, to provoke the resentment of all the officers in the fleet, and draw down their violence upon Lord Cochrane. And the question then is, Why did the Court refuse to Lord Cochrane † the sole means, that were afforded him, to prove, that the tale told by Lord Gambier, in his Defence, was totally unfounded?

Let the Charge be carefully examined, and connected, in any manner, most favourable for his Lordship, with the correspondence between the Lords Commissioners, and his Lordship; and then, let any one say, whether the officers of the fleet, or any of them, were directly or indirectly, positively or by inference, in

* This fact is established by the President, in more than one instance. When Captain Newman noticed, that he would have mentioned to the Court, the conduct of any particular officer, the President said: "No, that would "have been improper; you can speak only as to the Commander in Chief. "IT IS ONLY THE CONDUCT OF THE COMMANDER IN CHIEF, THIS COURT IS "CALLED UPON TO ENQUIRE INTO." (p. 218.)

† Vide the Resolution of the Court upon Lord Cochrane's address.

any manner, or in any way whatever, implicated. And if not, we submit, that in examining witnesses upon the subject of any part, of the conduct of those officers: whether in praise or condemnation, as the principle is the same, the Court quitted the line of conduct pointed out by the Charge; and violated their own rules, and the rules of evidence generally.

When the President examined, as to opinion and *appearances*, did not his conscience smite him, did it not tell him that he was then also, departing totally from the rules, he had laid down, to govern the proceedings of the Court, at the period, when he rejected the testimony offered by Lord Cochrane, and concluded that rejection, with the following legal and perfectly correct doctrine: "It is from *facts*, that the Court must form "their opinion?" The public will view these matters in their proper light.

CAPTAIN BERESFORD.

THE first question put to this gentleman is of the imposing kind: it is to shew, that he was in Aix Roads, on the 12th, and therefore capable of giving an opinion in favour of the Commander in Chief; but it carried its antidote with it, as the answer produces shews, that Captain Beresford was not in Aix Roads in the morning, but the afternoon of the 12th, as he says, "the "Theseus' signal was made about 5 o'clock." (p. 161).

With such information, to regulate the examination of Captain Beresford, we are at a loss even to frame a conjecture, on the possible reason, that could have induced Lord Gambier to ask him the following question: *Q.* "Had I sent in line of Battle "ships, on the morning of the 12th, were any ships of the enemy, "in a position to rake and injure our ships, as they advanced?" To answer positively, was totally out of Captain Beresford's power; as he must have been, at all times, previous to 5 o'clock in the afternoon, nearly five miles distant from the enemy's ships, that were afloat: and a still greater distance from those that were on shore; he therefore merely offered an opinion, regarding the two ships, that were afloat—he could do no more. Nor do his ideas, as to what two of our own ships, in a similar situation, would have done against an enemy, in any way advance that opinion towards certainty. "Indeed," said he, if two of *our ships* had been placed, as they were, "I think we could have "defied an enemy's approach; for the approach *must have* "*been going end on.*" Our ships are, in the long established habit of beating the enemy, whenever allowed to come in contact with them; so that no conclusion can be drawn from Captain Beresford's comparison.

The President then produced Mr. Stokes's Chart, and thus dictated*. "Captain Beresford *must* say, whether the ships are

* We shall take this opportunity to express our astonishment, that the President should have presented such a paper, to any witness, as an authentic document: by which his recollection was to be refreshed or his own ideas cor-

" marked upon *that Chart*, as they appeared to him?" Captain Beresford, however, very properly declined compliance with the President's mandate, and spoke of his own knowledge, and we wish others had followed his example—" Those two ships ap-

rected; as the manner, in which it was originally brought forward, and the conversation that took place on the subject, between the President and Mr. Stokes, the contriver of it, must have been fresh in the President's memory. And it is the more astonishing, that he should have exhibited it to Captain Beresford, as he immediately followed Mr. Stokes, who by his evidence had falsified it. But as it is our sole object, that the public should decide on every matter we state, relative to Lord Gambier's Court Martial, we shall, to that end, submit in the present instance, the following facts. Mr. Stokes was the first witness, who appeared before the Court, (p. 23), and was desired to " produce a sketch, or drawing of the anchorage at Isle d'Aix: with the re- " lative situations of the British and French fleets, and other particulars, on " and previous to the 11th of April last. (The witness produced it)."

Q. " Did you prepare this drawing, and from what *documents*, *authorities*, " and *observations*; and are the several matters and things, thereon de- " lineated, accurately described, according to the best of your judgment and " belief?—*A.* I prepared that drawing *partly*, from the knowledge I gained " in sounding to the southward of the Pallés shoal, and the anchorage of the " Isle of Aix: the *outlines* of the Chart, are taken from the Neptune Fran- " çois: the *position* of the enemy's fleet from *Mr. Edward Fairfax*, and " from the *French Captain of the Ville de Varsovie*; and the *British fleet* " from *my own observations*.

Q. " Are the matters and things, therein delineated, accurately described, " according to the best of your knowledge and belief?—*A.* They are. There " is one thing it may be necessary to explain, respecting this Chart: it can- " not be expected, that from the opportunities I had of sounding in this " place, I could accurately point out the distance BETWEEN THE SANDS: " therefore, for any thing respecting *that*, I must *refer* the Court to the " Chart, which *I copied from a French Manuscript*, which will be produced " here; and that I take to be correct.

President. " There was a large Chart *you lent me*?—*A.* Yes; that is the " Chart I allude to; *this Chart*, I produce, as containing the various positions.

This Chart, then, is declared to contain "the relative situations of the Bri- " tish and French fleets, on and previous to the 12th of April;" we have an- nexed to these Notes, a *fac simile* of it, as given in the printed Minutes, published with the name of Mr. Gurney, and published, as we are informed, at the instance, or with the sanction of Lord Gambier. We will now turn to Mr. Stokes's deposition, under the examination of Lord Gambier.

Q. " State the situation of the Enemy's fleet on the morning of the 12th of " April?—*A.* At day-light, I observed the whole of the Enemy's ships, ex- " cepting two of the line, on shore; four of them lay in a group, or lay " together, on the western part of the Pallés shoal, the others on the eastern

" peared to me, from the position, in which I saw them to be
" at the mouth of the Charauté, *guarded by the battery*." (p.
162).

" side of that shoal; some off the Fouras, and within Madame. The
" frigates had entered the Charanté, except the Indianne, which was on shore
" near Ennette Isle. The three-decker was on the NORTH-WEST edge of the
" Pallés shoal, with her broadside flanking the passage, the NORTH-WEST part
" *nearest the deep water*." Here we intreat, that this parole testimony, may be compared with the Chart; and it will lead to the discovery, that they are at fatal variance with each other: the former placing the enemy's vessels on " the *Western*" and " *North-West* part of the Pallés shoal;" and the latter places them on the EAST, and SOUTH-EAST part of the shoal.

Immediately after Mr. Stokes had delivered this evidence, the President, as if impressed by the contradiction it offered to the Chart, which it was, no doubt, intended to support, thus expressed himself: " I observe, in the *Chart* " *I had from you*, the situation of the OCEAN particularly, is NOT MARKED ON " THE 12TH; *she is marked on the* 13*th*, as advanced up the Charanté?" This observation must have greatly embarrassed Mr. Stokes; if we may judge from the following incoherent explanation. " The ONLY, SHIP " marked in the Chart on the 12th, ARE THOSE THAT ARE DESTROY-" ED: the reason I marked *her on the* 13*th* is, that a particular attack was " made on her, by the bombs. *I observed her* from the mizen-tops of the " Caledonia, and I also had an *observation from an Officer*; so that I have no " doubt, her position is put down within a cable's length." What had his observation *from the mizen tops*, and *from an Officer*, to do with the omission remarked on by the President? And why so much anxiety, to lay down such premises, such miserable premises, that could only afford a wretched conclusion, altogether foreign to the subject, and on every consideration inadmissible?

But from the incongruous mass, we obtain an important fact, necessary to the furtherance of truth and justice; and we trust sufficient to justify the astonishment we expressed in commencing this note: First we have a Chart (23 and 24), avowedly made up of shreds and scraps; the patch-work of various hands, and referring to a French Manuscript Chart, which never made its appearance, to ascertain one of the most, if not the most essential component parts of it, that is to say, " *the distance between the sands*." And this Manuscript Chart, which came from God knows *where*, and into Mr. Stokes's possession, God knows *how*; seems to have been sufficiently authenticated to satisfy the Court, with no other evidence than the following equivocal words which Mr. Stokes carelessly uttered, " and I take *that* to be correct:" Secondly, we have Mr. Stokes's completely falsifying HIS CO-PARTNERSHIP CHART, by his own evidence, (p. 147); we then arrive at the last stage of that Chart's turpitude; and find, that *instead of being a Chart of the* 12*th*, IT IS A CHART OF THE 13TH OF APRIL, as it contains the position of many of the enemy's ships on shore, not only *those that were destroyed*, but *those also that* ULTIMATELY ESCAPED: whereas, Mr. Stokes says, the ONLY SHIPS *marked in the Chart of the* 12*th*, " are those that are DESTROYED." And as this closing of the scene

Q. by the President. "Is the description of them upon that "paper, similar to what you saw, when you saw them there? This question, which, we submit, is an extraordinary reiteration of its predecessor, evidently embarrassed Captain Beresford—he answered it very cautiously.—*A.* "That strikes me to be, as "nearly the position, as I can speak to." And why, as nearly as he could speak to? He gives the best reason in the world; because, "I did not *go into the inner Road, 'till they moved up.*" (p. 162).

Lord Gambier, not at all nonplussed, by this reasoning, which does Captain Beresford great credit, and which seems to have silenced the President, resumed the Examination himself.

Q. "Could two or three line of battle ships, on the morning "of the 12th of April, when two of the enemy's ships lay afloat, "at their anchorage, have advanced to attack them, by passing "near the Boyart, and putting their helms a-lee, bearing in "mind, how the wind was that morning, their fore and main "top sails being to the mast, having thus brought their heads "to the NE. Could they, by these means, have been able to "bring their guns to bear with effect upon the enemy's ships, "AND BE THEMSELVES, OUT OF THE REACH OF SHOT "*from the Isle of Aix?*"—Captain Beresford says, "CERTAINLY NOT;" and we, judging from Mr. Stokes's Chart, say "also, certainly not."

But would those ships have been exposed to imminent danger? That was a question, Lord Gambier did not think proper to ask of Captain Beresford, whose answer, as it stands, does not yield even the shadow of advantage. Indeed, the question, which is in itself highly improper, and equally absurd, contains two dis-

resulted, in fact, from an act of the President, we cannot refrain from repeating, that it is astonishing he should ever afterwards have allowed it to be shewn to a witness, as a document, worthy of more than common credit; or, rather, that he did not instantly pronounce it worthless and disgraceful. But it is for the public, and not for us to decide: we do not profess to be sufficiently calm: our passions have been roused, by the mass through which we have waded; but the public deliberate calmly, and therefore decide justly.

G G

tinct propositions; and Captain Beresford's answer must be received as given to *one* of them *only;* but to which, it is difficult to determine. Such questions we have frequently met with, coming both from the Court, and from his Lordship.

Taking every other consideration out of the case, such questions are highly improper; because by getting a negative, or an affirmative to the former or latter part, might appear to be an answer to both, and by such means, and for want of sufficient time for deliberation, the Court might be led to erroneous conclusions. We say this with the more confidence, from having been ourselves imposed on by answers to questions, similarly constructed: and by some of the bold statements contained in Lord Gambier's written defence; and we have only been able to detect the fallacy both of the one, and the other, by a strict and minute investigation.

Precisely circumstanced with the answer, just noticed, is the answer to the following question from his Lordship.

Q. " Could any line of battle ships have run to leeward of " those two ships, and have had space enough to anchor, and " by such means have attacked them?" (p. 162.) *A.* " I should " not like to have risked it myself: and it appeared to me, that " there was scarcely room for a friend, to have passed between " them and the shoal, setting aside all idea of an enemy firing " in passing; for *the smoke alone*, besides the ship being crippled, " must have caused you to be entangled, and the ship must have " gone ashore, and been lost." (p. 162.)

Knowing the extreme difficulty of ascertaining distances, of the description before us, we are at a loss to conceive Captain Beresford's reasons, for venturing on the details, he has given, flimsy as they are, of the situation of the two ships belonging to the enemy, that remained longest at their anchorage, and of the shoal in their vicinity; and to surmise, that there was scarcely room for a friend to pass between them. He was several miles from the spot, to which he made allusion: the ships he mentions were in the intervening space; and there was, from nine to fifteen feet at low water on the shoal. We do not dispute the impression upon Captain Beresford's mind; but appearances, in such cases, are deceitful. It was not possible, to speak to the point advanced, with any thing like certainty; and therefore Captain Beresford says, as any other person might have said, who founded an opinion upon appearances, at five miles distance from the spot, "there was scarcely room for a friend to pass "between them, and the shoal."

Yet how "the SMOKE *alone* must have caused" our ships "to "be entangled" is altogether unaccountable; it is certainly a danger, that never entered the mind of even Lord Gambier. But as hypothetical reasoning, and deductions drawn from appearances, cannot be received as evidence, Captain Beresford's answer, like many others, that speak much, but mean nothing, is altogether nugatory.

We have referred, in another stage of our notes, to that part of Captain Beresford's testimony, which treats of a conversation, that passed between him and Lord Cochrane; and we shall therefore pass it over in all possible haste. We feel it, however, incumbent to say a few words on the subject.

Q. By Lord Gambier. "Did you ever understand, by whose "orders the Calcutta was set on fire?"—*A.* "The only thing I know, "with respect to the Calcutta being fired, was by a conversation "between Lord Cochrane and myself, in the presence of Captain "Bligh, Captain Maitland, and others."

Here the Court and Judge Advocate rendered themselves eminently conspicuous, not for their impartiality; but for the striking difference, in the conduct they observed, between Lord Cochrane and Lord Gambier. The only thing Captain Beresford knew of "the Calcutta being fired," "was by a conversation with Lord "Cochrane" in the presence of other officers. (p. 163.) The President therefore, whose former decision, on evidence similarly complexioned, seems to have hovered over his recollection, asked: "Is this strictly evidence, Mr. Judge Advocate?" the Judge Advocate answered: "YES; I *think* it is; because *I conceive* it

" is to affect the evidence of Lord Cochrane; in that point of " view, *I think* it is LEGAL EVIDENCE." In this answer the Judge Advocate must have rebelled against his own conviction; and advised the Court, contrary to his own understanding of the fact: as he well knew, that Lord Cochrane, in speaking of the fate of that ship, merely noticed, that she was set fire to. But how, and upon what grounds could he have conceived, that such evidence was to affect the evidence of Lord Cochrane, we cannot imagine. And as the President had taken exceptions to it, why did he not refer to that part of his Lordship's testimony, which he conceived it was meant to affect? He must have known that to do so was no more than performing an incumbent duty: not only to the Court, but to justice and to his country. He also knew, that the matter was not connected with the charge, therefore immaterial; and consequently could not have affected the testimony of Lord Cochrane. He likewise knew, that the Court had decided, that *hearsay* and *conversation with, or in reference to, Officers,* was not evidence. A fact, that must also have been in the recollection of the Court; or if not, why did they not make the necessary enquiries, instead of pinning their faith on the *conception* of the Judge Advocate? Why did they not either turn to Lord Cochrane's evidence, or desire Lord Gambier to point out the part, to which Captain Beresford's answer referred? Why was Captain Beresford asked, in consequence of that answer, and in consequence of having stated Lord Cochrane to have said, that the ship had been fired by a youngster; why was he asked " whether he thought, the ship might have been brought off? (p. 163.) The Judge Advocate did not pretend, that, that question also, was proposed with a view of affecting the evidence of Lord Cochrane. No! he knew well, that it did not, but he well knew, that both question and answer were intended to create a prejudice, injurious to the professional character of Lord Cochrane, and to lower him, in the estimation of the public; HE WELL KNEW, that they could not possibly have any other tendency or bearing; shame! shame! How could the Court reconcile such proceedings with the dictates of honor and the principles of justice? How expect to justify them, if called upon by their country? Had they any jurisdiction given to them, over Lord Cochrane, further than as a witness subpœned, to give his testimony, respecting the charge they were assembled to try, between our Sovereign Lord the King, and Lord Gambier*?

Where did the Court or the Judge Advocate find the Law that gives authority to try a man in his absence; against whom no charge had ever been preferred; and who, it was determined, should not be permitted a hearing in his defence? Did they not all know, that by our glorious Magna Charta, no man can be called before any Court, until a charge has been regularly preferred; nor put upon his trial, until regularly arraigned; nor tried, until he shall have regularly pleaded to such an arraignment? And did they not also know, that every witness produced against him, must deliver his testimony in his presence; and that he, or his Counsel, has full liberty to cross examine him? And above all, did they not know, that *before a man be condemned, he* MUST BE FULLY HEARD IN HIS DEFENCE! DID THEY NOT KNOW ALL THESE FACTS? Facts, that form a part of a BRITON'S BIRTHRIGHT, and of the benefits of which, thank GOD! no power can deprive him. Was Lord Cochrane present, when these and other enquiries, tending to his condemnation, were pursuing by the Court, aided by the advice of the Judge Advocate: when they thought proper to take his character into their hands, and mangle it, at their pleasure?

We hope, and trust, not on account of Lord Cochrane only, but for a general good, that the public will consider, those extraordinary and extremely alarming acts, which we have enumerated, and pass on them that judgment which their delinquency shall appear to deserve†. We know not how they may be regarded

* We do maintain that the Court, in this instance, and they acted the same way on many other occasions, had entirely quitted the object, for which alone, they were convened; and were actually and positively trying Lord Cochrane; the only witness on the part of the Crown: the Charge—setting fire to a ship, that might have been brought off, thereby in breach of his duty, injuring the nation. And Capt. Beresford was the witness brought forward to give that charge support. Let the Court deny this, if they can; and if they cannot, *Fiat justicia ruat cœlum!*

† Such proceedings were not resorted to, nor any indulgence shewn, in the case of the gallant Sir Robert Calder, nor in that of the equally brave Admiral Harvey, to soften the rigours of the prosecution, that was conducted against them. They have been consigned to retirement; and their country doomed to regret the loss of their services.

in the eye of the Law, as acts of a Court, but were such to occur in private society, we believe they would approximate pretty closely to a conspiracy.

To return to the Examination of Captain Beresford—*Q. By Lord Gambier.* " Did you go on Board the Imperieuse, on the " afternoon of the 12th of April."—*A.* " Yes."

Q. " What was her situation, and what passed between you and " Lord Cochrane *?" 163. On this question being asked, the Judge Advocate, turning to Lord Gambier, said, " I take this to effect the " same purpose I mentioned just now: otherwise, it is not evidence. " I must beg to ask, whether it is to produce a contradiction to " Lord Cochrane; because, in THAT CASE ALONE, would it be " evidence." And how could it, we may ask this man of legal distinctions, even in that case, be evidence? Was Lord Cochrane before the Court? or were there Counsel for the Crown, on the behalf of which, Lord Cochrane had deposed, before the Court, to cross-examine Captain Beresford? For admitting, as we do, the most honest intention, on the part of that Officer, still to give his evidence any validity, it was necessary, that he should have been open to the cross examination of Lord Cochrane, whilst deposing to any point, that implicated his Lordship's character. Were it otherwise, a man, with every reason to think

* The situation of Lord Cochrane in the afternoon of the 12th, may be very easily imagined. He had been actually employed from the time of his first joining the fleet in Basque Roads; but particularly so on the 11th, when he had to make his arrangements, and prepare the explosion vessels for the attack of the enemy, the conduct of which having been solely, confided to his direction. He could not, in the nature of things, have taken any repose during the whole of that night: and his sufferings, under the pressure of loitering anxiety, from the period at which the first signal was made, that the enemy was on shore: until two o'clock, were infinitely more insupportable. At two o'clock he fell down, without orders, upon the enemy's ships, and engaged them, until about four: he was afterwords occupied in those avocations, that give ample employment, after an engagement. In the midst of these, in the midst of hurry and confusion, and when his Lordship was every way exhausted, Captain Beresford held the conversation with him, that Lord Gambier had called for, and with so much address obtained. If his Lordship had no personal knowledge of Lord Cochrane's situation, he might have faintly imagined it; and that it would have been both cruel and inhuman, to enquire into any expressions, Lord Cochrane might have used, in any conversations he held, so harrassed, and so borne down as he was, and when, in fact, he was not himself.

himself in perfect security, might have his fame blasted, and his character ruined for ever!

Even when the Attorney General, by virtue of his office, moves for leave to file an Information, he must serve a rule upon the party to be affected by it, to shew cause against it: and the Judge Advocate must know, that proceedings of a Court Martial, much as they may differ, from Courts of Record, dare not violate the Law of the Land; nor the rights of individuals. And that all evidence, taken by the Court, without giving to the party interested in it, an opportunity to cross-examine the deposing witness, is *ex parte*, and therefore null and void.

Of Captain Beresford's answer to the question, now discussed, we have little further to say, than, that if it were admissible, it does not establish any fact of the least consequence. "I told "Lord Cochrane that Lord Gambier seemed to me, to be most "anxious to act with his *fleet*; but, that if he had sent *them* in "there, it clearly appeared, that few would have returned, if any. "I think, were my expressions, and that it would have been "madness to have done it. His Lordship said, that three sail of "the line might have been lost, which, in his opinion, did not "signify. My reply was, that even *one* sail of the line *being lost*, "would in my opinion, have been A DISGRACE to the *enterprise* "and *to England;* this passed in the presence of Captains "Bligh, W ooldridge and Maitland, Colonel Cochrane his Brother, &c. 165.

This evidence, whilst it furnishes further instances of that conduct of the Court, and Judge Advocate, which we have just noticed; tends to prove, that Lord Gambier, in his written defence, had most materially exaggerated, when he mentioned Lord Cochrane to have said, that had he, Lord Gambier, "complied "with the signal "Seven sale of the line on shore, half the fleet "" can destroy them," he calculated on the loss of three or four "sail of the line." Lord Cochrane, according to Captain Beresford, alluded to the WHOLE FLEET going in; and Captain Beresford's evidence is supported by Captain Bligh (157,) or taking those Gentlemen in the order in which they stand on the Minutes, the latter was supported by the former. Without adverting to the propriety or impropriety, of giving evidence of a conversation; although the Court seemed very tenacious, on that head, in the examination of Sir Harry Neale, we shall offer a few words, on an opinion of Captain Beresford, given in the course of that conversation, and which, to our judgment, not altogether ignorant of the havock attendant on daring enterprise, nor of the risks, that are absolutely necessary, and indispensably requisite, towards the achievement of a grand, and important object, is incomprehensible. How could the loss of one ship of the line, have been a DISGRACE to the enterprise, and to England, if by that sacrifice, eight or nine of the enemy's line of battle ships, had been destroyed? If the acquirement of glory be disgraceful to the Country, that is surrounded by its splendour, our Navy should be, at once, dismissed; whilst it exists, such disgrace will constantly accumulate, notwithstanding the endeavours, that have been made, to damp the ardent spirit of its ambition, and check the prowess of its energies.

Did the Heroes, who have fought our Battles on the ocean, never lose a ship in an action, in which they captured only, two or three of a large fleet belonging to the Enemy? If they did, was the event considered as a *disgrace* to the enterprise, and to England? Those Heroes, many of whom are no more, but whose names are preserved in the grateful bosom of their country, certainly, entertained very different sentiments; or they would have sunk unknown into their graves, and their names would never have been heard of. We have, however, one consolation: the opinion in question will not be productive of any serious consequences; its influence will never extend beyond the Minutes of the Court Martial, in which it lies entombed.

We shall add, in conclusion, by way of explanation, that when Lord Cochrane spoke of the loss of ships, he calculated (and his calculation was well founded, as it arose out of Captain Beresford's own suggestions), on the coming in of the whole fleet; in which case, such loss would have been very probable; as it is in evidence, that although there was safe anchorage for half a dozen sail of the line; there was not room for double that number and, which was also double the number, that was, at any time required.

In common with others, Captain Beresford was asked by Lord Gambier, if it appeared to him, that there was "any neglect "or unnecessary delay, on the part of his Lordship, in taking "effectual measures to destroy the Enemy?" he answered, "None whatever," (164) and that "the proper time of the tide "for sending ships in, was at the time, that would ensure their "coming out again, *in case of accidents*," (164.) This evidence is purely a matter of opinion; and, in fact, has no definitive meaning. The tide that would have carried the ships into Aix Roads, could not have brought them out again; unless they had gone in at about a half flood, and come out again at high water. And what possible benefit could have accrued from an excursion, that would not have extended beyond an hour? If such should have been Captain Beresford's meaning, it proves both negligence and delay, on the part of the Commander in Chief, who ordered the ships in, about half past two o'clock, when the water had begun to fall (212) (150).

As to the accidents, which Captain Beresford speaks of, that were to be provided for, by the circumstance of the tide, what were they? The *loss of masts*, and the *destruction of rigging!* what else could have been the nature of those accidents? Not taking the ground, when the tide was ebbing: nor the sinking of the ships; in the last instance, the tide would not have been of any service; and if the masts and rigging had been materially injured, with the wind, as it was, how could they have beat out? These are of the texture of the arguments, urged by Lord Gambier, and some of his witnesses, on the same point; and we hope his Lordship will not be displeased, if we make use of his own weapons. Captain Beresford's answer, then, becomes every way inefficient.

The questions by Admiral Young, in relation to Captain Beresford's *recollection*, of a circumstance, that had been made known to him, by his first Lieutenant, or by his signal Lieutenant, for

H h

Captain Beresford could not recollect which, (p. 164,) is really ludicrous; and can only be exceeded, in that respect, by his promoting Captain Beresford to a flag, and making him Commander in Chief of the fleet at once, (p. 165.) in order to learn his opinion, of what was to be understood, by Lord Cochrane's signal of "half the fleet can destroy the enemy," and what he, as Admiral and Commander in Chief, would have done in consequence of such signal, having been made to him, by one of his Captains. Captain Beresford, thus elevated, answered: "At "the time the signal was made, I would not have sent in one "ship."—Admiral Young should not have made him Commander in Chief.

Q. "If you had had the command of a fleet, and a captain "under you, had informed you, that half your fleet could destroy "your enemy; what proportion of your fleet should you send "in?"—*A.* "I think, to make sure of it, I should have been "inclined to send in more than half." (p. 165.)

Here Captain Beresford is again himself*, and this answer knocks down its predecessor, for the arrogance it too presumptuously uttered; notwithstanding they were children of the same parent. The question being in substance, and nearly so in words, precisely the same.

We are disposed to think, that Admiral Young would much better have employed his time, had he asked Captain Beresford, (who, by the bye, had no local knowledge of the inner road of Aix) whether in circumstances of so critical a nature, which offered to our embrace a very important object, that depended only, upon the promptitude of decision, and the vigour of execution, it was not the bounden duty of the Commander in Chief knowing that every minute lost by us, was so much of advantage gained

* Had Captain Beresford been really Commander in Chief, he would not have acted, as Lord Gambier did—two people frequently form a different opinion on the same object—and if we know Captain Beresford, his would have led him into the Roads of Aix, on the signal being made, that the enemy could be destroyed.

by the enemy, to have moved the fleet instantly, on the signal being made, to the ground which he afterwards took up, as "best "calculated to observe the motion of the enemy, and to send as- "sistance to the attacking ships," and thence proceeded himself to the station, at which Lord Cochrane lay, to remove every doubt, if any doubt he had, as to the grounds on which his Lordship made the signal, "Seven sail on shore; half the fleet can destroy "them;" leaving orders for the fleet, to be in readiness to obey any signal, he might make, at the moment it should be observed. He might then have examined minutely, and at no very great distance or risque, the state of the fortifications of Aix, and of the enemy's ships; as well the two, that were yet afloat, as those on shore. Had Admiral Young pursued such course of examination, to the extent which reason, dwelling on the numerous facts and circumstances that lay before him, would have suggested, the Minutes might have been considerably contracted: the whole truth would have been revealed; and the demands of justice gratified.

And we will ask, why did not Lord Gambier thus act, and thus discharge his duty, in a crisis, that loudly demanded all his attentions: instead of remaining on board his ship, at anchor in Basque Roads, calmly listening to the report of signals, repeatedly making by Lord Cochrane, that the enemy were within his power; and that a part of the fleet could destroy them? He states that he could not comply with those signals: because of the force of the batteries; and because TWO of the enemy's ships lay at anchor, flanking the passage, which was otherwise guarded by those of the grounded vessels, that were sufficiently upright, to annoy ours. But how did his Lordship know all this? Only by appearances, that were observed at a distance of several miles. Had he gone into the roads of Aix himself, he might then have been capable of forming an accurate judgment; and convinced himself, in all probability, that he had been deceived by appearance; which is particularly delusive, when circumstanced as the scene was, that lay before him.

What were Lord Gambier's exertions, and how was his zeal manifested, during the whole of the eventful period, between six o'clock in the morning and two in the afternoon? What melancholy questions! that leave a blank, which his Lordship has not attempted to supply: either by any statement in his written Defence: or by the depositions of his witnesses; yet the Court Martial seem to have been contented with it, when they pronounced his most honourable acquittal. Surely some kind of information was necessary, even for the sake of decency, to shew that his Lordship was doing, or thinking to do, something, in consequence of the signal after signal, that was made by the Imperieuse.

Did he imagine, that Lord Cochrane was wantonly making those signals? if he did, why did he not instantly recall him, instead of waiting until the next day? if he did not think so, it was his duty to have sent in that force, which his Lordship had signified would destroy the enemy. Why did he not, we repeat, repair, himself, to the scene, and ascertain, by his own observations, how far Lord Cochrane was, or was not correct in his judgment; and form his plans, and pursue his measures accordingly? He would then, have been enabled to know the extent of the dangers to be encountered, from " the batteries:" from " the two ships " afloat," and from those on shore, that " were sufficiently up- " right to have annoyed our ships on their approach;" instead of depending upon the variegated opinions of others, equally uninformed as his own, that served only to embarrass and confuse him. But during the course of *eight hours!* every moment of which was precious, he was, as far as we can collect, from such parts of his conduct, as he has condescended to submit to the public, wholly idle: was wholly idle when he knew, that the enemy was on shore, and might be destroyed!! when he must have known, that they would attempt to make their escape, and probably succeed in that attempt, as the flood tide should make! and when he was, from time to time, informed of the progress, they were making, to extricate themselves, from their deplorable situation, and get beyond our reach! (p. 33.)

Was this " taking effectual measures?" Was this doing all that could be done, to destroy the enemy? Or does it not argue, with irresistible force, that EIGHT HOURS were spent in the most profligate waste, " in unnecessary delay," in total " negligence?'

Had our's been the situation of the enemy, would the French Commander have lain *eight hours*, in a state of apathy, after he had been told, by his advanced frigates, that our ships were on shore; and could be destroyed? Would he have remained totally inactive, forming idle chimeras, and suffering himself to be led away, by fears, and apprehensions, of imaginary dangers, for the lengthened space of *eight hours?* Would he have rewarded the vigilance of his officer, by treating the important information he was constantly acquiring, and constantly giving to him, with silent contempt! leaving him, for *eight hours*, full of anxieties, the most painful that can be imagined? Will an injured public, injured by such conduct, be satisfied with the sentence of the Court Martial, when they have abundance of facts and circumstances before them, on which to form their own opinion, and pronounce their own judgment? To those opinions and to that judgment we look for justice.

Had Admiral Young, and the Court, taken into their consideration the several points, we have noted, and framed interrogatories to meet them; they would have rendered most essential service to their country. But they adopted a very opposite line; and their chief object appears to have been, to criminate Lord Cochrane, a witness on the part of the crown, compelled to appear before them: to establish that his Lordship's signals were improper; (p. 164,) and that Lord Gambier would not have been justified, in acting on the information they offered. In fact, the interrogatories administered to Captain Beresford, in reference to those signals, were calculated to shew, that Lord Gambier had neither judgment, nor discretion; but was bound to send in the precise number of ships, that Lord Cochrane had suggested would be sufficient, to destroy the enemy. And this too, in the very teeth of his Lordship's own acts, or rather omissions, which evidence, in the most perspicuous way: that he was fully sensible of the authority he possessed; and that he was bound only, to act as he pleased. And whatever became of his judgment, he convinced Lord Cochrane, that he was determined to exercise his discretion; and, therefore, instead of sending in half the fleet, he would not send in a single ship, for the anxious space of eight hours.

Why, then, did the Court torture Captain Beresford, and all the other witnesses, to learn their opinion of the "number "of ships, that ought to have been sent in, upon the signal "made" by Lord Cochrane: and whether, had they been Commander in Chief, they would have sent in half the fleet, or more, or less?

We have extended our remarks upon the evidence of Captain Beresford, to save repetition, as they apply to the testimony of almost every witness examined, during the whole proceedings of the Court Martial. Captain Beresford's evidence is founded entirely on *report*, *hearsay*, and *appearance*, and of course, cannot be considered as "FACTS" on which the Court were to "form "their *opinions*," (p. 50.)

CAPTAIN KERR, OF HIS MAJESTY'S SHIP THE REVENGE.

We have shewn, on various occasions, that Mr. Stokes's Chart is altogether erroneous, and that it is falsified, even by himself. Yet to this Chart, Captain Kerr's attention was called, by the first question, that was given to him: to which he said, " I think the " situation of the enemy's fleet, on the morning of the 12th, is " marked upon it, *as nearly as it can be.* I recollect the situa- " tion of the enemy's fleet *perfectly, seven sail on shore, and two* " *sail of the line afloat*;" (p. 166,) of course his answer, as resting on a fallacy, is totally unfounded. He, however, spoke positively only to the latter part of it.

Examined upon the general question, of the dangers to which our ships would have been exposed, had they been sent in, when Lord Cochrane, made his signals for that purpose: passing over the batteries of Aix, he observes, that the *two ships afloat*, were certainly in positions to have *raked* and *crippled* any ships, in advancing: " the *three decker* was likewise in a situation, that a part " of her guns *would have borne upon the ships, going down.*" This coalesces a part of Lord Gambier's written defence, in which, as a justification of his *confessed* delay, his Lordship enumerated opposing dangers: amongst others, the menacing situation of the *grounded ships, sufficiently upright, and so situated as to be able to bring their guns, to bear upon the entrance,* (p. 125.)

Q. " Were the *three ships* of the enemy, that were on shore, " on the Pallés, and which afterwards got off, AT ANY TIME in " a situation to be attacked by us."—*A.* " CERTAINLY NOT, " they were advanced further than the Tonnére; and the Re- " venge's shot just reached her," (p. 167.) It is to be recollected, that *the three decker* was *one* of those three ships: and Captain Kerr had before deposed, that SHE *was capable of annoying our ships,* (166,) although he is here seen to state, that *she was not within reach* of them. The question that led to this answer, is in conformity to that part of Lord Gambier's defence, in which he asserts, that "three out of the seven, of the "enemy's ships aground, on the Pallés, were, from their FIRST "*being on shore, totally out of the reach* of the guns, of any "ships of the fleet, that might have been sent in: and at NO "TIME, either *sooner* or *later*, could they have been attacked;" and "that the *other four*, of the *eleven* ships, of which the "enemy's fleet consisted, were never in a situation to be assailed, "after the fire ships had failed in their main object," (p. 157.)

Such is the defence of Lord Gambier, and such the evidence brought forth to support it. Fact opposed to fact. The grounded ships, that afterwards got off, *were never near enough to be attacked:* yet so near, that *they could have raked ours*, had they been sent in! We must submit this extraordinary assemblage to the public judgment; the Court Martial have already pronounced theirs, by their most honourable acquittal of Lord Gambier.

With evidence of such a description, to encourage enquiry, Lord Gambier proceeded.

Q. "Could any more of the enemy's ships have been destroy- "ed, than were destroyed, had any of the King's ships been "sent to attack them sooner, than they were ordered in for that "purpose."—*A.* "No—It is my firm belief, that had any ships "gone in sooner, they would have been crippled; by which "means, the French ships, that remained afloat, *would have dis- "covered* the strength of their position: of course remained, in- "stead of going up the river; and prevented the four ships that "were afterwards destroyed, from being so." (p. 168.)

This string of conclusions, drawn from two ships, placed in the most forlorn situation, is certainly surprizing.

On this head, we have already trespassed in detail, to shew, what indeed, is generally known: that those ships had thrown the far greater part of their guns overboard, and were intent only on seizing upon the earliest opportunity, that should offer, to cut and run: and consequently, were in no circumstances or disposition, to oppose two or three sail of British ships of the line; nor to remain where they were "instead of going up the river." And it will here be recollected, that only *three* of the enemy's ships were destroyed *by us*, the other having been burnt *by themselves*; a circumstance that was indisputably occasioned by our ships, at last, going in; and gives us a right to assume, "that *more* of the enemy's ships *would have been destroyed, than were destroyed*, had any of our ships been sent in earlier, than they were ordered in for that purpose." In this conclusion we are further strengthened, by the following testimony of Captain Broughton.

Q. by the President. "Would not the ships so sent in have "been exposed to the fire of the two ships, that remained at an- "chor, the French Admiral's ship, and the batteries of Aix, at the "same time."—*A.* "Certainly: but I considered they were "partly PANICK STRUCK; and on the appearance of a force "coming, might have been induced to cut their cables, and try "to make their escape up the river." (p. 221.)

But Captain Kerr does not seem to have been aware, that the Cassard, one of the two ships that remained longest afloat, and which, in his opinion, would have dealt such destruction amongst our ships, "had they been sent in earlier than they were," cut and made sail for the Charante, at *ten minutes past one*; and that the other, the Foudroyant, followed the example of her consort *ten minutes* afterwards. This is what Mr. Stokes and Mr. Hockings have asserted positively; and as they *noted the time by their watches*, we are to suppose, that they were correct.

When, therefore, all the dangers to be apprehended from those two ships, had been removed, could not our ships have proceeded towards the grounded vessels? And, if our ships had been so ordered, *ten minutes after one*, instead of ten *minutes after two* o'clock; might it not have added to the dismay and terror of the fugitives, and been the means of their running on shore also? This, at least, was possible. Captain Malcolm says, "when those two ships quitted their stations, *then*, there was *no obstacle* to prevent the small ships from going in, by which I mean frigates, or even seventy-fours, if they had been light.

" but the fire from the Isle of Aix, which they could nearly " avoid by keeping near the Boyart." (p. 208.) It is further to be remarked, that "*the three-decker*, which was in a situation, " that *part* of her guns (pp. 209, 204,) could have *borne upon* " *our ships*, coming down*," and was, *of course*, assailable, did not move, until about twenty minutes, or half an hour *after those two ships* had sailed (p. 158), which corresponds with the testimony of Lieutenant Hockings, the Signal Lieutenant of the Caledonia, who says, " she hauled off about *two o'clock*." (p. 232) And was it not *possible*, that the three-decker might have been prevented from warping off (p. 211), " had any of the King's " ships been sent in to attack sooner than they were ordered in " for that purpose?"

There were also two other ships, that hauled off about the time, that the three-decker did (p. 22), and which, together, were the three ships that Lord Cochrane speaks of, as " heeling " inwards," so as to " give them the *appearance* of having their " masts and yards locked together," and a part of the " groupe" that Mr. Stokes says " *lay together*;" (p. 147) and which Mr. Fairfax has told us, were " not a ship's length from each " other." (p. 146) Indeed, so close were they together, that Mr. Fairfax could not say, in day-light, whether their yards, were or were not locked, (p. 144) though he distinguished, that " *they were separate at night*." And was it not possible, that those ships, or some, or one of them, might have been destroyed, " had any of the King's ships been sent to attack them, " sooner than they were ordered in, for that purpose?" (p. 160) How then could Captain Kerr take upon himself to say, he really believed that "*no more of the enemy's ships could have* " *been destroyed*, had any of the King's ships been sent to attack " them sooner than they were ordered in for that purpose?" And when he was asked: " Under all the circumstances of the wind " and tide, did it appear to you, that on the morning of the " 12th of April, or at any time, when the enemy's ships were on " shore, when the signal had been made, that 'half the fleet " 'could destroy them,' there was, on my part, any neglect or

* P. 163, 150, 152, 166, 209, 210, 211, 221, &c.

"unnecessary delay, in taking effectual measures for destroying "them*:" How could Captain Kerr say, "I *thought*, that "every thing was done, that could possibly be done;" and, "that had the ships gone in sooner, I am *confident*, a number "must have been lost?" (p. 188) And when questioned by the President: "From the first attack upon the ships of the enemy, "to the final cessation of hostilities against them: was every "thing done, that could be done, to effect their destruction:" How could he, with the several circumstances we have just referred to, pressing on his senses, answer positively "EVERY "THING?" (p. 168.)

It is a gloomy fact, furnished by the evidence before us, that those ships, the three-decker and others, were allowed to warp off; and that Lord Gambier remained an inactive spectator of their operations. His Lordship recollected, no doubt, the proverbial appeal, "as you are strong be merciful," and acted accordingly. Here finishes Captain Kerr's deposition, upon his first examination; although we might have remarked on other points of it, that have an equal claim on our attention; but they all found themselves upon nearly the same reasoning and allusions, as those we have noticed.

On the following day, after the examination of several witnesses, Captain Kerr was again called in, and asked by Lord Gambier, "if he had, on the evening of the 12th, when the Revenge "was in a state of considerable danger, obtained any information from Lord Cochrane, either directly or indirectly, of a "secure anchorage to the Southward or Westward?" To which he answered: "The only communication I had, with Lord Cochrane, was through the Master of the Revenge, who, in passing "the Imperieuse, asked Lord Cochrane"——

The Judge Advocate here interrupted him—

Q. "*You were not there?*"—A. "No, I was not."

* Why did not his Lordship ask Sir Harry Neale the same question? and why did he not interrogate him to every other part of his conduct? Sir Harry was, perhaps, *too near* an observer!

Judge Advocate. "The evidence cannot be taken from Captain "Kerr; if it is necessary to produce it, the Master of the Re-"venge must be called." (p. 202.)

Yet, notwithstanding this plausible rectitude, the testimony thus objected to by the Judge Advocate, was, upon the most absurd surmise of Lord Gambier, instantly afterwards allowed; but in a shape, and colouring, somewhat different.

Q. by Lord Gambier. "Perhaps Captain Kerr can answer "without referring to this *?"—*A.* "I felt the situation of the "ship to be dangerous; and I sent him (the Master) to sound. "On his return to me, he told me, that Lord Cochrane had in-"formed him, he did not know, but that he believed there was "water to windward." (p. 203.)

When the unprejudiced man shall have considered the circumstances we have in this manner placed before him, according to the principles of justice: he will not hastily yield to them his approbation; nor advocate the cause of the Court, in an act, which their own judgment previously condemned: an act, contrary to the rules of evidence and justice; and against which the Judge Advocate had loudly objected. He will naturally ask: Why was not the Master of the Revenge called, as the Judge Advocate suggested; instead of attending to the wish of Lord Gambier? Does it not evince, in the strongest, the most forcible manner, that the Master did not dare to verify, by an oath, the inconsistent, and indeed palpably absurd Report, he is said to have made to Captain Kerr.

Extraordinary as those things may appear, they are, however, surpassed by the proceedings of the following day; when he was again called before the Court, somewhat unaccountably, for the third time; and the business was rather aukwardly managed.

President. "It is UNDERSTOOD, that you IMAGINED, the

* How could his Lordship thus conjecture, when he had, only a moment before, heard Captain Kerr aver, that the *only communication* he had, with Lord Cochrane, was through his Master!

"Court had stopped you, where you had SOMETHING MATE-"RIAL, to add to your evidence?" (p. 208.)

How this *something* could have been *understood* by the Court, to have been *imagined* by Captain Kerr; and why it was not *understood, previous to the commencement of Captain Malcolm's evidence*, is not mentioned. But this *something* turned out to be *nothing*, or *something* WORSE than *nothing*. It afforded, however, an opportunity, to attempt the injury of Lord Cochrane, upon a point not embraced by, or connected with the charge; and consequently a point, of which the Court had no jurisdiction. We will give Captain Kerr's own words: "I have ONLY "to say, with respect to the Master's communication, with Lord "Cochrane, that I sent him to sound: he applied to his Lord-"ship to know, whether he knew of a depth of water, to place "the ship; and he said *he did not know;* he believed up to "windward:" (p. 208) Which proves this and no more, even, if the Master had reported truly: that the Master, instead of acting in obedience to the orders he had received, thought it would be saving trouble to apply to Lord Cochrane: that is, if he ever did make the application, which is a matter of fair doubt, as we have not his oath to the fact, which the learned Judge Advocate seems to have known was the *best evidence;* and he must also have known that the law requires the best evidence, and with which it will not dispense *.

Here Captain Kerr paused; but the President, not allowing him to know the extent of *his own grievances*, occasioned by his

* This examination, if it may be so called, is the more extraordinary, as all that which Captain Kerr had ONLY *to say*, had been said by him, the preceding day, and stands thus: "The *only* communication, I had with Lord "Cochrane, was through the Master of the Revenge, who was sent to sound, "immediately on the ship's anchorage. In passing the Imperieuse, he asked "Lord Cochrane"—(p. 202). Captain Kerr was here interrupted; and he was, after some discussion, allowed to proceed. "I felt the situation of the ship "to be dangerous, and sent him to sound round. On his return he told me, "that Lord Cochrane had informed him he did not know, but that he be-"lieved there was water to windward."

Q. "To the windward was to the Northward?"—*A.* "Yes, under the bat-"teries." (p. 203.)

having been "stopped when he had something *material* to add to his evidence" or "*imagining*" that he might have forgotten *something*, said: "we UNDERSTOOD you had SOMETHING to add, "respecting the damage of your ship," (p. 208.) Captain Kerr, in consequence, resumed "*that is known to the Commander in "Chief.*" Which is a tolerably strong proof, that he had finished all that he had to say, when he repeated the report given to him by the master, which he prefaced by the very impressive words "I have ONLY to say, &c." The President, however, *still not satisfied*, asked him: "whether the ship did not sustain damage "from the batteries of Aix and Oleron, and what was the amount "of it?" Captain Kerr, stated: "that *one* shot, from the batteries of Aix, struck the ship, under the main chains, on her passage out, on the 13th: that on the 12th, her bowsprit was "severely wounded: great part of the running rigging, and sails "cut to pieces; five planks of the quarter deck cut through; "and a quarter deck beam entirely carried away: a number of "shot in different parts of the hull; three men killed and fifteen "wounded, two of which afterwards died." (p. 208, 209.)

The remainder of the examination of Captain Kerr by the President was not of the least consequence. To us the *tout ensemble* is strange, and appears in a very questionable shape; yet we collect from Captain Kerr's evidence, materials, by which to form a pretty accurate idea, of all the destruction said to have been produced by the batteries of Aix, of which Captain Kerr, in the former part of his evidence, has said so much in apprehension, had our ships gone in earlier, than they were ordered in for that purpose.

The damage done to the quarter deck of the Revenge must have been from a *falling*, or *lobbing* shot, which proves, that Captain Kerr was barely within range, of the batteries of Aix; notwithstanding all that has been said of their dangers; indeed, by a Chart published in the Naval Chronicle for the month of July 1809, sent by Mr. Fairfax * to the editor of that work,

* With a Letter from Mr. Fairfax, which will be found in p. 49, of that Register. See page 141 of Mr. Fairfax's evidence.

it appears, that the Revenge, when she attacked the grounded vessels, was a mile and an half from those batteries. Again, it is to be considered, that Captain Bligh has stated in his Evidence, that the Revenge anchored the "Northernmost and Easternmost ship, about " three cables length, within the Imperieuse; and APPEARED TO " DRAW THE FIRE of the batteries of the Isle d'Aix, *from the* " *frigates, to* HER;" (p. 156) and Captain Kerr says himself, in another part of his evidence, after noticing, that the island *was one continued chain of works, connected* with the fortifications, that the guns of which *never ceased to act upon the Revenge*, during the whole time, *from her going* in, till her *coming out again;* and that during the whole of the time of her being in Aix, the guns continued to play upon her. (p. 226.)

After Captains Malcolm and Broughton, had given their evidence, which was strongly in support of the Charge, Captain Kerr was for the fourth time called in, at the request of Lord Gambier.—" I should wish," says his Lordship, " Captain Kerr " might be questioned, as to his *opinion* of the effect of the bat- " teries of the Isle d'Aix, *as he passed?*" Which was requiring the information, he had already given, in answer to a question from the President, and expressly upon that subject, namely, that the ship " was struck from the batteries in the Isle of Aix, " on her passage out on the 13th." " It was *only* ONE *shot* be- " tween wind and water, under the main chains, which struck " her."

Q. " Were you coming off with a leading wind?"—*A.* " About " a point free." (p. 208.)

Hence it is evident, that neither reason, nor propriety could have been consulted by Lord Gambier, when he resolved on this further examination of Captain Kerr. And what will be said of the Court, in suffering such further examination, and in permitting, nay soliciting, hearsay evidence; after having rejected it in the instance of Lord Cochrane: after having declared, as they did, on that occasion, that " it was from FACTS the Court were to form their opinion;" (p. 50) and after they had been fully informed, by their President, in a kind of caution to Lord Gambier, on his Lordship expressing a wish, to call Captain Kerr, "that that Gentleman had been pretty closely examined on that "point, in the morning." (p. 224.)

If we look into the testimony given by Captains Malcolm, Seymour, Newcomb, and Broughton, particularly the former, and the latter, Lord Gambier's REAL reason, for his repeated application to Captain Kerr, will no longer remain unintelligible. Captain Malcolm stated, that "if there had appeared no other "chance of destroying the ships, that were aground, but by "sending in a force, *while the two ships* REMAINED AFLOAT, "he certainly thought, it *ought* to have been done:" (p. 211) but, he exclaimed, "the moment, that the *two ships quitted* "*their defensive position*, THE RISK WAS SMALL, *of sending* "*ships in; and, of course, I would have sent them in instantly.*" (p. 212.) Captain Broughton said, "the fortifications appeared "to him in a very different state, to what he observed them, "when serving two years before, under Sir Richard Keates; he "thought they were repairing the works, from the QUANTITY "OF RUBBISH that was thrown up;" (p. 218) he thought the "RUBBISH was the REMAINS OF THE OLD WORKS, that had "been *taken down.*" (p. 219.)

When interrogated, whether he observed the batteries, on the South end of the Isle of Aix, after answering to customary *ifs* and *buts,* relative to sending in ships to attack the grounded vessels, in the face of the two ships, that were afloat, Captain Broughton said, "a ship or two might have been placed, in my "opinion, against the batteries on the Southern part of the Isle "of Aix, *so as to take off their fire and* SILENCE *them.*" (p. 221 *.) Captain Broughton was then asked; "how near ships "of the line might approach the batteries, on the Isle d'Aix, "on that part where he would have recommended an attack?" and he answered, "about two cables length."

We will now return to Captain Kerr.

* Vide Captain Kerr's evidence, p. 225 and 226 of the "Minutes," &c.

Q. *by Lord Gambier.* " In the course of your evidence you " have stated, that your ship received considerable damage from " the batteries of the Isle d'Aix: I desire you will state, what, " from your experience of the effect of the batteries, would have " been the fate of the Revenge, and any other seventy-four gun " ships, had they been anchored, within two or three cables " length, with a view of engaging those batteries, *until you had* " *silenced them?*"—*A.* " I certainly should have expected from " the heavy fire they kept up, both in going in and coming out, " that the ships, anchored there, must have been completely dis- " masted, and suffered a severe loss of men." (p. 225.)

To proceed further, on this enquiry, would be superfluous.—Lord Gambier's object, in so frequently calling upon Captain Kerr, here stands too manifest, to admit the shadow of doubt —it was to invalidate the *testimony of his own witnesses!* an act, not very delicate in its nature, nor suffered in practice.—Twice was Captain Kerr's evidence closed, and yet he was brought forward a third and a fourth time!!

There was one question proposed to Captain Kerr, that must not escape without some note—It came from Admiral Young: " Did you observe the batteries on the South end of the Isle of " Aix?" (p. 221.) He had been previously asked the same question, by the same person, upon his first examination, when he answered positively, " NO; *I did not,* the situation of the Re- " venge was so critical, that I was otherwise taken up." (p. 168.) In his answer, however, to the foregoing question, it will be perceived that he began to change his language—" I did not make " any PARTICULAR observations; *the officers* REPORTED to " me, that they saw *a number of guns,* on the South-West side, " and I SAW *a number of guns.*" The subject was pursued, and his answer to every question increased our surprise.

Q. " Is the battery you saw near the water edge, or at a dis- " tance from it?"—*A.* " Not a *very great* distance:" " it is not " *close* to the water's edge; *but the guns* WOULD HAVE BORNE " upon any ship *within a cable's length* of it!!" " They were " *not covered* batteries!" " there were *different tiers of guns*:

K k

" not *one battery* IMMEDIATELY ABOVE THE OTHER; but " OF DIFFERENT HEIGHTS!!"

Q. " Was the battery low enough to admit of being destroyed " by guns from ships, on the South side?"—*A.* " I THINK " NOT; on *the South-West* side, the guns from the ships would " have *borne on the* batteries!"

Q. " Did you see any other batteries on the Isle of Aix, that " would have borne on ships, sent in to attack the enemy?"—*A.* " None, *but those immediately connected with the works;* " ALTOGETHER, IT WAS ONE CONTINUED CHAIN OF " WORKS, CONNECTED WITH THE FORTIFICATIONS OF THE " ISLAND, EXTENDING FROM THE WESTERN ROUND TO " THE SOUTHERN SIDE of the island!!!" (p. 226.)

When the public recollect the former deposition of Captain Kerr, when, on being asked by Admiral Young, " Did you ob- " serve the state of the batteries on the Isle of Aix?" he answered, " No, I DID NOT; *the situation of the Revenge was " so critical,* I WAS OTHERWISE ENGAGED."—When the public recollect this, we are fearful, lest they should hesitate in believing, that we have transcribed faithfully; indeed we can scarcely give credit to our own eyes.

Here is a more particular and precise account of the fortifications, than any of the witnesses have given, and such certainty, as no person would have imagined, could possibly have come from Captain Kerr, after having declared, that he did *not* observe the state of them, assigning a very strong and amply sufficient reason, " the situation of the Revenge was so critical, that " he was otherwise taken up;" (p. 168) and after having, even on his last examination, deposed, " that he did not make any " PARTICULAR observations" (p. 225) upon those batteries: that the extent of those observations were confined to a number of guns; and that he would not have made even those, had not his attention been directed by his officers. " The officers re- " ported to me, that they saw a number of guns on the SW. " side, and *I saw a number of guns!*" (p. 225.)

How unfortunate it was, and how much to be lamented, that Captain Kerr did not *make,* on the batteries of Aix, what in his calculation were OBSERVATIONS: and if he had given to them only an hundredth part of that attention, which others profess to have done in theirs, how would the public have been enlightened by his information!! Likening it to a problem in the rule of three: we might thus state it—If NOTHING produces SO MUCH, what will SOMETHING produce? But taking it as it actually stands, we may fairly say, that the quadruple testimony of Captain Kerr is totally invalid, and nugatory; such, as is contrary to the rules of evidence, and to every principle of equity: and such as common sense disclaims, and justice condemns.

Were such testimony to be sustained, the rights of an officer, as secured to him by the laws of his country, would be trampled on; he would never be able to defend them; and innocence itself would be branded with crimes, that connect only with guilt!

Respecting the consistency, and impartiality of the Court Martial, on the occasion, we do not think it necessary to express our sentiments further, than to suggest, that there is something singular in the line pursued by one of the Members. Admiral Young can alone explain his reasons, for having proposed a long string of interrogatories to Captain Kerr, on the state of those batteries: Whether he did not observe the batteries on the South end of Aix? Whether the battery he saw, was near the water's edge, or at a distance from it? Whether it was low enough, to admit of its being destroyed, by the guns from the ships: and whether he saw any other batteries on the Isle of Aix, that would have borne on ships, sent in to attack the enemy? When he, Admiral Young, knew, of his own knowledge, that Captain Kerr had not any information on the subject; having declared upon a former examination, in the most positive manner, in answer to a question proposed by Admiral Young himself, that he had not made any observations on those works, the critical situation of his ship having occupied his attention *.

* That we may be the more clearly understood, and that the Admiral may not mistake us, we will again state the fact to which we allude, as it stands on Captain Kerr's first examination.

Q. *by Admiral Young.* "Did you observe the state of the fortifications on "the Isle of Aix?"—*A.* "NO. I DID NOT! the *situation of the Revenge* "was so CRITICAL, *I was otherwise taken up.*"

The conduct of the President, however, gives the climax! Upon the second examination of Captain Kerr, that gentleman made his appearance before the Court seemingly without knowing the cause. The President, explained it; yet in the most mysterious manner. " *It is* UNDERSTOOD, that you IMAGINED, the Court had stop- " ped you, when you had SOMETHING MATERIAL to add to " your evidence." And what was this material something?—a mere thing of hearsay, which even had it been admissible, was altogether insignificant. But if it had been *understood* in the sense, in which the President stated it: after Captain Kerr had said all that he had to say, and more than he had ever thought of saying, according to his own declaration: why should the President have tortured him further, by the following suggestion, which he ushered in, by a part of his former extraordinary exordium:—" We UNDER- " STAND that you had SOMETHING to ADD respecting the damage " to your ship?" and after having been informed by Captain Kerr, that, *that was known to the Commander in Chief:* why did he go on examining him to a point, on which Captain Malcolm had began to depose, when the course of his examination was broken in upon, by this further examination of Captain Kerr?—Captain Malcolm had said: " when those ships," that is, those of the enemy, " that remained longest afloat, had quitted their stations, there " was then no obstacle to prevent the small ships from going in. " by which I mean frigates, or even seventy-fours, if they had " been light, but the fire from the Isle of Aix, which they could " nearly avoid, by keeping near the Boyart." (p. 208.) And, as the questions, on the intermediate examination of Captain Kerr, were directed to obtain information, that there was the utmost danger to be encountered, from the batteries of Aix: *it is evident,* that *Captain Kerr was called in, to invalidate the testimony delivering,* by Captain Malcolm; as he was for the fourth and last time, to invalidate that which was afterwards delivered by Captain Broughton, whom he immediately followed. And if such be the fact, a more irregular, and unjust proceeding never was heard of. And if such proceedings are allowable before a Naval Court Martial, we most fervently hope, that some Members of Parliament, would take the steps, that may be necessary, towards reforming a system, pregnant with the most destructive consequences to modest merit and unprotected worth. The character of an officer, embraces every thing that is dear to him; and every security, compatible with the safety of the state, should be given to shield his fame and honour; for if party prejudice, and party spirit, be once roused against him, they imply the height of a powerful accusation. And what must be his fate before a Court Martial, who will say to him: We will not receive such and such evidence: it is mere conversation with officers, it is hearsay: "it is "upon matters of fact only on which the Court are to form "their opinion;" and the next instant receive the self same description of evidence from the witnesses of his adversary. Or who will prevent the most important facts, from being disclosed, merely, because a question had not been asked on the subject; and instruct a witness, contrary to the clear and express direction of the oath administered to him, that if he be not asked a SPECIFIC QUESTION, his oath would *only oblige him* to ANSWER SPECIFICALLY.

It is certainly to be understood, that a Court Martial, either naval or military, cannot be governed by all the rigid maxims and niceties of the law: nor even by every mode that obtains in our Courts of Equity: but there are certain rules that are within the most limited comprehension; and an impartial adherence to rules, when once laid down, becomes the bounden duty of every man.—At Military Courts Martial, there is a Judge Advocate, who is, or ought to be, conversant with those points of law, and those principles of equity, that are essentially necessary to aid the dispensations of justice, and defeat the odious influence of partiality and prejudice. He is the adviser of the Court, and we have witnessed, with pleasure and admiration, the present Judge Advocate General*, with noble and dignified perseverance, combating the opinions of a Court Martial with the honourable purpose of securing for the parties before the Court a direct and constitutional course towards just and impartial decision.

* The honourable Mr. Ryder, in the course of Proceedings, held some time ago at Chelsea.

CAPTAIN NEWCOMB.

Of this gentleman, much has been stated on the Minutes, provoked by Lord Gambier, aided by his Secretary, and sanctioned by the Court; and in such a manner, and to such ends, that even his Lordship's friends must blush for his conduct, and lament the motives, by which it was operated. But whatever might have been his Lordship's views, he certainly failed to produce any effect on the manly feelings, and honourable integrity of Captain Newcomb: who was not to be biassed by insinuations; nor influenced by considerations, that connected only with self.

Captain Newcomb appears to have conducted himself with that true zeal for the good of his country, and that well directed energy against her enemies, which gives effect to intention; and without which, judgment and ability are negative characters.—He saw an object, that demanded his immediate attention, and he did not wait for orders to pursue it. Being under weigh, on the 12th of April, and "it being reported to him, that a signal had "been made by the Commander in Chief, that the frigates should "go to a ship, making signals of distress in such a quarter; he "felt it his duty to proceed on to the Imperieuse, in Aix Roads; "she being the ship pointed out by the signal." (p. 196.)

Prompt and decided measures, animated by enthusiastic spirit, have hitherto been considered, as characteristic of the British sailor; and while thus pointed, the British Navy will ever maintain its proud pre-eminence.—Were we persuaded, that, on the present occasion, the tribute of our praise would be acceptable to Captain Newcomb, we would cheerfully offer it.

We have already had reason to notice, the sympathetic feeling that Lord Gambier has displayed, in defending the conduct of Captain Newcomb, against an attack, unjustly insinuated to have been made on it, by Lord Cochrane. But was such defence, the uncontaminated result of benign philanthropy? Was it as pure in its nature, as it professed to be in appearance? Were there no secret workings of the little passions, that sometimes wind themselves through the mazes of plausibility, in search of gratification for private resentment? Was it not, we ask this in tremulous diffidence, was it not, with a view to injure the good name, and ruin the reputation of Lord Cochrane, that originated *this shew* of defending the conduct of Captain Newcomb? These are questions, in which Mr. Wilkinson is somewhat interested; as they partly grow out of his own statement.

The language held by Mr. Wilkinson, when on his examination; and the gentle manner, in which he delivered himself, that spoke at once his anxiety and his modesty, were well calculated to rouse the indignation, and infuriate the resentments of an officer, whose character is dearer to him, by far, than existence. They were well calculated to rend asunder the ties of friendship, that had long subsisted between two men, who mutually regarded and esteemed each other: they were calculated to sow dissentions, and promote quarrels in the Navy; to the disturbance of individual harmony, and the injury of the public service? They were well calculated also!—but it would be endless, were we to pursue the matter to its utmost extent; we shall therefore only add, that Mr. Wilkinson insinuated more than he proved; and that his proof contradicted his insinuations.—He makes Lord Gambier extol the conduct of the Beagle, as having excited the admiration of himself and the whole fleet. And we heartily concur in the sentiment: not only from what we have seen in the Minutes: and what we have heard from others; but from what we, personally, know of Captain Newcomb's merits.

Having done this, Mr. Wilkinson made Lord Cochrane raise objections, and say;—I have a great regard and esteem for Captain Newcomb: and from his having been an old messmate of mine, (p. 179) it may be supposed, that I should say every thing in his favour; but, my Lord, I cannot make any exception respecting—respecting what? "Not the conduct of the Beagle: "not the conduct of Captain Newcomb;—but respecting the "conduct of *the officers commanding* GUN BRIGS:" (p. 181) vessels that are always commanded by Lieutenants; Captain

Newcomb commanded a sloop of war, which is always given to a Master and Commander.

Admiral Gambier, at a subsequent period, commenting upon the text of his worthy Secretary, in an address to the Court, says: " As all the Captains of the in-shore squadron, have been " before the Court, with the exception of three, I would claim " your indulgence, so much further, as to call in those officers, " intending to ask them a very few questions; one of them is " Captain Newcomb. As his name appeared yesterday, in evi- " dence, and it may lead to an inference prejudicial to that me- " ritorious officer, if I did not notice his conduct, I beg leave to " assure the Court, that he acquitted himself, in the command " of the Beagle, in Aix Roads, in a manner highly honourable " to himself, and certainly satisfactory to me." (p. 181.)

What man is there with a spark of sensibility in his bosom, having read the deposition of Mr. Wilkinson, can reflect upon these, his Lordship's hints and suggestions, without evincing an honest indignation? And where is the man of honour, and liberality, who would not exert himself to expose the hypocrisy that lurked beneath this pomp of benevolence and rectitude? Upon an abstract consideration, and a cursory view of his Lordship's feelings, as he has thus expressed them, any one might be induced to suppose, that Captain Newcomb's name had been brought forward by accident, or traduced by an enemy, who had seized an opportunity suitable to the purpose; and that Lord Gambier, influenced by pure Christian charity, had generously stepped forward to advocate his cause, and protect his honour? But on referring to a few facts, we shall trace the motive, by which his Lordship was actuated, to another source.

Lord Cochrane, in his evidence, repeated a conversation, that had passed between him and Lord Gambier, regarding the affair of Basque Roads, which he censured; at the same time, " he " submitted to his Lordship the necessity of still doing some- " thing more; and suggested, *that it would be impossible, things " remaining as they were, to prevent a noise being made about " it, in England;*"—to which, says Lord Cochrane, his Lordship replied, "if you threw blame, it would appear like arro- "gantly claiming all the merit to yourself." (p. 64.) Of this part of Lord Cochrane's deposition, Lord Gambier has taken notice in his written Defence; and endeavoured to turn the concluding sentence to his own purpose, in a way peculiar to himself. And if there should be found but few, to compliment his ingenuity on the occasion, we may venture to say, there will be still less to applaud its object.—His Lordship says: "I, however, "trust the Court will not conceive, the expression of 'casting "'blame,' has any allusion *to my conduct.*" His Lordship's allusion had reference only, to *the several officers who acted with him*, in Aix Roads; upon whom generally, *he cast blame.* (p. 135.) And on another occasion, "Lord Cochrane in presenting him- "self to me, after the action, was general in his complaint of "the officers, who commanded the other ships engaged." Having thus attempted to refute the statement made by Lord Cochrane, he naturally concluded, it was essentially necessary, that he should support his naked assertion, by a witness; and therefore, called upon his Secretary, Mr. Wilkinson, who, in his deposition, which was called for, by questions proposed by Lord Gambier himself, stated, that Lord Cochrane had spoken of Captain Newcomb in terms, that reflected on his character.

Thus it was that Captain Newcomb's name was mentioned; and thus originated the "evidence," that his Lordship has said "might lead to an inference, prejudicial to that meritorious offi- "cer." So that, after having studiously and deliberately, most wantonly and improperly brought forward Captain Newcomb's "name in evidence," in a manner, that might subject it "to an in- "ference prejudicial to that meritorious officer;" he affects to be all alive to that officer's situation, a situation in which he had himself placed him: and to feel most keenly for inferences, that might be prejudicial to him! Inferences, for which he, himself, had laid the foundation; and therefore, tells the Court, that he means to call upon Captain Newcomb, as a witness. (p. 184.)

We say nothing of the candour and magnanimity, or of the piety and rectitude of such proceedings. They will best speak for themselves: but we repeat, that they were adopted to render

L L

Lord Cochrane odious in the eyes of his brother officers; as a man, who had endeavoured to magnify his own merits, by depreciating theirs; and that, therefore, those officers were, as far as possible, bound to make a common cause against him. The more particularly, as his Lordship had pretty plainly told them, that it was principally to defend their honour, against Lord Cochrane's "insinuation," that he had demanded a Court Martial; because "had he tacitly acquiesced in those insinuations, he would have compromised, not only his own honour, but also that of the brave officers and men, serving under his command." (p. 106.)

So much, apparently generous and disinterested conduct, must have excited, as his Lordship, no doubt, imagined, the most lively sensations of gratitude, in the bosom of every officer under his command; and roused a proportionable resentment against Lord Cochrane. And if such influence, and some other of equal force, although of a different complexion, be not obvious in the Minutes, our senses have deceived us, and our conceptions have been extremely erroneous. Be that as it may, Captain Newcomb has certainly delivered himself, in his evidence, according to the honest dictates of his heart, and the best of his judgment and belief. And if he sometimes errs in his opinions, it must be attributed to the general confusion of the times; certainly not from any intention. In speaking to the question of neglect, or misconduct, in the Commander in Chief, he says, he does not know of any, "save and except, had the Commander in Chief "thought proper, from his situation, to have sent vessels in "EARLIER, THAN THEY WERE SENT;" (p. 200), although there might have been a great risk in doing so, there was a possibility of annoying the enemy, more than they were annoyed.

Q. by the President. "Under the circumstances of the an-"noyance, which the ships earlier sent in, would have been sub-"ject to, from the two French ships remaining at anchor: and "from the batteries of the Isle of Aix: and considering the "state of the winds at the time; would you, had you been "Commander in Chief, have sent the ships in earlier to attack "those of the enemy, on shore, than they were sent in?"—

A. "The risk, I *think*, as the wind was, and the tide, rather "too great." (p. 201.)

The President then supposes a case to meet the evidence of Captain Seymour, who threw out, that ships might have been sent in at 11 o'clock; but the answers he received from Captain Newcomb, left things rather worse than they were; as he shewed that the multiplied dangers, which the case held out, depended, in his idea, upon a mere fortuitous occurrence, "if any "unfortunate chance-shot, had crippled her masts and yards," (p. 201) then, indeed, there might have been a probability of "great danger." Nor was the question, as to every thing having been done, that was practicable, to destroy the enemy, more successful. Upon the whole, Lord Gambier, instead of obtaining any support from Captain Newcomb's testimony, has, by bringing it forward, contributed much towards sustaining the Charge.

CAPTAIN RODD, OF HIS MAJESTY'S SHIP THE INDEFATIGABLE.

This gentleman was brought forward upon "what may be "called the Prosecution," in consequence of Mr. Bicknell's proceedings, towards the conclusion of it: (p. 69) and Mr. Bicknell commences his examination, with a sprout of his "general "question," (p. 70) by asking Captain Rodd, "when he knew "of any anchorage, on the Isle of Aix, for line of battle ships, "out of the range of shot and shells?" "Not until I saw the "*frigates*, after the action, *move to the anchorage they took* "*up*," (p. 87) was Captain Rodd's answer, which drew forth the following remark from the President: "Seeing of *frigates* "there, would be *no proof*, that the *line of battle* ships could "*lie there*." Captain Rodd corrected himself—"I never knew "that line of battle ships could lie there; for I DID NOT KNOW "THE DEPTH OF WATER!!" (p. 88.) In another part of his examination, he was asked by the President, "Whether every "thing was done, that could be done, to effect the destruction "of the enemy?"—*A.* "I believe every thing, with *safety* to "his Majesty's ships."

To relieve his testimony from such ambiguity, Admiral Young very kindly asked, "*if he* MEANT, *without being exposed to any* "*danger, or without their being exposed to more danger, than* "*the circumstances would justify*." (p. 88.) His answer was in the affirmative, and in the very words, of the last part, of the question.

Thus shewing his sense, of such the Admiral's bounty towards him, by carrying it in his memory; and therefore, when he was some time afterwards questioned: "Whether the anchor-"age, where the Indefatigable lay, was in a situation, in which "ships of the line could have been placed, for the destruction "of the enemy's ships?" he again answered, "Not with SAFETY "to the ships;" and immediately added, "*I* MEAN *not without* "*the* RISK OF THE LOSS OF THE SHIPS." (p. 89.)

Q. "Was there any other situation, in the Roads of Aix, in "which ships of the line might be placed to destroy the enemy, "*without risk of being lost?*" On this question, he again became confused.—*A.* "I *think not*, WHERE THE ENEMY "WERE; they were *surrounded with shoals*, or upon a shoal," he did not know which; and we may say, without the hazard of a contradiction, that he could not have had any information, on the subject, *of his own knowledge;* and he has given his own confessed uncertainty and ignorance of the fact, as, reason for *thinking*, that there was no situation in which ships of the line could be placed, to destroy the enemy, *without the risk of being lost.*

The Court, notwithstanding, allowed such evidence to stand on their Minutes, without the slightest comment, or a single question, to ascertain from what "*data*" Captain Rodd delivered his opinion; though Admiral Young might have continued the examination, somewhat in this manner:—"Captain Rodd, you have stated, that when your ship swung, at half a cable's *length* distant, you had only, from four and an half, to five fathoms water: that, had you gone FARTHER IN, your ship must have run aground; and that your anchor was nearly in seven fathoms. (p. 89.) Now as the water deepened so rapidly, *in so short a distance* as half a cable: are you quite sure, there was no deeper water, at a quarter of a cable's length beyond your anchor?" Some such question, drawn from such given premises, might have produced a very satisfactory and highly important answer; but Admiral Young did not pursue the subject, and we are sorry for it. Leaving those objects at a moment in which Captain Rodd had opened a field, that promised much information, to a well directed examination, the Court called Captain Rodd's attention to the fortifications of Aix, &c. of which he could not give them any other certain, or satisfactory account, than he had given them, regarding a safe anchorage for ships of the line——"The enemy "certainly moved their guns from one part to another:" at least he thought so; "the works were evidently under repair:" "it appeared by the Log, that the Indefatigable weighed, at half "past four in the morning of the 13th:" "that Lord Cochrane

" had hailed him; but he could not hear distinctly what he " said:" " did not know, that had he remained in Aix, that he " could have destroyed any more of the enemy:" " did not think " he could have got up with them:" " two of the enemy's ships " were afloat, and they got under weigh, or slipt, and ran up:" " did not know, that our line of battle ships would have ground- " ed; but that they must have been wholly disabled, by the bat- " teries and the ships afloat;" for that he " counted thirteen " guns, as he passed, on the battery!" (p. 90.)

The Court then turned to a matter, no way connected with that in issue, and asked: " Whether the *Calcutta had struck to " the Imperieuse,* before Captain Rodd anchored, and com- " menced the action?"—*A.* "MOST ASSUREDLY NOT; *several " broadsides were fired at the Calcutta,* from the Indefatigable " and Valiant: when Lord Cochrane, or some person from the " Imperieuse, hailed me, and said *the Calcutta had struck;* and " we then desisted firing upon her." (p. 91.) Here the President might have introduced some pertinent interrogatories, premising, in the language he used, when he observed upon a part of Captain Kerr's evidence, that "seeing the frigates at an anchor" in a certain spot " was no proof, that line of battle ships could lie " there"—" that *the firing of those broadsides, was no proof, that " the Calcutta was not, previously, in our possession.*" To establish that she was not so, it would be requisite to shew, that those *broadsides were returned,* either by broadsides, or some guns, or a gun: or that her people were in the act of preparing to fire; more especially, as the Indefatigable and Valiant desisted firing upon her the instant, they were informed, from the Imperieuse, that she had struck. But the President allowed such extremely fallacious reasoning, to pass unnoticed; as if it had carried conviction, instead of absurdity, on the face of it.

He might possibly have been thinking of something else, and attending only, to the first part of Captain Rodd's answer, which was as strong, as a negative could be conceived, concluded that the insinuation of Lord Gambier, that the Calcutta did not strike to the Imperieuse, had been clearly and decidedly established; and that therefore, any thing further would be superfluous *.

We however, contend, that Captain Rodd's reason, on which he founded a positive assertion, carries upon the face of it the strongest presumptive proof, that totally ignorant of the situation of the Calcutta, the Indefatigable and Valiant had been throwing away their shot upon her, when she was already our own; and when "the Imperieuse's boat was actually on board of her." (p. 42.) Indeed Captain Rodd himself seems to admit the strange blunder, and to apologize for the commission of it, when after stating, that Lord Cochrane had hailed him, and said the Calcutta had struck, he says: "I could only see her at INTERVALS, "*through the smoke:* we then desisted firing upon her, and "turned the whole of our fire, upon the Varsovie." Of one fact, we are assured, that on Lord Cochrane's information, the Indefatigable and Valiant instantly ceased firing on the Calcutta.—Until then, they were pouring their broadsides into her, and we may presume, that left to themselves, they would have gone on firing broadsides, until they should have torn her to atoms. When all these facts and circumstances are taken into consideration, is it not astonishing, that Captain Rodd should have allowed himself to declare, so *decidedly*, and in terms so *positively*, that the Calcutta HAD NOT STRUCK to the Imperieuse—"MOST ASSUREDLY "NOT." And is it not astonishing, that the Court should have allowed such testimony, to have had weight, against the official report of Lord Cochrane, on the subject of the Calcutta, when the information, on which that testimony solely rested, was derived from his Lordship, and which is in full confirmation of such his Lordship's report? Or was it determined, right or wrong, to withhold every credit from Lord Cochrane; that, right or wrong, Lord Gambier should be MOST HONOURABLY ACQUITTED.

We have stated that Captain Rodd was called in, in consequence of an occurrence, in the course of "what may be termed the pro-

* Why was not Captain Newcomb asked the question, on the subject: his boat accompanied that of the Imperieuse on board the Calcutta: his examination followed that of Captain Rodd? Why were not others, who were present examined, besides Captains Rodd and Bligh, between whose testimony there is a considerable difference?

" secution," as he was a witness summoned on the part of the Defence: he was afterwards called to support it: but Lord Gambier observed, on the instant he appeared in Court, that the question he meant to have been proposed to him, was not considered by the Judge Advocate, as strictly applicable; and that therefore he should not have occasion for him.

On the testimony of Captain Rodd, there is very little more to be said, than that it is confused and embarrassed in some parts; and wholly inconsistent in others: that to the last question asked him, upon his first examination, he spoke positively, as of his own knowledge, when in fact, and so it appears from his own deposition, he had no knowledge on the subject, to which he was deposing; and that sometimes, his memory failed him, of which his answer to the following question, by Admiral Young, is an instance:

Q. " Did you, on the morning of the 12th of April, see the " Imperieuse, inform the Commander in Chief, by signal or te- " legraph, *that half the fleet would be sufficient to* destroy the " enemy?—*A.* " I did not, PART of the signal made by the " Imperieuse, about that time, was reported to me: which was, " *that seven sail of the enemy's line of battle ships were on* " *shore;* but I do not remember the OTHER signal.

It is very extraordinary, that Captain Rodd, should have recollected the *least important part,* " seven sail of the enemy's line of " battle ships were on shore," and forgot, that which was most essential, and which of course, ought to have made the deepest impression on his mind, namely, that those seven sail " could be " destroyed by half the fleet;" and the more so, as those pieces of intelligence, were not given at two distinct periods, but were the compound parts of the same signal, and given in one and the same moment. But he has given his reason, and it is fair we should state it here—" I was under weigh, at the time, and oc- " cupied in working the ship:" which would infer, that in the bustle of his duty, on board his own ship, he had no opportunity for regarding exterior transactions; and that he caught a PART of the signal by accident. Unfortunately for his reasoning, it was, as he says himself, "*reported to him;*" so that his attention was not much required. Captain Rodd, however, says, that it was only PART of the signal that was reported to him. Is it to be supposed, that the person who made the report, would have made it by halves; and if he had: how does it happen, that as Captain Rodd says, "he did not remember the OTHER part," as the very expression implies he *once* knew it?—Again, how did he know that it was only a PART of the signal, that had been reported to him?—In whatever way the circumstance is received, it involves doubt and suspicion, improbability and inconsistency.

In going over the evidence of Captain Rodd, we have selected from it, the more prominent points only, and this, in fact, is and must be the case, with the evidence in general—To have taken up every point, that called for review, would have swelled these Notes into volumes—Some of the interrogatories administered to Captain Rodd are leading, and exceptionable; and were consequently a waste of time. The public will perceive, that the answers they received, do not amount to the weight of a feather; not one of them is either positive or certain, so as to take from the force of the Charge, or carry any thing to support the Defence.

M m

CAPTAIN HARDYMAN.

Of Captain Hardyman's evidence, there is little further to be said, than that he appears to have followed the dictates of his conscience, and delivered an honest testimony. At the same time, the guarded manner in which he answered irrelevant questions, that jumbled together distinct periods of time, and circumstances, foreign to each other, to serve particular purposes, furnishes the best compliment, that can possibly be paid, to a deliberative mind, and a watchful judgment. His testimony, however, is not of any the least weight. He did not go into the Roads of Aix, until about three o'clock in the afternoon of the 12th; although the queries put to him, would infer, that he had been there during the whole morning of that day.

In his answers he adhered closely to opinion, founded in appearances.—Speaking to the conduct of the Commander in Chief, he said: "I *do not know* of any neglect or unnecessary "delay;" and to the question: whether every thing was done, that could be done, to effect the destruction of the enemy? he said: "*I think* there was." (p. 188.) The Court, in the course of Captain Hardyman's examination, observed the same unwarrantable line of conduct, as they did towards almost every other witness, exhibiting a long string of interrogatories, in reference to the conduct of the officers commanding vessels, in the roads of Aix, over whom no authority had been given to them; and with whom, consequently, they had not the smallest right of interference.

CAPTAIN WOOLF.

Captain Woolf's evidence is, in point of importance, inferior even to Captain Hardyman's, and was delivered without that gentleman's circumspection or prudence. As far as it goes into fact, of his own knowledge, it rather defeats than maintains the Defence set up by Lord Gambier; particularly, with regard to the conduct of several of the fire-ships; which he shews was extremely bad. (p. 266.) He speaks of two spots, on which our ships might have anchored; one of them capable of containing five or six sail of the line, clear of the enemy's batteries. (p. 86.) We give Captain Woolf credit for good intentions; and if he has committed errors, we can believe them to be wholly of the judgment, in which design had no share. The questions that were asked him, might have confused any man. We will select one subject, to which they were directed, as an example. He had shewn, that he did not take soundings in the roads of Aix; and therefore, the Court must have been convinced, that, on that head, he could not give any information: still however he was, not only examined, but closely pressed, in relation to it.

Q. by the President. " During the time, that you remained " at the second anchorage, had you an opportunity of ascertain- " ing, what was the rise of the tide on spring tides?—*A.* " Upon " the average of the time, we were there, I suppose the rise and " fall was, from fifteen to sixteen, seventeen and eighteen feet."

Q. " During the time, that you continued at this anchorage, " did you cause soundings to be taken, between *the Pallès and* " *Boyart Shoals?*"—*A.* " I received orders from Lord Gam- " bier to assist Mr. Stokes, the second Master of the Caledonia, " with boats, and whatever Mr. Stokes might require in survey- " ing the anchorage."

President. " I more particularly allude to the supposed shoal " water, there is between these two shoals; if what you are " going to mention comprehends, what I particularly allude to, " you will proceed—*Would the casting your eye upon this Chart*

" *give you a clearer comprehension?*"—*A.* "No; I have it all
" in my mind; I received those orders to assist Mr. Stokes, in
" surveying the anchorage, which was done, with the assistance
" of our Master and others, whomever Mr. Stokes applied for."

Q. "What was their report of the depth of water, at any par-
" ticular time of the tide, in the situation I have pointed out, *be-*
" *tween the Pallés and the Boyart*, if you have a recollection
" of it?"—*A.* "I do not recollect any particular remark of Mr.
" Stokes, or our Master; excepting Mr. Stokes having said, he
" had found DEEP WATER, and a little more room, farther to the
" Southward."

President. "I believe what you are stating applies more to
" the anchorage, than to that, which I am enquiring about; it
" appears BY THIS CHART *, as if there was a SHOAL *between*
" *the road of Aix and this other situation* (pointing it out);
" what I wish to know is, what water there was upon this BAR
" OR BAY † (shewing it upon the Chart)?"—*A.* "That does not
" come within my knowledge; in the particular part to which the
" question alludes, with the exception of the Cæsar having
" grounded much about the spot pointed out in the Chart shewn
" me by the President, I will not take upon me to say the exact
" situation of the Cæsar's grounding: I speak within *half a*
" *mile.*" (p. 86.)

We will not comment upon the very extraordinary efforts, that were made, to prevail on Captain Woolf, to give information upon a point, of which he had expressed his total ignorance. The public will decide upon the candour and impartiality they convey.—The shoal noticed in the question, is no where to be found, but in Mr. Stokes's disgraced Chart, and it was there laid

* Mr. Stokes's Chart: and it will be recollected, that Mr. Stokes referred to another—a MSS Chart, for the soundings.

† Although the President, in examining Captain Broughton, was equally desirous to obtain his evidence, on this point: he did not produce this Chart to him; and why not!! he contented himself with stating: "It is marked " in *some* of the Charts, that *between the Boyart and the tail of the Pallés*, " *there is a bar.*" Vide Captain Broughton's evidence as we have extracted it. The distinction made between the two witnesses, is worthy of remark: it means more than it unfolds.

down to unite the Boyart and Pallés, for the purpose of demonstrating, that our ships could not pass to the anchorage, that lay behind them; and the Cæsar, to which Captain Woolf refers, grounded nearly a mile from the shoal, or, as the President has it, " bar or bank," to which Captain Woolf was examined, as is ascertained by the testimony of Admiral Stopford.

CAPTAIN SEYMOUR.

The evidence of this gallant young officer calls for more attention, than time and circumstances will permit us to give it.—Indeed, painful occurrences, of a private nature, has compelled us to leave much of our original plan unfinished; and prevented us from condensing the rest, to one half of its present size.—Captain Seymour is mistaken in one point; but it is of no consequence whatever. In every respect, he delivered his testimony with a manliness, that must reflect the highest credit upon his character: nor did he permit language, that carried with it something of menace, nor the diversifying of questions, to direct him from his honourable purpose.

After the Court had asked him two or three questions, of no material import, he was about to be dismissed. His sense of rectitude then manifested itself, and he exclaimed, "Am I not "bound, by my oath, to relate every circumstance which comes "within my knowledge, relating to the proceedings of the fleet?" The President suggested, that he was bound to do so only, when questions were asked him; (p. 190,) and he appeared disappointed. His appeal to the Court, however, led to various other questions; in the course of which, he was desired to state his observations on "the conduct of all the vessels, of every description, employed against the enemy." (p. 193.) He asked, from what period; and was evidently hurt, when he was told, by the President, that he was not to go back to the night of the 11th, which Captain Seymour probably considered, as it doubtless was, a period of considerable importance—that is, if it had been admissible, on the part of the Court, to make enquiry into the conduct of officers, not named in, or noticed by the Charge.

Asked by Admiral Young, "Whether he perceived any neg- "lect or misconduct, on the part of the Commander in Chief?" prefacing his answer in the most modest terms, he said: "From "what I afterwards saw, I think the ships might have floated in "sooner; and that they might have gone in, in the last half of

" the flood tide;" (p. 193,) " that they might have gone in at " 11 o'clock:" " that his opinion was formed from the depth of " water, found in going in: and from seeing the Revenge go " out, at a corresponding time of the tide, on the following " day." (p. 193.)

Q. by the President. " Do you mean by your answer to say, " that there was water sufficient, for the line of battle ships, to " have gone in at 11 o'clock; but of the expediency of such a " measure, you do not form any judgment?"—*A.* " I meant to " say, it is a point, on which the discretion of the Commander in " Chief might be fairly used; it is impossible for me, to foretell " the event of such an attack." (p. 194.)

After some further cross-questions from the Court, Captain Seymour was desired to give a short answer: and the following question was proposed by the President: " Did you, at the time " you made these observations, think that the line of battle ships " *should* have gone in?"—*A.* " I cannot give an opinion upon " that; I was not in the possession of the Commander in Chief's " information, that would allow me to form any judgment, as to " the propriety of it." (p. 195.)

Throughout the whole of Captain Seymour's evidence, that we have gone over, the utmost respect and diffidence were conspicuous; yet Admiral Young seemed displeased with it; but, upon what ground, we do not venture an opinion. He said: " This general question is not meant, to subject the general con- " duct of the Commander in Chief, to the opinions of all the " officers, *serving under his command;* because it cannot be sup- " posed, that all officers, *serving under his command*, can be " competent to form opinions of his general conduct; but it is " quite within the capacity of any officer, *serving under his* " *command*, to state a particular instance of misconduct; and if " you think this, of the two ships not going in so early, as you " think they might have floated, is an instance of neglect, or de- " lay in the Commander in Chief: it is your duty so to state it: " that WE MAY ENQUIRE INTO IT, and HEAR ANY OTHER " EVIDENCE UPON IT?"—*A.* " I have already stated, that

" I cannot say it was misconduct: I STATE THE FACT, " AND LEAVE THE COURT TO JUDGE."

Q. " You state an opinion, that the fleet would have floated " in, at 11 o'clock?"—*A.* "Yes, that THERE WAS WATER " ENOUGH."

Q. " *Is that all you mean to say*—that there would have been " water enough for them to have floated in?"—*A.* " Yes; that " is all I have said."

Q. " When you say, that the ships of the line would have " floated in, at 11 o'clock; do you mean to speak to the depth " of water alone, without taking into consideration any other " circumstances, which would have prevented, or impeded their " getting in?"—*A.* " *I confine myself to the meaning of the " words—that there would have been water enough, for the line " of battle ships to have floated in—that is all I mean to say. " The opposition they would have met with,* THE COURT " HAVE AS MUCH BEFORE THEM AS I HAVE." (p. 195.)

After Admiral Young had said, the general question was not meant to subject the conduct of the Commander in Chief, to the opinions of ALL *the officers, serving under his command,* which is a contradiction in terms, when regarded with the examination of almost every witness on that point; what could he have meant, when he said, in allusion to neglect, or delay in the Commander in Chief, in not sending in the two ships at eleven o'clock: " it is your duty to state it, that we may ENQUIRE " INTO IT, and hear ANY OTHER EVIDENCE upon it?"

We leave this, and the examination that followed, to the candid and liberal consideration of the public; submitting, that the Court had, at the time, examined almost all the witnesses, that were summoned, to the very points to which Captain Seymour was giving his testimony, and some of them more than once; and that Captain Seymour's evidence completely supports the Charge. His manliness and his judgment, and the spirit of daring enterprise, which he discovered on the occasion, give a fair promise, that he will one day be an ornament to his profession, and to his country.

CAPTAINS DOUGLAS, BALL, BURLTON, AND NEWMAN.

In the common occurrences of society, we often witness, a variety of inconsistencies and absurdities, that cannot be reconciled with reason, and we pass them by as matters of course. But in those assemblies, where the judgment is called upon to exercise her best faculties: in Courts of equity and honour, whence every passion should be banished, and decorum and propriety go hand in hand with impartiality and justice, should incongruity and frivolity intermix with the solemnity of the proceedings, conducting in the prosecution of truth, and to the furtherance of justice, the feelings are naturally roused into indignation, and turn from the scene with disgust.

Captains Douglas, Ball, Burlton and Newman, who do not appear ever to have been in the Roads of Aix, were notwithstanding, examined by Lord Gambier to points, that could not have been understood, without a tolerably intimate knowledge of those Roads; and without having been in them, on the MORNING of the 12th of April.

Q. to Captain Douglas. "Had I sent in any ships to Aix "Road, at day light, or soon afterwards, on the morning of "the 12th, to attack the enemy, were any of the enemy's "ships in a situation, to enable them to rake and injure our ships, "as they advanced?" (p. 171.)—*A.* "Certainly: I think they "were."

Q. "At what time could our ships have returned, during that "day?"—*A.* "The wind blowing very strong, into the harbour "of Aix, they could not have returned until the ebb; and then "they must have worked out, and probably been disabled by the "batteries, or the ships they must have engaged."

Q. "If any of the ships advancing under such circumstances "had become crippled: what would have been the consequence?" —*A.* "The impression made upon my mind, at that time was, "that *they would have been burnt with* RED HOT SHOT."

N N

We have already said, that Captain Douglas had never been in the Roads of Aix: consequently, could not have known, that there were furnaces on the Island, by which the shot could be made RED HOT, that were to burn our ships: it is therefore surprising, that such an impression could have been made on his mind. All that can be said of it is, that it was a red hot answer, to a terrific question! The question, however, was followed up by another, that appears, to have grown out of the answer remarked on.

Q. " Under all the circumstances of the wind and tide: Did it " appear to you, that on the morning of the 12th of April, or at " any other time, when the enemy's ships were on shore, when " the signal had been made, that half the fleet could destroy " them, there was on my part, any *neglect, or unnecessary delay,* " in taking effectual measures for destroying them?"—*A.* " On " the contrary, *I think the happy time,* for effecting it, was *chosen* " *by the Commander in Chief.*"

And to another question, regarding the general conduct of the Commander in Chief, Captain Douglas said: " In my opinion, " every thing was done, that could be done, under the circum- " stances."

We have been induced to notice the testimony of Captains Douglas, Ball, Burlton and Newman, upon two considerations; first to shew, that notwithstanding witnesses, on the part of the defence, had it not in their power to state any one fact, in support of it, they were examined, as if they had been conversant with every fact; and secondly, to shew the inconsistency of asking them questions, relative to his Lordship's conduct, when it is more than probable, that, with the exception of five minutes, when they were receiving their orders, they did not even see his Lordship during the whole day; although the Court were, at the same time, withholding such questions from Sir Harry Neale, who never left his Lordship a moment; and had exclusive opportunities, of observing his conduct, and forming the most accurate judgment upon all his acts. Sir Harry Neale was not only the best, but perhaps, the only man, that could have given an account of his Lordship's measures, and of his zeal and exertions in the whole of the memorable 12th day of April 1809; yet Sir Harry Neale, with all his means of giving essential information, was not required to say a word, on the subject of Lord Gambier's conduct, the grand object of the investigation of the Court; and Captains Douglas, Ball, Burlton and Newman, who had no information at all, were particularly examined to it. In some cases, for example, in the examination of Captains Malcolm, Seymour and Broughton, who entertained sentiments very different to those uttered by Captain Douglas, we have seen the Court, sounding with particular attention, the depths of such witnesses knowledge: penetrating the means by which he acquired it: and endeavouring, by well pointed questions, to learn the reasons on which he founded his opinions; but Captain Douglas's was not one of those cases: He proceeded in his short career, without a single interruption, or any thing, that resembled a cross question from the Court: and all that he stated was received as gospel, though the Court must have been convinced, that he could not have known any of the matters to which he was interrogated, "of his own knowledge," and of course, all that he could assert, would amount to no more, than naked conjectural opinion: a species of evidence, that the President had previously rejected, in the most decided manner; and declared, that "it was from *facts*, that the Court must form "their opinion." (p. 50.) The questions then, that were put to Captain Douglas, were frivolous and absurd; and of course his answers idle, and totally insignificant.

Under all the circumstances of the case, then, and with the knowledge that Lord Gambier possessed, of Captain Douglas's total ignorance of the most material facts, on which that case founded itself, the introducing of Captain Douglas, as a witness, is altogether unaccountable; unless, as we have before observed, Lord Gambier imagined, that he could supply the deficiency in evidence, by the number of the witnesses he brought forward; for amongst his Lordships witnesses, there was a very great number, no better qualified than Captain Douglas. In that number, we may very safely class the Gentlemen, whom we have named with him, Captains Ball, Burlton, and Newman. To each of those gentlemen the following questions were exhibited, alternately, by the President and Admiral Young, the fact is curious.

Q. by the President. "From the first attack upon the "ships of the enemy, on the evening of the 11th of April *, to the "time of your leaving Basque Roads, according to your judgment, "was every thing done, that could be done, to effect the des- "truction of the enemy's ships?"—*A. by Captain Burlton.* "I think there was."—*A. by Captain Ball.* "I think there was "every thing done."—*A. by Captain Newman.* "Perfectly so."

Q. by Admiral Young. "From the time the Commander in "Chief arrived in Basque Roads, to the time of your quitting it, "can you state any instance of neglect, misconduct, or inatten- "tention to the public service, in the proceedings of the Com- "mander in Chief?"—*A. by Captain Burlton.* "I know of "none."—*A. by Captain Ball.* "No, I cannot."—*A. by Captain Newman.* "None †."

* Here the President commences his examination on the 11th of April, and from what has been seen of the principle, by which he professed to be governed on another occasion, it might naturally be concluded, that the witnesses had been with the fire ships in the Roads of Aix, on that evening: and had an intimate knowledge of every transaction, that was going on, and every measure that had been suggested on board the flag ship, and were by such means *immediate spectators*; because when Captain Seymour was examined to the conduct of Officers in the Roads of Aix, he was not suffered to give evidence of the evening of the 11th.—"No," said the President, "I take it from your "going in on the 12th, because then you became an immediate spectator," (p. 193.) The truth, however, is that those Gentlemen never were in the Roads of Aix; and that they knew no more of the conduct, or plans of the Commander in Chief, on board the Caledonia, than of those of the Commanding Officer of Isle d'Aix.

† This kind of negative answers, to questions of the same description, give the sum total of the evidence that supported Lord Gambier's Defence, and are such as any witness, who had neither curiosity to examine into his Lordship's conduct, nor the means of acquiring information, by which alone, a sound opinion could be formed, could have given with the greatest safety. But there is the affirmative evidence of Lord Cochrane, and Captains Seymour, Malcolm, Broughton, and Newcomb to the contrary—the four former of those witnesses, after critical examinations, and rigid cross-examinations, do support and substantiate the charge, and such evidence is corroborated by the fact, of ships of the line and frigates, going into the Roads of Aix, and the attack upon the enemy's ships which they destroyed, and suffering only very triflingly, from the tremendous and destructive batteries of Aix, which is declaredly one of the causes, that produced the neglect and delay of eight hours, which, his Lordship has confessed did take place. The public may, therefore, be considerably embarrassed to discover the ground, upon which the Court Martial declared, Lord Gambier most honourably acquitted.

Captain Newman added, "From the nature of the oath, I "have taken, or even if that had not been the form of the oath, "I should feel it necessary, if I had observed any conduct, of "any particular officers and men, however humble their situation, "to have mentioned it to the Court." The President, however, thus admonished him. "No: that would have been improper, "you can speak only as to the Commander in Chief, *it is only* "*the conduct of the Commander in Chief, that this Court is* "*called upon to enquire into.*"

Here the President returns to the path of his duty, and marks precisely the jurisdiction of the Court. Judging him then, by his own doctrine, what shall we say of his conduct, and of the conduct of the Court, and Judge Advocate, through almost every part of their former proceedings, in which they deviated into a totally different course; and unjustly and cruelly examined witnesses to the conduct of Lord Cochrane, and to the conduct of the Officers, who acted with his Lordship, in Aix Roads, by which to affect his Lordship's character in his Lordship's absence; and afterwards refusing his application to be heard in his defence *.

But what would Captain Newman have said, had he been allowed to go on. Why—"Having observed some conspicuous "conduct of the brigs, I was about to have mentioned that"—which, in all probability, might have cleared, that particular point, which Mr. Wilkinson had so embarrassed, and confused by his testimony; and to this point, Captain Newman must have been highly competent, as he appears to have been informed by his own observation.

But Captain Newman was called on, to speak to points, to which he was not competent; whilst others who were, had not been allowed to deliver their testimony: amongst these, and certainly the foremost, is Sir Harry Neale, who, as first Captain of the Caledonia, and Captain of the fleet, should have undergone a very strict examination as, well in explanation of his own conduct, as

* Vide his Lordship's Letter to the President and the President's Answer, (p. 228, 229.)

in illustration of that, of the Commander in Chief; and we witnessed that he was prepared for such an examination, and desirous of meeting it.

It was not to be supposed, that he would have looked with indifference on an enemy, within our power, without ever offering any advice, as to measures, that might be pursued, to sescure them. The public who know him, know that he would have given opinions, and urged the adoption of some eligible plans, towards the capture of them; and it was therefore, an injustice to the public, and to the character of that gallant Officer, that he was not allowed an opportunity of speaking to the question, and as fully as others.

There seemed to be an apprehension, from too deeply probing Sir Harry Neale: and therefore, caution was used to prevent his examination, from extending beyond the very circumscribed limits, that were assigned to it. In the commencement of it, the Court advised him, upon the relations between his confidential situation, and his oath: and after Lord Gambier had finished with his Examination in Chief, and the Court had entered upon, "what might be called," their cross examination of him, his Lordship hastily interrupted them, by suggesting, that "under the peculiar circumstances, in which Sir Harry Neale "stood, as his confidential friend, and first Captain of the Cale- "donia, he did not think it was proper, to ask him any further "questions."

Was such language ever before held, by a defendant to the Court, by whom he was trying, upon alledged offences, against the interest and honour of his country—"most certainly not"—or if it had been attempted, would the Court have suffered it, and allowed it to stand on the face of their proceedings, as an apology, for their neglect of a public duty, due to their Country and to justice? most certainly not. Lord Gambier's experience must have taught him to understand, by what sacred ties the Court were bound, under the oath, that had been administered to them, to render strict and impartial justice, unbiassed by favour, uninfluenced by affection.

The Court also, must have felt the truth of all this, deeply impressed upon their minds; and that, in the dispensation of justice, and where the "*salus populi*" was interested, individual considerations, and individual feelings, could be allowed no weight, in their deliberations. Yet they suffered such the dictatorial language of Lord Gambier to prevail.

CAPTAIN MALCOLM, of His Majesty's Ship DONEGAL.

This Gentleman, by his evidence, corroborates the testimony of Captain Seymour. He saw every thing, that appeared in the Roads of Aix, with the eye of an experienced officer; and glowed with the genuine ardour of a seaman, anxious to attack the enemy. He said "when the two ships," those that remained the longest afloat, "quitted their stations, there was then, no obstacle "to prevent the small ships from going in: by which I mean *fri-"gates,* or even SEVENTY FOURS, if they had been light, but "from the fire of the Isle d'Aix, which they could nearly avoid, "by keeping near the Boyart," (p. 208). The evidence of Captain Malcolm was here broken in upon, by the examination, for the third time, of Captain Kerr, partly with a view to refute the testimony he had just delivered, (p. 209.) After which Captain Malcolm was again called in, and observed, "that about noon the Ocean "was heeling considerably." And having undergone one of the severest examinations possible, in questions and cross questions, the President thus interrogated him. "You have stated it to be "your opinion, that half flood, was about noon; and that the "enemy's ships got off, at about two P. M. and you have in the "answer to the preceding question, stated, that any ships sent in, "previous to the removal of the French ships, that got off, would "be liable to considerable annoyance from them, as well as the "Isle d'Aix; would you then have sent ships in, before the two "ships were removed, and the three decker got off?"—*A.* "Had "it appeared to me, that there was no other chance of destroy-"ing those ships, but by such an attack, I certainly think it "ought to have been made: but it was understood, that they "must all again ground, in the mouth of the Charante, where, it "was the received opinion, they could be attacked by bombs, "gun vessels, and fire ships again, without risk, bombs particu-"larly; and had there been a reserve of fire ships, I think some "of them would have been destroyed, on the flood tide of the "12th. There were fireships prepared with all expedition, but "they were too late." (p. 211.)

Subsequently to this answer, he was again examined very closely, upon a variety of points, when he said, that "had the enemy's "ships been attacked by ours, *they could not, in his opinion, have been warped off from the shore;* as it was necessary so to do, "to lay out anchors, to heave them off," and he noticed a remarkable incident, in speaking to the hour in which "the two ships "first went away," namely, that "*the ships differed very much* "*in time, that day,*" (p. 211.) "That the moment, the two ships "quitted their defensive state" which was considerably before 2 o'clock, "the risk was then small:" that he had been on the station before, and had used various means to acquire a knowledge of the soundings; and that he had consulted pilots and charts: that he did not know, that he had made known to the Commander in Chief, that by passing near to the Boyart, the ships might have gone in; because the Chart shewed it.

The evidence of Captain Malcolm was, for the most part, given upon a very well conceived cross-examination, and re-cross-examination, under which he was supported by his fortitude and his truth, which were both equally and essentially necessary auxiliaries: or confusion, and its attendant, contradiction, must have been the inevitable consequence. An independent mind, however, on the one hand, and conscious rectitude on the other, preserved his consistency, and enabled him to pass the ordeal in safety. If we were to notice any misconception, in the course of his evidence, we should add, it is surprizing that he steered so clear of error. As it stands, it is extremely interesting, and maintains the charge, both in the neglect and delay, that is objected to the conduct of Lord Gambier, not by assertion merely; but by reasoning founded upon positive fact. It does equal honour to Captain Malcolm's prudence and to his bravery: he was sensible of the risk, that would have attended an attack upon the enemy; but he was equally sensible of what was due to the honour of his country, when he said, "had it appeared to me, "that there was no other chance of destroying those ships, but "by such an attack, I certainly think it ought to have been "made."

CAPTAIN BROUGHTON.

Captain Broughton had previously been in Basque Roads, under Admiral Sir Richard Keates; at which time, he was very actively employed against the enemy; and his remarks shew, that his exertions to acquire information, were directed by an enlightened understanding.

He stated the fortifications of Aix, to be very different to what they were, when he had formerly examined them; and conceived, the enemy were repairing the works, from the quantity of rubbish, that was thrown up: he thought, from such comparison, that the fortification was not so strong, as they had been supposed; and he reported accordingly, to Lord Gambier: (p. 218) that he made such report on " the first of April;" and that the rubbish, he saw, was not for the purpose of constructing new works, but was the remains of the old works, that had been taken down. (p. 219).

Q. *By the President.* " From the first attack, on the ships " of the enemy, on the evening of the 11th of April, to the time " of your leaving Basque Roads, (according to your judgment), " was every thing done, that could be done, to effect the de- " struction of the enemy's ships?"—*A.* " I think it would have " been more advantageous, if the line of battle ships, frigates, " and small vessels had gone in, at half flood, which I take to be " about 11 o'clock, or between 11 and 12."

Q. " Were the two line of battle ships remaining at anchor, " in Aix roads?"—*A.* " Yes, they were: this memorandum was " written at the time, to which, I suppose, there is no objection " to my referring: there were nine sail on shore, with the " frigates; the Rear Admiral and Commodore remained at their " anchorage."

Q. " Did you take notice of the position of the French *three* " *decker*, when she was on shore?"—*A.* " Yes, I did."

Q. " At what time did the two ships, that remained at anchor, " remove to the entrance of the Charante?"—*A.* " I cannot " speak positively, as to time; but it was soon after noon, that

" the French Admiral, and two more, got off, and moved towards " the Charante.—I beg pardon: I was thinking of the ships, " that were on shore: the two ships at anchor went first." On a further question, as to the time in which he thought the ships ought to have gone in: he thus corrected himself—" I would rather " say 11 and 12 o'clock, and which, in my judgment, was the " most advantageous." (p. 220) That " he conceived the enemy " partly panic-struck; and, on the appearance of a force coming " in, might have been induced to cut their cables, and try to " make their escape up the river."

Questioned upon the supposition, that they might not have been panic-struck?—He answered, that, in that case, " a ship or " two, might have been placed against the batteries, to take off " their fire and silence them;" and that he had, early in the morning, mentioned to Sir Harry Neale, when the signal was made for all Captains, that they were attackable. In the event of injury to our ships, he pointed out, " with the wind as it was," a secure anchorage, "particularly where the Aigle afterwards lay," out of the range of shot and shell; and " in thirty or forty feet " water." (p. 221) He was then cross-questioned on the possibility, that the batteries might not have been silenced; and our ships obliged to retire.

President. " I say, there being a necessity to retire from the " batteries; there could not be a necessity for retiring, if they " were silenced?"—*A.* " It would depend upon circumstances. " There would be slack water about two o'clock, or between " two and three, (it cannot be supposed that the action would " be over in a moment), with the wind moderate, for the wind " was moderating fast, at that time: in the morning they would " be able to reach that anchorage, in my opinion."

Q. " In a crippled state?"—*A.* " Yes, in a crippled state: I " only speak, as to the conviction in my mind, of the possibility " of silencing the batteries—not going to the above conse- " quences."

This, however, did not satisfy the President, and he proceeded.

Q. " Are we to understand then, that you would have recom-
" mended the measure of sending ships in, against the batteries in
" the Isle d'Aix, upon a presumption, that the batteries must
" be silenced; without adverting to what would befall
" the ships, in case they should not be silenced? — *A.*
" I did not give it that consideration, at the time: I only
" speak to my opinion, that I conceived it was practicable to
" acquire that anchorage, although disabled; and I heard my
" Lord Gambier, the same morning, state, it had been his intention
" to have gone against the batteries, I now speak of, with the
" Caledonia and some other ship; but, as the enemy were on
" shore, he did not think it necessary to run any unnecessary
" risk of the fleet; when the object of their destruction seemed
" to be already obtained." (p. 222).

Such an answer, anyone would have supposed, was sufficient to have roused the feelings of the Court, and opened their eyes towards the groundless insinuations, and assertions of Lord Gambier, relative to his anxious desire, to attack the enemy; and to the obstacles that opposed him. It clearly, positively, and decidedly shewed, that his Lordship, not only never intended to attack the enemy, but, that he had actually determined to the contrary; perfectly satisfied, that the object of their destruction seemed to be already obtained. The Court, however, did not appear to be affected by it, in the slightest degree; but went on with the cross-examination of Captain Broughton, in the most rigid manner, as to the French Charts, of which Captain Broughton spoke in high praise; and, at length, came to a grand point, connected with the Chart, fashioned by Mr. Stokes.

Q. " Do you know, that from the anchorage in Aix roads, to
" the anchorage you have just now described, there is any shoaler
" water, between the Boyart and the Palles Shoal; I mean in
" the entrance to this anchorage, that there is a bar goes across?"
—*A.* " No; I do not know any thing of it, whether there is or
" not. I sounded from the wreck of the Varsovie, to that
" anchorage, and found no shoal there."

President. " That is not the place. *It is marked in some of*

" *the Charts, that between the Boyart and the tail of the Palles,* " *there is a bar ?—A.* " I sounded, as I came in from the fleet; " but I did not find out any bar." (p. 223).

The former witnesses, who had been examined on this important subject, had deposed indirectly, from opinion or hearsay: nay, Mr. Stokes, himself, would not venture to touch on it positively; he rather chose to refer the Court to some MSS. Chart never put into evidence, and never afterwards heard of; but here we have the positive testimony of a man, who obtained his information by actual soundings: one whose professional researches armed him at all points. " I sounded," says he, " from the wreck of the Varsovie to that anchorage; and found " no shoal." " That," said the President, " is not the place. It is " marked in SOME OF THE CHARTS, that between the Boyart " and the Palles there is a bar." Captain Broughton had sounded there also; but " did not find out any bar." The least curious person will naturally ask: what Charts are those, on which such a bar is marked? Why did not the President produce, or, at least, name them? Why did he not produce to Captain Broughton, Mr. Stoke's famous Chart, on which, and which only, this *imaginary bar*, is marked? he shewed it to others; and to some of them dictated, that they must speak to particular points of it. (p. 162). Why, then, withhold it from Captain Broughton: one who had evinced superior intelligence, and a well founded information? The reason, as it appears to us, is very obvious; but if our conception should be erroneous, the public will penetrate it, and in their decision upon it, render justice, where justice shall be due.

The Court asked Captain Broughton " if he would have " attacked the enemy, moored in two close and compact lines:" (p. 223) which was, certainly, an extraordinary and altogether a superfluous question. But whatever might have been its object, Captain Broughton shewed by his answer; that although brave and enterprizing, he was governed by prudence and discretion: his answer was " Most certainly not." To other questions he said, that, in his opinion, two ships would have been sufficient, to silence the batteries of Aix; and that five or six sail of the line, of the least draft of water, should have been sent in to the attack of the enemy's ships.

The evidence of Captain Broughton was, throughout the whole of his examination, clear, distinct, and decided. An examination, and cross-examination, that was, in every respect, as severe and close, as that of Captains Seymour, and Malcolm; and his conduct under it was at once, manly and respectful, bold and decorous. Those who shall peruse it, for we have given only passages from it, will find in it the traits of a noble daring spirit, such as characterises the true sailor; and of that sound discriminating judgment, which marks the excellent officer, and the cultivated man.

It is remarkable, although not extraordinary, that Lord Gambier should not have offered some cross-questions to Captain Broughton, on that very important part of his deposition, in which he shewed, that his Lordship, NEVER INTENDED ANY ATTACK UPON THE ENEMY, ON THE 12th OF APRIL. But when he was asked by the President, if he had any question, he said "No: " I have *no question to ask Captain Broughton: I could wish,* " *Captain Kerr might be questioned, as to his opinion of the* " *effect of the batteries, on the Isle of Aix, as he passed out, in* " *the Revenge!!*" Captain Kerr was, for the fourth time, called in accordingly, to invalidate the testimony of Captain Broughton: but he failed.

Mr. HOCKINGS, Signal Lieutenant of the Caledonia.

This Witness delivered to the Court, the Signal Log of the Caledonia, and deposed, that the contents were written by the Mate of the Signals, UNDER HIS INSPECTION; and that they were TRUE, to the *best of his knowledge and belief.* (p. 21.) On his second examination, however, he shewed, that it could not have been written under his inspection: of course he could not have had any knowledge of the certainty, or uncertainty of its contents; and as to his belief, so founded, we shall leave it to its own miserable situation.

Q. by Admiral Young. " Are you Signal Lieutenant of the " Caledonia?"—*A.* " Yes, I am."

Q. " You will then be able to speak to ALL the signals, that " were made by the Imperieuse, *on the morning of the 12th?*" *A.* " YES, I CAN."

Q. " Can you say *positively*, that the telegraphic communica- " tion mentioned, was, HALF the fleet is sufficient to destroy the " enemy. I particularly mean to press the word HALF, upon " your mind?"—*A.* " I cannot answer as to *that signal;* be- " cause I was coming on board the Caledonia, from the Impe- " rieuse, and was not there until seven o'clock; and the signal " was made at five. I had been in one of the fire-ships." (p. 176.)

On his third examination, for even Mr. Hockings was examined four times, he was questioned by Lord Gambier.—" Do " you know, on what day the Regulus, which was on shore, " under the town of Fouras, got off and went up the Charante?" *A.* " It appears on the Log Book, that at day-light, on the 29th, " the enemy's two-decked ship got off, and removed to the " *Westward.*" It ought to have been Eastward.

Having previously remarked, in the course of these Notes, upon this answer, and in doing so, compared Mr. Hockings with

Mr. Wilkinson, we shall merely notice, that we have here a proof, that the contents of the Signal Log of the Caledonia, were not so immaculate, as Lord Gambier had endeavoured to prevail on the Court to believe.

The error is certainly of a trifling nature, and became known by an accident; if the Log had been annexed to the Minutes, we might have been enabled, to point out errors of greater magnitude, and of infinitely more consequence. But his Lordship, at least the Editor of those Minutes, has carefully provided against detection by suppressing it, and every other, except those of Lord Cochrane and his Master. Of the unfairness of such conduct, we have a just right to complain; and we repeat, that the whole of the Logs should have been published, or no one; and have we not also a right to assume, that the suppressed Logs, have been so withheld, on the conviction, that they bore internal evidence in support of the Charge? If not: why were they not produced; or why were the Logs of Lord Cochrane, and his Master, detached from all the rest? Was it not in the hope of inducing the public, to draw conclusions unfavourable to his Lordship? Is this the correct mode of dealing out evidence? Did not Lord Gambier, or the Editor, know, that to give one part of a piece of evidence, and keep back the other, is both unfair and unjust? Have not the public an equal and indisputable right, to have both sides of the question submitted to their judgment? What decision can be given upon a partial statement of facts? And is not Lord Cochrane's character equally dear, in the consideration of the public, as that of Lord Gambier?

Mr. Hockings was further questioned by Admiral Young:—
" Did the Imperieuse, at any time after you returned on board
" the Caledonia, inform the Commander in Chief, by signal, that
" any smaller part of the fleet, than one half, could destroy the
" enemy?"—*A.* " *I do not recollect!*" (p. 176.)

Yet this is the person, who told the Court, without any hesitation, and most positively, that he could speak to ALL the signals, that were made by the Imperieuse, on the morning of the 12th; and here is a second instance in which he has contradicted that assertion. On the first occasion he attempted an excuse—" he was out of the ship," which was no excuse at all: here, however, he was in the ship; but then his recollection failed him. So that whether in the ship or out of her, the case was not varied; and the truth is, he knew nothing of the fact, of which he had deposed he knew every thing.

Upon the examination of Mr. Hockings, although very short, notwithstanding he was often called upon, an opportunity was afforded to the Court, to manifest their indulgent attention and particular regard towards Lord Gambier; and they embraced it with apparent gratification, as the following occurrence will evince. Finding that Mr. Hockings could only speak from the Log, as to the time, that the Regulus, which was on shore, under Fouras, got off and went up the Charante, Lord Gambier, without a cause assigned, or reason given, and with an eagerness that must have surprised every one, thus addressed the Court: " I " only beg to remark to the Court, that it appears by the evidence " of Captain Woolf, who commanded the squadron upon that " service, that he received from me all the assistance he required, " for carrying it on." The President very courteously observed, " that is in the perfect recollection of the Court. It was not " upon that ground, that the Court wished to see Lieutenant " Hockings." (p. 184.)

What must have been passing in his Lordship's mind at the moment, when he could thus fly from the object he was pursuing, to one of a nature altogether foreign, may perhaps be imagined. We leave the conjecture, together with the feelings of his Lordship, in the strong colourings they received, from such an extraordinary appeal to the Court, and the cheering sympathy shewn by the Court on the occasion, to the judgment of a discerning public. We admit that Captain Woolf did depose as quoted by his Lordship; but when did he command the in-shore squadron? When there was, according to his Lordship's own statement, no possibility of carrying on any further operations against the enemy. But the answer of Captain Woolf was given to a general question, that embraced the whole of Lord Gambier's conduct, " from the first attack of the enemy's ships,

P P

„ to the final cessation of hostilities against them:" (p. 87) and on that consideration, the Court appeared to receive it.—Connected with the ignorance of Mr. Hockings, it is inexplicable.—We have said, that Captain Woolf did not command the in-shore squadron until the business to which he was interrogated had terminated; we will, however, for the sake of argument, suppose it otherwise, and that he commanded the in-shore squadron on the 11th and 12th of April. What then? What would such an answer establish? Nothing. Captain Woolf has not stated even, that he ever made any application for assistance: nor does it appear that any was ever rendered to him: or that in the nature of things he could have required any; and, therefore, his statement, that "every application he made to his "Lordship, to effect the destruction of the enemy, was always "complied with," was saying nothing. Again we will suppose, that he had asked and received assistance; still the circumstance does not furnish any argument, that such assistance was other than trifling, or that Lord Gambier had been equally attentive to the general claims of the service, which were "to effect the "destruction of the enemy." But as we have above remarked, the necessity, that called for any such assistance could only have existed, after the enemy's ships had moved beyond our reach: after the grand scene of the 12th had passed away—the exhilirating scene, which held out to our exertions the capture of the whole, or the greatest part of them. What then, had the Court to carry on their perfect recollection, as arising out of such an answer, so inefficient and indefinite; in fact, so inapplicable, vague, and nugatory, referring to a period so unworthy of notice: or what could have induced his Lordship to have pressed it upon them with so much impassioned anxiety. It was a straw, at which no man, unless in the last stage of despair, would ever think of grasping. And yet, if we are to form our opinion on the manner in which the President expressed himself, the Court regarded this shadow of an equivocal circumstance as a matter of importance in favour of Lord Gambier—"That is in the "perfect recollection of the Court." If the Court, indeed judged by comparison, they were not very far wrong, in attaching consequence to it; as it is nearly as essential to Lord Gambier's Defence, as any part of the testimony, of any other witness produced in support of it.

We shall here close our Notes on the examination of Lord Gambier's witnesses; submitting, that the evidence of Captains Seymour, Malcolm and Broughton, is in corroboration of the testimony, delivered by Lord Cochrane, and of each other: somewhat aided by the evidence of Captain Newcomb: so that by the concurrent testimony of five witnesses, the charge of neglect and delay is fully established. The evidence of Captain Broughton in the most material part, is irrefragable: as it is fortified by the authority of Lord Gambier, himself, and demonstrates, that the defence set up by his Lordship, in justification of that neglect and delay, was totally without foundation; he having declared, on seeing the ships on shore, as Captain Broughton has positively deposed, that he would not attempt any thing against them. "I "heard," says Captain Broughton, "my Lord Gambier, the "same morning state, it HAD BEEN his intention to have gone "against the batteries, with the Caledonia and some other ship; "but as the enemy were on shore, *he did not think it necessary* "TO RUN ANY UNNECESSARY RISK OF THE FLEET, *when* "*the object of their destruction* SEEMED TO BE ALREADY "OBTAINED." Captain Broughton's evidence gives also, another fact of great importance; because it proves, that the BAR, marked in Mr. Stokes's, otherwise falsified Chart, was an invention, for the purpose of shewing, the impracticability of our ships retiring to the back of the Palles; where, according to the same Chart, there is good anchorage.

We shall now say a few words on the subject of the Charts, delivered to the Court by Lord Cochrane, intended by his Lordship to shew the soundings* in the roads of Aix, and the position

* These were laid down in the printed Chart, of which the sketches, containing the position of the enemy, were copies; but without the soundings marked on them.

of the enemy's ships, at different interesting periods. These have been rashly called fabrications, by those who knew nothing of them, or were determined by prejudice to calumniate them, and who have insinuated, that they were framed to mislead the Court: than which, nothing can be more inconsistent, absurd and untrue. We saw them in the hands of Lord Cochrane. They were *fac similes* of the Neptune François, and the printed original accompanied them; the whole were, however, refused by the Court, who said they were not evidence: and therefore, no one can possibly say of what nature or description they were; and consequently, every assertion on the subject, must be unfounded, and equally illiberal as unjust. When Lord Cochrane delivered in the Charts above-mentioned, namely, the printed Chart, and the copies, scarcely any notice was taken: but shortly afterwards, the following examination and discussion took place.

President. " I think your Lordship said, just now, that you " thought there was water enough for ships, of any draft, at any " time of the tide?"—*A.* " Yes."

Q. " Have you an authenticated chart, or any evidence which " can be produced, to shew, that there is actually such a depth of " water?"—*A.* " *It was actually from the soundings we had, in* " *going in*, provided the tide does not fall more than 12 feet, " which I am not aware of; I do not think it falls more than that; " I studied this Chart some days before. The tide appears, by " the French Chart, to flow at three hours twenty minutes, full " moon: the rise and fall of the tide is, I understand, from 10 to " 12 feet: it is so mentioned in the French Chart. I have no " other means of judging."

Judge Advocate. " This Chart is not evidence before the " Court, BECAUSE HIS LORDSHIP CANNOT PROVE IT IS " ACCURATE."—*President.* " No; *it is nothing more, than to* " *shew upon what grounds* his Lordship forms his opinion of " THE RISE AND FALL OF THE TIDE*." (p. 35.)

* Yet Mr. Stokes's Chart was readily received as evidence, without any proof whatever. We make this assertion upon the best possible grounds: the statement of Mr. Stokes, when laying his Chart before the Court. (p. 23) We have referred to it in another part of our Notes: and quoted the passages that were applicable.

In another part of his Lordship's examination, the President resumed the subject.

President. I beg permission of the Court, to ask one or two questions. *Q.* " When did your Lordship first discover, that in " the inner road of Aix, or of Basque, there was anchorage suffi- " ciently capacious, to contain six sail of the line to ride, without " being in range of shot or shell?"—*A.* " I had been in possession " of the French Charts, *which I have not found to be defective,* " *in any material point,* for a period of years; and from those " Charts, I had, at all times, drawn my conclusions, with respect to " the depth of the water, or other circumstances, which relate to " navigation upon that enemy's coast."

President. " That coast of the enemy, I suppose you mean?" —*A.* " I refer to the French coast: The Spanish Charts also, are " exceedingly good: I always go by them, and on them, as in this " case, and in all others, I placed my dependance. I went in: " on my way I found them correct. *I knew by the Chart,* that " when in pursuit of the Calcutta, *I was to find a bank;* I FOUND " IT, and anchored upon it, and this I did, knowing what I was " about.

Admiral Young. " *Was the bank the anchorage?*"—*A.* " I " could not get so close, as I was desirous of going."

Q. " When did you discover that there was this anchorage in " deep water?"—*A* " I have said, that, in going in, *I found the* " SOUNDINGS CORRECT, *in my track, close by the Boyart;* " and that, in fact, I had that CONFIDENCE IN THE CHART, " that I had said to Admiral Keats, when we were off there, " and to Admiral Thornborough, that there could be no difficulty " in going in there, and destroying the enemy's fleet; and I took " the Chart on board Admiral Thornborough's ship. I was at " that time, that the Plan* went to the Admiralty, for destroying " the French fleet. I will only say, by which it has long appeared " to me, that this anchorage might, if any object was in view, be " taken."

* This appears inserted on the face of the Minutes (p. 18) entitled: " *Situa-* " *tion of the enemy's squadron, under the Isle d'Aix,* (23 *April,* 1807), *with* " *a proposed mode of attack*: and signed, " R. G. KEATS."

President. " In the Chart, that your Lordship consulted, " upon this occasion: are the soundings so marked, as to afford " a space sufficient for six sail of the line, not within range of " shot or shell?"—*A.* " That conviction was upon my mind, " and is upon my mind; but by referring to the Chart, which is " exactly the same as others which have been in my possession: " those soundings are marked, the Court can, by referring thereto, " decide the question.

Q. " When you found, by experience, upon going into Aix " Roads, that the soundings were correctly laid down, in the " Chart you made use of, in which you state you placed great " confidence, and from whence you drew a conclusion, that there " was safe anchorage, for six sail of the line:—Did you make any " communication, of that important fact, to the Commander in " Chief?"—*A.* " The Commander in Chief had the same Charts, " I believe, as I was in possession of, upon which, as I have " already stated, I founded my conclusions, with respect to the " anchorage above alluded to; HE had also French Pilots on " board, upon whose reports, from previous experience I knew " the Commander in Chief to rely, above all other authority. " In reconnoitring the fleet, the first day, when so near, as " to induce the enemy to open a fire from, almost his whole " line, I reported to the Commander in Chief, the ruinous state " of the Isle d'Aix: it having the inner fortifications com- " pletely blown up and destroyed, which I not only ascertained " from the deck, WITH PERFECT PRECISION, as to the side " towards us; but also, as to the *opposite side*, from one of the " tops of the ships. There were only thirteen guns mounted." (p. 58).

Admiral Young. " Will you consider, my Lord Cochrane, be- " fore you go on, how far this is relevant?"—*Lord Cochrane.* " I am only going to say, the impression which I knew was upon " his Lordship's mind: *notwithstanding I vouched for these* " *facts with my own eyes;* and notwithstanding these French " pilots had not been there, for several years. There were only " thirteen guns mounted on that side, on which I had formerly " seen, to the best of my recollection, about fifty. In making " these observations to his Lordship, for his information, he "stated his *perfect reliance* upon the opinion *of the pilots,* and "assured me, that the Isle d'Aix was exceedingly strong; and "that (I think) it had three tier of guns mounted, towards the "shipping. I then observed to his Lordship, that the circum- "stances I had related, FELL WITHIN MY OWN OBSERVA- "TION, *which did not alter his Lordship's opinion!!* I noticed "also the *little confidence,* which was to be placed in *these pilots;* "and said to his Lordship, as well as to Sir Harry Neale, that I "never yet had a pilot."

Judge Advocate. "Can this relate to the *question which is* "*asked?—Lord Cochrane.* "Yes; I conceive so, AS MY REA- "SON FOR NOT COMMUNICATING TO HIS LORDSHIP."

President. "Lord Cochrane states this as his reason for not "taking a particular line of conduct?"—*Lord Cochrane.* "I have "felt that if I had answered YES, or NO, to all the questions "which have been put to me, I ought to be hung; and that if a "Court Martial was held upon me, and only the answers YES, "or NO, appeared to those questions; I should be hung for "them."

Judge Advocate. "I believe nobody has desired your Lord- "ship to answer merely yes or no?"—*Lord Cochrane.* "I an- "swered, that I never yet knew a pilot, particularly a French "pilot, WHO DID NOT FIND A SHOAL WHEREVER THERE "WAS A GUN; and his Lordship, on the day of my leaving "Basque Roads, which was the 16th, or the 15th, still continued "of the same opinion, with respect to the Isle d'Aix; notwith- "standing my assurances then, when I had had full time to "make my observations upon every part of it. And as the "whole of the frigates, with the exception of the Pallas, had "withdrawn; and as it was evident, to the knowledge of his "Lordship, as well as to the knowledge of every one of those "officers, that those frigates might have continued, where the "Imperieuse and Pallas then were; I held their being placed in "that situation, a matter for his Lordship's decision. I naturally "conceived, that as even these were not ordered to return (I con- "ceived in my own mind, for I did not express it to any body), "that as those were not ordered back again, his Lordship did "not require any information, of which he was not possessed."

Admiral Young. "It should seem, from a part of your an-

"swer, that your soundings, to discover the position for six sail "of the line, was after the burning of the enemy's ships?"—*A.* "By the soundings which I made, I was *only confirmed in* "*my opinion, of the* correctness of the French Charts; ours are "abominable, and not fit to be delivered out."

With the minute information, thus furnished, it might be imagined, that the Court would have been tolerably well satisfied with the Charts, delivered by his Lordship; and that the result of the following examination, would have fixed the judgment in their favour.

Admiral Sutton. "Are the Charts produced in Court by your "Lordship, namely, No. 2, and No. 3, copied, or taken from "the Chart No. 1, which your Lordship produced in Court?"—*A.* "They were copied by a pencil, and afterwards a pen passed "over, to make black lines."

Q. "From No. 1.?"—*A.* "Yes; from No. 1. The soundings are not marked upon *this;* it was merely to shew the po-"sitions of the fleets; there was a large sheet of black paper put "between, and it was scratched over."

Q. "Do you mean by black paper, oiled paper?"—*A.* "I do "not know, it is such paper as they have for copying letters."

Q. "Are these two Charts a fac simile of No. 1.?"—*A.* "They were taken from that, by a person whom I paid for the "purpose: his name I do not recollect; but he is a common "chart-drawer in London; and I marked the positions of the "French ships upon it when he had done."

Q. "Did he do that in your presence *?"—*A.* "He did some "of it, at the table with me; and he took one home with him. "I have one, which he sent down to me, by the mail, drawn "from a copy, which he took himself; but *these are two,* which "he did *actually take from the Chart itself.* I put in the po-"sitions of the French ships (which ships were, at the hour men-"tioned on these Charts, in the positions in which they appear)

* Whence could have arisen the necessity of questions of such description. The Court had the original printed Chart before them, and by placing the copies on it, it would in a moment have been discovered whether they did, or did not correspond together.

" as nearly as it was possible to do it; and the British fleet was " taken, as it appeared from the Imperieuse, when anchored at " the end of the Boyart Shoal, about half past 11 o'clock on " the morning of the 12th."

Q. " Are the representations of the ships marked by your " Lordship; or by the person who made the Chart?"—*A.* " Po- " SITIVELY they were MARKED BY MYSELF: he had nothing " to do with it: they were never seen by any body, who could " take advantage of inserting any marks; they were seen by " none, except those in whom I could place the most implicit " confidence. The frigates, which appeared to be near the Im- " perieuse, and close to the Boyart, had weighed with the Impe- " rieuse in the morning, and were, at that hour, with the fleet." (p. 75.)

Q. " There being no scale upon either of these copied Charts, " nor no marginal indication of degree: by what scale or rule " did your Lordship place the figures of the ships, as represented " here?"—*A.* " By the scale of the Chart, of which they are " copies, which is the same in size, and now before the Court, " marked No. 1.; the distance of the brigs from the Impe- " rieuse, I measured by the flight of shot; and I believe it to " be nearly correct. The distance of the Calcutta, Varsovie, " and Aquilon, was ascertained by the point blank range; our " shot did not reach the Tonnere."

Admiral Sutton. " I only asked your Lordship, by what rule " or scale it was done; I do not wish to go further, than the " question I put, and that is answered?"—*Lord Cochrane.* " I " wish to shew the mode, in which I measured the distance; and " what I measured by the eye."

Admiral Sutton. " Certainly, if you think it will explain it." —*Lord Cochrane.* " Our shot did not reach the Tonnere: which " the enemy kindled themselves: the three-decker was towards " the North East, a little further off: she having warped over by " hawsers, and got into that position, by the force of sail and " other means; for she had a parcel of boats a-head of her " pulling her along, perhaps she might have hawsers also. " When I say the Aquilon was within point blank range, she " might be a little otherwise, but I remember to have brought

" the horizon above our guns: the people were firing right " over."

Admiral Young. "There are references, but there are no " marks?"—*Lord Cochrane*. "I had some doubt, as to the pro- " priety of laying them at all, before the Court, and I have not " marked them; there is one marked, I think, and the refer- " ences would be the same to both."

President. "There are several references there, without any " mark to shew to what they apply?"—[*Lord Cochrane made the marks upon the Charts.*]—*Lord Cochrane*. "I did not intend " that these Charts should represent the soundings at all *."

President. "No, so we understand, merely as outlines, to " mark the positions." (p. 76.)

We have said, it might be imagined, that the result of this examination, coupled with that which preceded it, would have decided the Court in favour of the Charts, introduced by Lord Cochrane, and of course, that they would have been allowed to stand as evidence, as far so they went, and for the object they had in view; but that was not the case. They were thrown aside, on the close of his Lordship's examination, and never more brought forward. Mr. Stokes's Chart, the outlines of which were said to have been taken from the Neptune Françoise, that was never produced: the distance between the sands, from a pretended MSS Chart, that never made its appearance; and the position of the British and French fleets, from the information of two different persons, was received as evidence, and with all solemnity offered by the Court to the witnesses, as an authenticated document worthy of the highest credit.

As a contrast, and a very striking one it is, we will look at the foundation on which Lord Cochrane's Charts rested. In the first place a *printed Chart*, the work of the ablest men in France, framed for the use and security of the French navy, and containing all the soundings, the correctness of which, Lord Cochrane as-

* His Lordship had here reference to the printed Chart, which accompanied the copies taken from it. The former having the soundings marked upon it, of course they were omitted in the latter, which were merely to shew the positions of the enemy's fleet.]

serted, he had proved by experience: and, secondly, two copies *from that printed Chart*, on which his Lordship had marked, with his own hands, from his *own personal observations*, the several positions of the enemy's ships on the 12th of April—observations that were not made at several miles distance, "partly from the mizen-top "of the Caledonia, and from an Officer," as was the case with Mr. Stokes; but upon the very spot, in which his Lordship continued from the 11th, until the 13th: not only an anxious eye witness; but a zealous and conspicuous actor.

Upon the whole, "under all the circumstances of the case," the conduct of the Court, in rejecting the Charts delivered by his Lordship, and at the same time, receiving the Chart, that was invented and fashioned by Mr. Stokes, is extraordinary: it is unaccountable; it is incomprehensible!! Why did they not shew Lord Cochrane's Charts to the witnesses, at the time they exhibited Mr. Stokes's, and call upon each of them to say: which was the most correct, in laying down the position of the enemy's fleet, on the memorable 12th of April? And with respect to the situation of the shoals, and soundings: why did they not produce the printed Chart? They would not then, have had occasion to go so much into examination, relative to the "*shoal or* "*bar*," with which Mr. Stokes has, so artfully and fallaciously, united the Boyart with the Pallés Shoal! "A bank or bar," however, that the testimony of Captain Broughton has completely sunk and destroyed; and their non-existence is further demonstrated by the fact of the ships, passing between those shoals, on the afternoon of the 12th. We know, that the public will give their attention to matters of so much serious consequence; and we are persuaded, that they will not allow them to pass without the reprobation, they shall be found to merit.

In the course we have pursued, with the view we have taken of the Minutes, of the Court Martial, we have had very little recourse to Lord Cochrane's deposition: we rather chose to rest, principally, upon the witnesses produced by Lord Gambier; and we trust, that their testimony has amply supported Lord Cochrane's evidence, and fully established the charge. We heartily wish, that we could have included, in these Notes, the whole of his Lordship's examination: that the public might form their judgment upon the very harsh and severe treatment, his Lordship experienced from the Court; and also upon the conduct, that the Court and Judge Advocate observed towards him. But it was considered, that to have given his Lordship's examination, and excluded that of others, would have been acting upon the principle we condemned, when speaking of the annexation of Lord Cochrane and his Master's Logs to the printed Minutes, which insinuated that those only were incorrect, and the keeping back of all the others, which it was asserted were, to use the words of the President, as complete as any thing could be, in every respect *. (p. 29.) Unfortunately, however, Mr. Hockings, by an accident shewed, that the Log of the Caledonia was erroneous, the very Log regarding which the President had bestowed the panegyric, we have just noticed: and Admiral Stopford acknowledged that the entries in the Log of the Cæsar were not made correctly. (p. 71.)

There is yet one other point which we shall retouch, as Lord Gambier has strenuously endeavoured to establish it: certainly

* This was an extraordinary assertion, on the part of the President, and such as he could not, by any possibility have known, of his own knowledge: and such as we have shewn, by the deposition of the signal Lieutenant, was unfounded in fact.—What could have induced the President, thus to travel out of the path, traced for him, we shall not pretend to say; but we may observe, that such an eulogium, by such authority, must have impressed the world with high ideas, of the perfection of a thing, that was afterwards proved to be erroneous. As connected with this subject, we offer the following conversation, between the Court, the Judge Advocate, and the Master of the Cæsar.

Judge Advocate. " The signal Lieutenant of the Cæsar, is not here.

President. " No, but I believe it will be found, that the signals are entered " in the ship's Log."

A. " No: that custom has not been followed, in the time of Sir Richard " Strachan; nor has it, I believe, in Rear Admiral Stopford's command: they " are examined by the signal officer."

Judge Advocate. " You do not consider it to be material, to produce the " signal Log?"

President. " Is there any person to verify it?"

Judge Advocate. " No: I do not apprehend Rear Admiral Stopford, can " speak to every signal, which is inserted."

President. " The *Caledonia's* own signal Log, is *as complete* as any thing " can be, IN EVERY RESPECT."

Judge Advocate. " Then we will proceed to the Beagle."

not to his own justification; but with every appearance of intention, to injure Lord Cochrane. We allude to the explosion vessels and fire ships, on the night of the 11th. The former, Lord Gambier says, were, under Lord Cochrane's immediate direction, to precede the fireships in the attack; and that their explosion was *to point the proper time, for the officers commanding the latter, to set fire to their respective vessels,* (p. 123.) "The "situation in which, and the time when, those vessels blew up, "proved prejudicial to the enterprize in several respects. Their "premature explosion, contrary to the expressed intentions of "Lord Cochrane, that they should blow up in the midst of the "enemy's boats, to deter them from towing off our fire ships, in "their approach, served as a warning to the enemy, whose ships "were observed, instantly, to shew lights; and several of the offi-"cers, who commanded the fire ships, *not doubting*, that the ex-"plosion had taken place, *near to the enemy's fleet*, steered their "ships, and set them on fire accordingly; by which means, seve-"ral were in flames, at a greater distance from the enemy, than "was intended, *and so as to endanger our advanced frigates.* "In fact, had not Captain Wooldridge, and some of the other "officers, wholly disregarding the explosion, taken their fireships "in a proper direction for the enemy, it is more than probable, "that none of them would have produced any effect whatever, "on the enemy's fleet.

By these, and other averments and insinuations, Lord Gambier has endeavoured to make it appear, that the officers commanding fire ships, were to look to the explosion vessels *for the signals, by which to kindle their vessels;* and that owing to the premature explosion of the former, was to be ascribed the failure of the latter.—On this ground his Lordship entered into, rather, a singular examination of Admiral Stopford: he also examined, Mr. Fairfax, Captain Woolf and others: at once to shew, that the whole blame of failure, on the night of the 11th, originated with the explosion vessels; and that the officers, commanding the fire ships, who were to be guided by them, were consequently without blame and deserving every praise.—But, as we have already remarked upon such his Lordship's purposes, and noticed the conduct of the fire ships, we will not, now, go any further into the subject. Our present object is to demonstrate, that the fire ships were never intended to be governed by the explosion vessels, in any manner whatever; and that they were furnished with Orders, and particular Instructions, upon which they were to act, altogether independent of every other consideration or circumstance. In aid of this important proposition, we give the following General Orders.

" *Caledonia, Basque Roads, April* 11, 1809.

" The fire ships are to proceed to the attack, the ensuing " night. The exploding vessels *will close with the Imperieuse.* " The fire vessels will move from their anchors, at half past " seven o'clock. *In running in, they are to leave the two lights* " *of equal height (which will be shewn, on board a* VESSEL, " PLACED FOR THAT PURPOSE, *on the starboard hand; and* " *to leave the two lights perpendicular (which will also be* " *shewn, on board* ANOTHER VESSEL, PLACED FOR THAT PUR" POSE) *on the larboard hand.*

" *The Frigates, &c. which are to protect and receive the* " *officers and crews of the fire ships, will shew four lights per-* " *pendicular;* and the *Imperieuse will probably anchor near* " *the Boyart, and shew five lights perpendicularly.*

" If the wind should shift, before the fire ships proceed to the " attack, or from other circumstances it should be postponed, the " *Caledonia*, or the *Imperieuse*, will fire a gun and shew three " lights in a perpendicular position."

(Signed) " GAMBIER."

To the respective Captains, &c. &c. &c. [vide Min. 113.]

We will not stop here, to draw a comparison, between Lord Gambier's declarations in his written Defence, and his General Orders, issued to the fleet, until we shall have shewn, that, in addition to those Orders, each officer, commanding a fire ship, was furnished with Instructions, that completed the arrangement, and left him dependent only, upon his own discretionary judgment. They run thus.—" The vessels are to be divided into three divi-

" sions; preceded by three vessels to explode. The headmost " vessel, of each division, to be under the charge of a Comman- " der, or senior Lieutenant. The three divisions to be each about " half a mile apart: preceded by the vessels to explode. The " fuzes to be fixed, of two lengths; the longest on the starboard " side: the shortest on the larboard side; in order to be used " singly, as occasion may require. To fire the starboard fuze, " a port fire will be the signal. If the short fuze, a lanthorn hoisted " by the senior officer of each division, of the fire ships. The " of the ISLE OF AIX TO BEAR AT " LEAST, BEFORE THE TRAINS ARE FIRED; and the fire " ships, *to* BE IN THE HAWSE OF THE WESTERNMOST " FRENCH SHIP."

These Instructions were delivered to each officer, in charge of a fire ship, on board the Caledonia; and are what Lord Gambier alludes to when he says, in his Letter to the Secretary of the Admiralty:—" These preparations were completed on the 11th " ult. at night: and having previously called on board the Cale- " donia, the Commanders and Lieutenants, who had volunteered " their services, and who had been appointed, by me, to com- " mand fire vessels, I furnished them with *full instructions for* " *their proceedings*, in the attack, according to Lord Cochrane's " plan."—Lord Gambier was perfectly well acquainted with every one of those facts. How then could he venture, when speaking of the explosion vessels, to assert, what he has no where attempted to prove, that their explosion was *to point out the proper time, for the officers, commanding the fire ships, to set fire to their respective vessels.* (p. 123.) Is there, in his Lordship's General Orders, or in the Instructions connected with them, a single sentence denoting, that the explosion vessels were, in any manner, to direct or influence those officers, as to the time when they should fire their vessels? His Lordship's General Orders together with his Instructions, as to the only signals, that were deemed necessary, or to which they were required to give any attention, are in direct contradiction to that assertion.

And his Lordship, in a subsequent part of his written Defence, proves its fallacy. After having stated, that the explosion vessel, exploded prematurely, his Lordship says: "And several of the "officers who commanded fire ships, *not doubting* that the ex-"plosion had taken place near the enemy's fleet, steered their "ships, and set them on fire accordingly: by which means several "were in flames, at a greater distance from the enemy, than was "intended, and so as to endanger our advanced frigates." (p. 124.) This unequivocally shews, that the officers, *in setting fire to their ships,* did not do so, from any assurance, that the explosion was to be *the signal* for the act; but solely, in the exercise of their own discretion, from their own internal impressions.

If the explosion was to have pointed out the proper time for the officers, commanding the fire ships, to set fire to their respective vessels, they had no right to deliberate an instant: his Lordship, however, gives us premises from whence this, and only this, conclusion is to be drawn, namely, that the fire ships were kindled, because the officers commanding them had *no doubt,* that the explosion had taken place near to the enemy's fleet; but that had a *doubt* existed in their minds, upon that point, they would not have set fire to their vessels so early; and consequently, the explosion was not regarded by them, as a signal they were to obey.

If we look into his Lordship's Letters, to the Secretary of the Admiralty, we find a very different cause assigned for the failure. At 8 o'clock, says his Lordship, they proceeded to the attack under a favourable strong wind: "but OWING TO THE DARKNESS "*of the night*, SEVERAL MISTOOK THEIR COURSE AND "FAILED."

Second thoughts are, proverbially, the best; but with his Lordship, they have generally proved the worst. In his public Letter to the Admiralty, when every occurrence was fresh in his recollection, he laid down one fact; and at a remote period he changed it for another, of a different description: in the first instance, he had the best grounded right to be well pleased with the conduct of Lord Cochrane; in the second circumstances had varied, and was all wrath and resentment. The apology which Lord Gambier made, for the officers commanding the fire ships, in his written Defence, and in the course of the examination of his witnesses, can be likened only to the efforts of an extremely zealous, but equally injudicious advocate. Even had the explosion vessel been the signal, as pretended, his Lordship has shewn, that the conduct of the officers, commanding the fire ships, was extremely indiscreet, and very reprehensible; as they actually set fire to their vessels, *in the midst of our own advanced frigates*, so as to endanger them.

Now admitting Mr. Stokes's Chart to be correct in one particular point, and in that only he might have been correct, as might every man in the fleet, we mean the position of the advanced frigates, we shall find on referring to it, that those frigates were, upwards of a mile and a quarter, to windward of the Lyra: and nearly a mile and a half from the explosion, which Mr. Fairfax shews, took place a quarter of a mile, at least, nearer to the enemy. And was this a situation, in which to kindle fire ships, that were to destroy an enemy, who lay nearly two miles and a half from them? Did not those officers calculate the distance? If they did, by what justifiable motive did they set fire to their vessels, at the time stated, and in the midst of our own squadron? Did the "premature explosion" deprive them of the powers of reflection? did it stupefy all their faculties?

If we could suppose, contrary to the truth, that the explosion was actually "to have pointed out the proper time for the officers commanding the fire ships to set fire to their respective vessels;" and that the explosion vessel had, as was intended, blown up in the midst of the enemy's boats (and if their boats had been out), that would have been nearly the case, what would have been the difference: or how would the failure of the ships have been prevented? They were not near enough to take the advantage of the moment; they still would have been fired nearly two miles and an half from the enemy, and in the midst of our advanced frigates; of course the spot in which the explosion took place, was of no manner of consequence: whether in the midst of the enemy's boats, the centre of their fleet, or upon the Pallés Shoal. The officers commanding the fire ships, must, or at least ought to have known, that the enemy's fleet were two miles and an half from them: they must, consequently, have known, that they themselves were to windward of our advanced squadron: and that firing their vessels, in such a situation, endangered all around them, and would effectually frustrate their own purpose. Did they sail in divisions, with a leader, as pointed out by their Instructions? Did they pay any attention to the lights hoisted on board our advanced vessels, as directed by the General Order? Why did not his Lordship call upon some of the officers of those fire ships, upon the subject: those who behaved well, and amongst those, Captain Newcomb? Why did he not, and why did not the Court examine Lord Cochrane, and the officer, and people who were with him, in the explosion vessel?

The fact is, that, by some means, not accountable, several of the officers of the fire ships, lost their presence of mind; and confusion, which then succeeded, " steered their ships, and set fire " to them accordingly." Captain Woolf says, " I hailed five of " them, that came near us. Our own ship was nearly burnt by " two, that were badly managed: five behaved very well, and " one of them was commanded by Captain Newcomb—Lieute-" nant Cookesby, of the Gibraltar, was another, who begged, that " I would keep my eye on him, as he would not fire his vessel, " until amongst them, meaning among the enemy." " I did; " and saw him run on board of a two decked ship of the enemy." (p. 206.) Other two did not fire their vessels until they had passed him, which is at once a proof of their worth; and that they never considered the explosion, as pointing out " the proper time to set " fire to their respective vessels." To those who did behave well, great praise is certainly due; for the service they engaged in, was truly arduous. But Captain Woolf says, there were others, those for whom Lord Gambier has attempted to apologize at the expence of Lord Cochrane, who behaved ill, and had nearly burnt his ship. Admiral Stopford says, " every circumstance was ex-" tremely favourable to the fire ships acting; and therefore, I " took it for granted, that when properly placed, they must ine-" vitably go down upon the enemy's ships," (p. 80.)

In regarding the above facts and circumstances, it appears, that the explosion vessels were intended only, as Lord Gambier in one part of his Defence has correctly stated, " to deter " the enemy's boats, from towing off our fire ships in their ap- " proach," (p. 124.): but those boats, his Lordship says, were drawn away, by " the blowing weather," (p. 122): that the fire ships had no kind of connection with, nor were directed to have any reference to the explosion vessels; that they had their own separate and distinct Orders, and Instructions; and that they did not set fire to their vessels, in consequence of the explosion, that took place—a fact, that his Lordship has further established, by shewing, that the explosion occurred at *half past nine*, and that it was *ten o'clock* before the fire ships were kindled, and, even then, not the whole of them: (p. 9.) that many of the fire ships were badly managed; and that, owing to such bad management, the failure complained of is solely, to be ascribed.

THE END.

Printed by T. C. HANSARD, Peterborough-court, Fleet Street, LONDON.

Zeitfracht Medien GmbH
Ferdinand-Jühlke-Straße 7
99095 Erfurt, Deutschland
produktsicherheit@kolibri360.de